The BEING Leader:

Tracing the 'Inner Path' of Legendary Leaders

Sujith Ravindran

First Edition, July, 2014.

Production and publishing:
IngramSpark Publishing
ISBN 978-0-9937210-2-1

Cover Design: Hey Day Solutions
Back Cover: www.FabrizioBelardetti.com

Published by:
YOU-NITY PROJECT ACADEMY,
5056 Keith Road
West Vancouver V7W 2N1
Canada

"As human beings, our greatness lies not so much in being able to remake the world—that is the myth of the atomic age—as in being able to remake ourselves."

M. K. Gandhi

ACKNOWLEDGMENT

As I set out to put this work in writing, I quickly discovered how minute my role was in its creation. If putting fingers to keyboard is a reason to receive credit, I accept that.

There are numerous people and resources above the list of the real authors of this work. I will not name all of them, but my eternal gratitude goes to all of them.

My most heartfelt gratitude is for the four Being Leaders examined in this work; Abraham Lincoln, M K Gandhi, Dr. Martin Luther King Jr. and Nelson Mandela, who inspired and invigorated me for so many years. More than any man or woman alive, they have filled me with liveliness and purpose in all my organizational endeavours and beyond. Their energies are present fully throughout this book.

In the late nineties, I worked for Boyd van der Plas, a little acknowledged but mature leader. If he had not recognized leadership qualities within me and thereafter championed my leadership path within the multinational that I worked for, I would not have reached the leadership crossroads of my life so early in my life. I am indebted to him for his role in facilitating the early part of my formal leadership journey. I am also fortunate to have had a compassionate board in the same organization who let me go on my path fully knowing that the chances of I rejoining them after my own inner journey was slim.

A huge part of the credit for this work goes to my dear wife, Camilla, without whose presence this work could not have found its form. She uncomplainingly tolerated my long absences during the course of this work. She showed infinite patience with my creative process, and unhesitatingly created an environment of calm and love that helped open my inner doors.

My own life has been a series of experiments in consciousness. These experiments have been facilitated by numerous wise teachers and masters who have passed through the waters of my life, every time acting as mirrors that helped bring answer to seemingly confusing questions that life throws at every human. I willingly bequeath my life as an instrument for their mission.

I am also thankful to my friend Mark Vandeneijnde for being the consciousness partner with whom I am fortunate to facilitate 'being' leadership work among leaders in the business, political and non-profit environments.

This acknowledgment list would not be complete without the most amazing support I received from the team in the West Vancouver library and the Vancouver Central Library in BC, Canada. They accepted all my wishes as their command and made available to me all the literature I needed to compile all the stories and anecdotes seen in this work.

Finally, a special thanks to the three editors who have enriched this work and my life with their priceless input. Anja Hulskotter possesses an incredible eye for details invisible to any normal human being, and has an uncanny ability to feedback her thoughts in the clearest fashion. She is also a dear friend to me. Without Eugene Flood's input, I would never have been able to effectively shape the plot of this book. He brought valuable insights into how to stitch this work together in a way that takes the readers along the path of the Being Leaders. Lastly, Thomas Dachsel is the master of structure. He meticulously pointed out all the incongruence in the first draft of this work. He also carries an infectious passion for life that infuses me with enthusiasm for the unlimited possibilities surrounding this work.

"I have not the shadow of a doubt that any man or woman can achieve what I have, if he or she would make the same effort and cultivate the same hope and faith."

M. K. Gandhi

To those of you who choose to be guided by your truest *being*

0. INTRODUCTION:

Setting the Scene

I. DEPARTURE:

Walking through Fire

II. PASSAGE:

The Practice and Preparation

III. ARRIVAL:

Being in Mastery

0. INTRODUCTION:

Setting the Scene

INTRODUCTION TO THE BOOK

"In the end, it's not the years in your life that count. It's the life in your years."

Abraham Lincoln

"Name six business leaders you admire," Willie asked me. "They could be from any industry, any culture or any field, including politics, social organizations or the field of sport. They could be current leaders or past leaders. They could be real or fictional," she elaborated.

Willie was a Leadership Development Officer within a Fortune 500 firm that I had joined at the turn of the millennium. I was in my late twenties then. In her role as a Leadership Development Officer, Willie was responsible for grooming young potentials into future leaders.

Willie was a portly woman with a gentle, caring face, a lady who could put anyone at ease immediately. To me she seemed out of place in that formal, etiquette obsessed wing of the company premise. The talk among the emerging managers in the company was that it was a good fortune to be called into her office.

I was seated across Willie for my first assessment to be placed on a fast track to grow into a CEO. Just out of business school, I did not find her question difficult to answer. In business school, case studies were built around leaders who turned around failing businesses into raging successes and transformed large bureaucracies into nimble giants.

0. INTRODUCTION

In her presence, I made my list of inspirational leaders. The list included one popular leader from a well-known global conglomerate, two bankers, a news media mogul, a popular lady who founded a success story in the tech space, a business magnate and TV personality, and I even squeezed in a contemporary sports icon who had repeatedly won feats after overcoming setbacks.

Anyone in a managerial position in the West knows these successful men and woman. They have been pictured on the front cover of *Forbes* magazine, and most—if not all—of them have patronized the World Economic Forum in Davos, Switzerland.

"What traits best inspire you about these leaders?" Willie asked next.

I dug into some of the leadership case studies that I was exposed to in school and turned up a list for her. The list included leadership competencies such as the ability to discern strategies, develop deep business understanding, plan intelligent action and set challenging goals, communicate congruently, commit steadfastly, engage and mobilise people, focus uni-mindedly on the drivers of success, align those around in action...the list came long. I also added my wish list. The best leaders also ought to be go-getters, initiative driven, be ahead of the curve when it comes to industry developments, grasp the opportunity before others see it, I claimed.

"Excellent list," she enthused. Then she declared something that I already knew. "These qualities that you have listed are latent yearnings of your person."

This was the turn of the millennium, a time when multinationals were taking a more integrated approach to leadership. Leadership Development managers were driven by the view that there are certain common traits exhibited by successful leaders and given the right circumstances, emerging leaders can nurture those traits and put them to good use within companies.

∞   ☼   ∞   ☼   ∞

MY DEPARTURE

The above conversation with Willie kicked off a long leadership development process in my life that exposed me over the next many years to various schools of leadership and several leadership frameworks. I listened to various speakers on leadership and emulated best practices. To support me in my development path, I received the support of a string of leadership mentors and coaches.

Over the next seven and a half years, I was given various apprenticeship projects to develop as a leader and inherit the company values. I attended leadership workshops and conferences, and in best-in-class settings I learned about various leadership styles.

Eighteen months after my initiation into the Leadership Development track, I shaped my own leadership post within the company. I was responsible for drawing from the vast resource pool within the organization and shape the way forward for a new business opportunity. Another eighteen months later, I was posted with the exceptional leadership responsibility of mobilizing a large section of the organization to capture a lucrative market that my predecessors had repeatedly tried to capture but failed. I was told that I was specifically picked for this responsibility as I had demonstrated qualities essential to succeed in this challenge.

Through all these professional steps I found myself judiciously applying the leadership competencies that I had picked up from my leadership

0. INTRODUCTION

trainings. I role-modelled the leaders in my Inspirational Leaders list. I asked myself what my list of leaders would do in moments of adversity that I faced. I constantly obsessed with their outlook and values. And when things would not work out, I would go back to studying the examples from the lives of my list of leaders. Soon I was being recognized as possessing the finest qualities to lead the wider organization in the future.

Seven and a half years of emulating these business leaders, I reaped significant business success. The business opportunities I nurtured created great impact in their respective fields, and many individuals who I groomed achieved incredible success in their chosen fields.

And then in the summer of 2004, a turning point occurred in my life. In the midst of my meteoric growth, I started to notice something about myself. I was becoming increasingly restless and divided at heart. A gnawing doubt about my choices that had persisted in my gut all these years was turning into a realization that I was on the wrong path.

All the objective know-how that I had gathered from business school and the years of organizational experience felt outdated. The subjective intelligence that I so badly needed to make myself a better human and a leader was missing, and I had to pursue something new to claim it.

I often felt trapped inside a shell that seemed rosy and opulent, a deep sense of meaninglessness gnawing at my heart. All my success in my professional initiatives only compounded my sense of disillusionment. The more I was applying myself to a well-defined set of objectives, the more distant I felt from myself.

I felt trapped in an illusory life that involved actors who seemed to thrive in that setting, but who—like me—could not find a way out. I became increasingly irritated and impatient with many around me, and I started to belittle the narrowness of their dreams.

Introduction to the Book

One thought that went through my head was that I may have created plenty of value, but I have not created any legacy. I felt that I could leave my office and I would have disappeared from the memories of my colleagues and subordinates in no time. I may have had a positive impact on my employer's bottom line, but I have not made a difference in the lives of those I served. I may have fulfilled some customer needs, but I have not occupied a grateful space within their hearts.

And repeating over and over what I—and many successful business leaders before me—have already done was not going to change any of that. I felt I had reached the limits of my wisdom on how to elevate from being a good leader to become an exemplary human.

Burdened by the enormity of a role I was not suited to play, I became insomniac. My skin started to show signs of ill-health. Often I laboured for breath, as if my windpipe was kinked. The feeling started to grow within me that those close to me cannot understand my DNA, and they were just obliging me to remain in my good books. I could not shake off that feeling, and soon nature resolved a part of my dilemma for me. A few weeks before my planned marriage, I found myself separated and alone. I cannot exactly remember the nature and depth of my sadness, but there was a sense of freedom and tranquility that came from knowing that the time had come to take charge of my life.

Despite the generous support I received from my superiors, three months later I handed in my resignation. As I walked out of my office on my last day, I took one last look at a quote from Abraham Lincoln I left behind in my office; *"In the end, it's not the years in your life that count. It's the life in your years."*

0. INTRODUCTION

MY WALK

The last time I visited the teacher's *ashram*[1] was as a student twenty years ago. In 2008, my ongoing journey of self-uncovering drew me back to that *ashram*. As I entered the main hall I was once again struck by the tranquility inside. Everything inside looked exactly the same as they were twenty years ago, the colour of the curtains, the fragrance of the *agarbathi*[2], and the chanting in the distance.

For me, the previous five years had been tumultuous and revealing at the same time. I felt a greater clarity in life. Many of my inner conflicts were resolved. A lot of the darkness and disillusionment of having operated in an unauthentic and transactional manner for such a long time seemed replaced with a quiet and calm awareness. There seemed a lesser rush to do and a greater joy to just be.

I felt a greater certainty of what I stood for, what my unique gifts were and how I could live a life of meaning while making a difference in the world around. I felt more sure of my values and ideals, but felt only a dying need to impose my ideologies upon others.

Looking back, the steps I took all made sense in a mysterious kind of way. I could not rationally explain what caused things to happen in my life in the past five years, nor in all my years before, yet I felt that there were many subtle connections.

Only a few months before, a friend had asked me the connection between my first university degree and my current path. I could not give him an answer that satisfied his reason, but I knew that as a teenager I needed to be in that course in order for me to be where I was in 2008, however disconnected from each other both seemed. To get to a higher

---

[1] Monastery
[2] Incense

8

step, you must first step on the preceding step. The steps may not be connected to each other, but they have their respective places. The same goes with our life experiences. They are perfectly placed to give us the lessons of the moment.

As I entered the main hall of the *ashram*, the dark interior took me a while to get used to. As my eyes got used to it, I was struck by the same quality of that space that I experience twenty years ago, filled in space with silence and accommodation. At the far end of the room, I noticed the silhouette of the teacher seated in meditation. The sight of the dark interior spartanly decorated with colors gave the place a calming feel. I could feel my breath slowing into a soft and deep rhythm.

As I stood there, I once again registered the fragrance of *agarbathi* and a gong ringing somewhere in the distance. I quietly pulled off my shoe, and cognizant of the teacher in meditation, I tiptoed towards the altar. The rich fragrance of the *agarbathi* hit me strongly as I stepped to the elevated platform meant for those of us who wish to meditate. As I leaned forward to draw a meditation cushion from the stack, I heard the words of the teacher: "Welcome son, welcome back."

Startled by the sudden intrusion into the silence, I dropped my cushion, turned towards the teacher and greeted him with my hands held together against my chest in the traditional greeting of the Indian subcontinent.

"Namaste", I replied back.

I could clearly see his eyes shine through, and though there wasn't a smile visible on his face, I could see his smile radiate through his eyes. I smiled back.

"You have taken a while to get here." He let that remark hang in the air.

0. INTRODUCTION

"Yes, I decided to hike up here rather than take the jeep", I said. "I wanted to enjoy the walk and the fresh air."

"Good choice, the walk itself is your destination". He turned to look at some faraway spot on the ceiling. Then he added, "Yes, your walk took a while. The time you took to choose to walk was even longer."

"Yes, I was tempted to take the comfort of the jeep. Though the morning looked fresh, the prospect of walking such a distance was not inviting," I felt slightly defensive in the face of his statement.

"And how much time did you take to make the choice to take this path?" The teacher asked with a smile that felt disarming. Though the gleam in his eyes gave away the mischief in his question.

In that instant I knew what he meant. He was not referring to the trek I took to visit the *ashram*, he was referring to the choice I made to give up my life of certainty and opulence for a life of meaning and wholeness. I briefly shared my journey of the past years with him and quizzed him about leadership.

"Forget business", he suggested in a calm voice. "Look around, look in history, look in mythology, look at humanity in its face. Look wherever you can find inspirational leaders, leaders who have upheld the dignity of humanity and the world."

"What makes an inspirational leader?" I prodded as I felt in the mood for a readymade answer. After all, this mystic was knowledgeable in the ancient wisdoms of humanity. He has also been extensively speaking to and coaching leaders from the business and political spheres, so he should know something. He gave me a calm look and urged me to dig within myself to find my own truth.

After meditating with him for an hour I turned to leave. Bidding him my farewell, I asked. "How did you know that it took me long to get on this path?" He simply smiled at me, slowly nodded his head in a sagely manner. After a few seconds, what seemed like a minute, he spoke, "I can see it."

As he spoke, it felt as if the words floated in the chilly air within the hall. His words bounced off the wall and refused to fade away. As I stepped outside the *ashram*, I felt his words fuse with the slight hum in the background coming from somewhere outside.

MY RESURRECTION

During the mid 2000s, at the peak of my disillusionment with life, I embraced the four 'Being Leaders' examined in this work; **Mahatma Gandhi, Nelson Mandela, Dr. Martin Luther King Jr. and Abraham Lincoln**. I minutely studied and eagerly lapped up their life stories and lessons. This exercise was part of my rite of passage from my corporate life to a more choiceful life of leadership. Compared to my previous list, this time the list included leaders from the social and political realm, leaders who have withstood the test of time and captured our collective imagination. This list was not always this small. There were a number of other eminent personalities in the list, all of them famous. They have all tirelessly toiled to uphold the dignity of humanity or the planet.

However, as I started to apply their traits in my life, and later coach leaders in applying these traits in their lives, I started to notice that my reference list was narrowing. The closer I got to all these eminent personalities, the more I was becoming a witness to their truths. Some of the eminent personalities on my initial list have not yet been fully

0. INTRODUCTION

tested by time, and hence could not be held fully indefensible. I needed to afford them more time to continue their inspirational journey and finish scripting their noble legacies. Some other leaders, though populating our collective imagination with reverence, operated in contexts largely different than ours today. Though their lessons inspire us, their context falls outside the specific focus of this work.

Then there was a small group of leaders in my initial list who either dropped the ball at a crucial moment in history or have wilfully misrepresented themselves. They have denied the existence of their dark sides, camouflaged it or have even vilified those who examined their dark sides.

Over the years, I studied the four Being Leaders as I did the list of role models of my corporate times. I would lookout for examples of how these leaders tackled the challenges in their lives. When I was in a quandary, I would ask myself, "what would these leaders do?" Whenever the conditions of compromise were being discussed with me in this ever polarizing world of today, I would ask myself, "what would Gandhi do? Or Mandela? Or Lincoln? Or Dr. King?" When an adversary came upon them with tremendous force, what inner reflections went within them? When a moment of achievement arrived, how did they celebrate? In moments of crisis, how did they hold themselves up? When things turned sour with friends or family, how did they respond?

I would follow these observations with my own contemplation and experimentation. Through contemplation, I would see the similarities, the differences and the interconnections between their experiences and mine. I would notice that though the external situations of the Being Leaders were different—often vastly different—how I choose to respond to such events in my life could relate to theirs. Their lives reminded me that I had choices in every moment. After all, a true leader is a choice-maker, not a victim of circumstances.

Introduction to the Book

I would follow my contemplation with my own experimentation. I could experiment with my lessons during the setbacks I faced in my personal relationships. Though my life-setting was different from those of the Being Leaders, I noticed that I could choose to approach such adversities the same way as they did. That gave me great learning and enormous comfort. In the beginning, role modeling such eminent leaders felt artificial. It felt as if I was imitating someone unrelated to who I was, and hence being unauthentic. In hindsight, I can say that the way I felt during my practice was not surprising. After all, I was conditioned to respond to situations differently than them. Hence, to adopt a new response involved discomfort.

Yet, I continued to find inspiration in the life-lessons of these leaders to persist in spite of the discomfort. I consoled myself that the process of forming new habits involved pain. I cannot bypass the discomfort and turmoil that these leaders went through and hope to achieve the level of mastery these legendary leaders did. So I swallowed the pain. Note that there are no shortcuts to attaining such leadership as demonstrated by these icons.

After a period of such personal experimentation, I would go back to studying these leaders again. I would again dive into their life experiments and delve into their experiences. Then I would retreat into contemplation and experimentation again. This cycle has continued from the mid-2000s until today.

Along the way, I started to notice an important thing happen. I was finding my own voice. Yes, I was following the life examples of the Being Leaders, yet I was opening up to what I held precious within my own core. I was emulating less others' styles and values, and expressing what I felt was true about me.

The ghosts of chaos, confusion and self-doubt that were crowding my life before started to disappear, and a greater clarity of the purpose of my life started to appear. I began by noticing what I did not like to do, who I did not like to be, and how I did not like my life to be lived.

In time, a new awareness started to dawn within me. I started to become aware of the things that most inspired me, the people who most nourished me, and the kind of life that filled my days with most meaning. I started to see glimpses of the Being Leaders in my own life.

The four Being Leaders rapidly became my favourites. In moments of crisis, or when I needed guidance, I found myself automatically reaching out for a book, audio or video on one of these favourite icons.

All of this is not to say that these leaders were in total mastery of their lives. These icons were often torn between their public image and their private lives. They often struggled to carry the weight that history had cast upon them. What made them special though was that these leaders themselves have openly and repeatedly admitted to their shortcomings. And their whole life journey has been one long struggle of taming and integrating their dark sides, learning the lessons offered by their imperfections, and continuing to grow.

STRUCTURE OF THE BOOK

This book is as much about my evolving path of leadership as it is about the four legendary leaders. Yet, this work is not an exhibition of my journey, rather this work is an exhibition of the journey of the four Being Leaders who have profoundly impacted my life. Parts of my journey will be seen within this work, but that is only a reflection of the Being Leaders' journeys that I have followed. What you see about me is only a few steps I have taken along a path that have been walked by these Being Leaders.

Throughout this book, the expression 'Being Leaders' stand to mean the four icons, M.K. Gandhi, Dr. Martin Luther King Jr., Abraham Lincoln and Nelson Mandela. There are certain to be other leaders who are as accomplished and legendary as these four. However, these four have shaped my life in profound ways, and hence have earned my lifelong admiration and a place in my life and in this work.

This work is structured in four sections. Section 1, **INTRODUCTION: Setting the Scene**, creates the foundation for understanding this work and the four eminent Being Leaders. Using the words of those who have known the Being Leaders best, I have created an essential sketch of these leaders.

Every hero has had to go through a passage of stepping into hell, battling their demons, mastering their inner demons, and attaining inner clarity before they could elevate themselves into true mastery. This cycle is as true for real heroes as it is for our mythological heroes that leave us spellbound. Section 2 through 4 takes you through the cycle each hero must go through in order to reclaim their mastery.

Section 2, **DEPARTURE: Walking through Fire**, captures the beginning of the Being Leaders' journey. This phase includes the painful departure from people and things that they once held dear to themselves. In doing so, they had to endure the ordeal of confronting their past conditioning and wounds. The many life experiences that shaped the mindset and tendencies of the Being Leaders are examined here.

Section 3, **PASSAGE: The Practice and Preparation**, examines the steps of resurrection that the Being Leaders went through. The life workshops and the apprenticeship of life that the Being Leaders were exposed to are elaborated in this section.

0. INTRODUCTION

Section 4, **ARRIVAL: Being in Mastery**, captures the key essence of the Being Leaders that made them iconic. The clarity of spirit, the aligned actions and the empowered choiceful self that the Being Leaders embodied at the peak of their lives is portrayed in this section.

I invite you to follow the sections in the sequence presented in this book. Each section is filled with several life events and anecdotes from the lives of the Being Leaders. These events and anecdotes are meant to exemplify the consciousness examined in the respective chapters. The remainder of each chapter goes into the definition and description of the leadership quality or consciousness covered in that chapter. *Parts of anecdotes or certain life examples from the lives of the Being Leaders have been repeated on occasions in order to make a point or support a leadership trait.*

In this book, I also draw on the examples of numerous individuals who have demonstrated that by focussing on their Being, not only have they been in a more joyful and fulfilling place in their lives, but they have also made a difference in the lives of others, and as a consequence, to their organizational bottom lines. Numerous discussions and anecdotes from the lives of modern leaders are included in the text in order to make various points. *The names of the parties and their organizations have been changed to avoid any conflicts of interest.*

On rare occasions, I've shared parts of me and my life lessons. Extracts of some conversations that got me on this enlightened, ideals-oriented, purpose-led path are also presented in this work. These conversations and lessons are meant to convince you that each of us possess the resources to grow into magnificent leaders.

In a separate workbook, several practices and exercises will be made available to the Being Leader aspirant. These practices have helped me embed the various leadership lessons from the chapters included here. I invite you to use those practices also judiciously. They promise to help you grow in your self awareness and flourish in your leadership. That workbook will also include a priceless list of standards from the lives of the Being Leaders. That is a list for daily examination and application.

1. WHO IS THE BEING LEADER?

"An individual has not started living until he can rise above the narrow confines of his individualistic concerns to the broader concerns of all humanity."

Dr. Martin Luther King Jr.

To understand the Being leader, you must understand who the Being Leader is not.

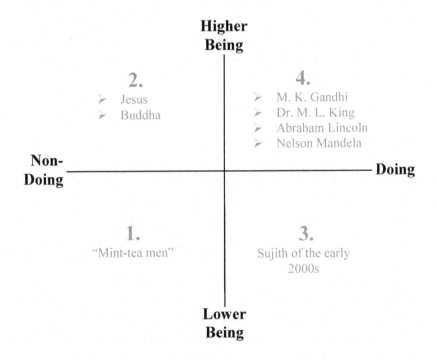

0. INTRODUCTION

The Being Leader is not a 'Non-Doing' leader operating from a place of 'Lower Being' (see quadrant 1).

Once a Sufi mystic shared with me the plight of some young men in his hometown in rural Turkey. Devoid of opportunities in life, these young men would gather each day at the neighbourhood teashop, sip mint tea all day and lament the misfortunes that have befallen them.

These young men constantly fretted over what would become of them, and they held others responsible for their state. They found fault with everyone other than themselves for their plight. Within them, they held a vast space for bitterness for those who had means, and they expressed anger and vengeance towards the way of life of those with means. They were indifferent to the outcomes of their actions and lacked self-belief. They were resigned to the belief that whatever they do would not uplift them. They sat there sipping tea, hoping that one day lady luck would marry them. The Sufi mystic called these men the 'Mint-tea men'. The 'Mint-tea men' do not see themselves as the choice-makers of their lives and live in a lower state of being.

x   x   x

Many masters of yesteryears were those who had renounced the world of 'Doing', choosing a monastic life instead, a life away from the worldly trials (see quadrant 2). Their primary purpose was to elevate themselves from their egoic conditioning and grow themselves beyond the patterns they had acquired in their years of upbringing. They did not choose for a life as a family man or woman. They did not engage in the trials of a common person, like taking a job or living in bustling cities or towns. Instead they spent their lives in meditation and contemplation, painstakingly penetrating through their stories and patterns, working through their wounds, and letting go of the actors of their past traumas. They forgave and forgot the perpetrators of their wounds, thus freeing themselves from all human bondage. These were exceptional human

Who is the Being Leader?

beings who were operating from their 'higher-Being' self while existing in a world of 'non-Doing'. Jesus, Buddha and the many spiritual masters of ancient times are such examples we remember. I grew up learning from and practicing with some such masters.

This manuscript is not deliberately preoccupied with those who operate in the 'non-Doing' realm. We live in a time that longs for heroes who have faced the trials and tribulations of worldly living. The ones I have examined in this work are such individuals. They all had families, and they all battled the daily struggles of bringing food to the table. In the midst of all that, they stood up for a greater good. In that process they embodied their greatest and inspired humanity to collectively lift itself.

x   x   x

The Being Leader is also not a 'Doing' leader operating from a place of 'Lower Being' (see quadrant 3). The leadership I practiced in the early 2000s was such a form of leadership. I disembodied myself from my true being, though unknowingly at that time, and exerted myself to the extreme. I managed myself and others through fear, and I looked at business matters as a survival issue. I had little connection with my inner voice, and as a consequence I was not bringing to bear my greatest gifts. I lacked clarity of my own goals and aspirations, hence I relied heavily upon a set of objectives assigned upon me. I was desensitized to my natural inclinations, so I mindlessly emulated seemingly 'successful' leaders in the blind belief that if I followed their recipe—as many of them have done before me—I would reach my goals. I was open to deviate from my values to find shortcuts to attain the summit. Such behaviour is symptomatic of a 'Doing' leader disconnected from the 'Being'.

Pure action is the realm of the 'Doing' leader. 'Doing' leaders are recognized and rewarded for productivity and performance. Doing a good job leads to a nice bonus package, lucrative retirement benefits and a golden watch! However, after the 'Doing' leader retires, even their successors struggle to recollect their contribution, and sometimes also their names.

The locus of leadership success for such leaders is external to them. Some external metric drives their lives. They hardly ever shape their own legacy. Such leaders seldom create breakthroughs within organizations. Research has shown that majority of the leaders of current times fall in this category.

There must be some reason why I had to be that type of individual during that phase of my life. Not only did it awaken me to the folly of impersonating other seemingly successful leaders—and in that process living an unauthentic life, in the years thereafter I have touched the lives of many other leaders who have operated from an identical place.

1.1.   SO WHO ARE THE BEING LEADERS?

I can never capture the greatness of the iconic personalities examined here with my limited human faculties, neither can I claim to have mastered a complete understanding of their magnificence. I do not know if I have the vocabulary to share the greatness of these legendary leaders. I can only say that I have been mesmerized by their greatness.

Such is the conviction of the ideals and the grandness of the Being Leaders' sacrifices that so many times when I was reading a bio or watching a documentary on these icons I would find tears pouring down my face. These tears came from my core being touched by the hard roads that these noble men choicefully travelled, and the miracles that they created.

Who is the Being Leader?

I first set out on this experiment of deconstructing the leadership traits of these Being Leaders in order to seek a way out of the vacuum that I existed in, and to fulfill my own need for elevating myself into a new realm of leadership. I wished to find within myself the same qualities of leadership found within these magnificent men...and to live them.

Many years ago, at the peak of my corporate life, I used to maintain a little journal. I used to take notes in this journal of the numerous immeasurable gifts that these icons possessed. Each morning as I would set out to my office, I would remind myself of studying this little journal and make a commitment to progress along—at least—one attribute.

After years of doing this, I discovered that in order for me to emulate the leadership traits of these Being Leaders, I had to quit focussing on *acting* a certain way with those around me. It was not an action of some sort that I must practice each day, rather it was a state of 'being' that I had to embody. This 'being' was not someone foreign to me, instead I knew that I had the qualities of this 'being' buried deep within me.

The Being Leaders go beyond the paradigm of 'Doing' to master the realm of their 'Being'. They have demonstrated great personal mastery, a very high level of self-awareness. They are amazingly self-authored, and they are individuals whose highest principles and personalities have merged. They have clarified for themselves who they were, with all their imperfections and strengths. They knew what their gifts were, what inspired them most, and why they were born.

In this book, we will examine the hero's path that these leaders undertook to get to that place. We will look at the choices that these leaders made that eventually led them to greatness. We will also study their ideals and sacrifices in-depth in the chapters ahead.

0. INTRODUCTION

1.2. "SO WHAT IS THIS BOOK?"

"So what is this book?" The lead editor of a popular North American publishing house asked. He removed his spectacles from his nose, carefully folded them, and used it to point at the copy of the manuscript in front of him.

"It is a map into the multidimensionality of the Being Leaders," I answered. "It bares open the building blocks that make for legendary leadership in any aspect of life."

As I looked over at the hunched figure of the lead editor, I remembered that he had a reputation as an editor sceptical towards work not considered strictly 'management' literature. I could sense that he did not know where to place this work and how his target audience would receive it.

"The leaders examined here lived during times of great sacrilege," he remarked pointing to the copy of the manuscript on his desk. "Humanity was struggling with big questions like slavery and colonization."

As he pursed his lips, I could see the scepticism on his face. "Compared to those times, there aren't many burning issues today that call for the making of such leaders," he added unconvincingly. "Doesn't that make this book redundant?"

I disagreed with him. "The issues humanity grapple with today are numerous," I gently challenged him. I went on to present to him a list of economic disparities, social injustices, moral violations, environmental challenges, societal malice and familial issues facing us today.

"And there is a grave dearth of transformational leaders to inspire us to resolve these issues and lead us towards light," I added. "Opportunities to step into greatness are all over the place. They are all around us. There is a lack of awareness and courage in the world we live in. We need such leaders today more than ever," I emphasized.

"Who stands to gain most from this book?" The editor reluctantly moved on.

"There are four types of leaders," I answered. "Leaders who are not driven by any noble purpose, leaders who chase ignoble goals, leaders who chase a noble purpose but through ignoble means, and the last— the most inspirational—category of leaders, those who chase a noble purpose through noble means." I gave him the context. "Those who are pursuing the noblest realm of leadership stands to gain most from this work."

Not looking fully convinced, he look over to the manuscript and asked, "Who is this book for? Who is the audience for your work?"

To answer his question, I had to search within myself and relate to the journey that I went through until I adopted the Being Leaders as my role models. I started with my own path that brought me to write this book.

"This book is for those aspiring to grow to the *highest* level of leadership in any realm; organizational, political or social." I emphasized the word 'highest'. "It doesn't matter which walk of life they are from," I added. I felt that this book was most suited for people who have achieved some success in their leadership roles and then discover a vacuum within.

"They are the ones who will most benefit from the essence of this book. They stand to gain most from digging into the traits of these legendary leaders."

0. INTRODUCTION

"And what is exceptional to these leaders?" He wanted to know.

"They all had a crucial quality beyond what other leaders had; self-mastery." I elaborated on my observations around their mastery of their true 'being'.

"Is this level of leadership associated exclusively with such legendary leaders as Gandhi and Mandela? How accessible is this to the leaders of today?"

I took a minute to answer that question.

"This level of leadership is available to all. Surprisingly, many who have embraced the lessons contained in this work are not hierarchically in senior leadership positions. So far, I've noticed only one common denominator among those interested in this work; they have a powerful yearning to undertake the same inner path taken by the Being Leaders. Those who are not suitable for such work are those limited by their own lack of calling."

"If this has been part of your inner process for nearly a decade, why did it take so long for you to write this?" He asked. I found his question reasonable.

"I was not ready to write it," I told him. "All these past years, I have been grappling with the divide that existed between my awareness and that of the Being Leaders. Unless I could resolve that inner turmoil I couldn't write. I had to overcome my ordeal of self-doubt and inner conflict before I could come out on the other side with clarity and write this book."

"Why are you the right person to write this book?" I felt that the editor was very meticulous in his assessment process of any work that came his way.

Who is the Being Leader?

"I never had the good fortune to join any of the above leaders in their endeavours," I admitted. "I never spoke with them, nor did I travel the hard roads with them. I never ate with them, nor did I get them refreshments. I did not work with them as their assistant, nor did I run errands for them. I wasn't a biographer for them, nor am I an author of any of the numerous dissertations on them. I am not a historian, a political scholar or social researcher."

"There is one thing though," I added passionately. "Like no other person on this planet, I have gratefully embraced the messages shared by these souls. For several years now, I continue to diligently hold my life to their set of standards. Every high standard[3] from the lives of the Being Leaders is part of my daily practice."

I felt it was important for him to understand my personal practice that nourishes this book. "This work is extremely personal to me because it relates to a hugely important phase of my life extending into this day. It bares open a precious part of my journey. So you will see some of my personal experiences and realizations creep into this work. That is because as I continue on that inner path, I continue to unlock and bring to life the true powerful nature that I have noticed in these eminent personalities and is innate to all."

In the subsequent chapters, I will take you down many roads; roads that are both abstract and subtle at times. While on that journey, I urge you to keep the leadership question in mind. Be critical and ask how this topic relates to leadership. Keep a sceptical mind, because these

---

[3] A Being Leader workbook with practicum and standards from the lives of the Being Leaders will be released following this work

0. INTRODUCTION

legendary leaders did so. Incessantly ask how a certain bit of information relates to you and your path.

And when you have something to share that will enrich the conversation and enlighten others, please do share it with me at <u>Sujith@beingatfullpotential.com</u>.

2. INTRODUCTION TO THE FOUR BEING LEADERS

"My life is my message."

M.K. Gandhi

∞ ☼ ∞ ☼ ∞

The leaders that I examine in this book need no introduction. They have filled our collective imagination with their ideals and valour. As heroes, they have become fixtures in our children's bedside stories, and have tickled our children's fantasies. These men have become the idols we turn to when we seek strength and conviction in our daily toils of life.

We know the Being Leaders well. Still, as a brief introduction, I find it valuable to capture the essence of these leaders in this chapter. This chapter is not about covering all the crucial plot points of these leaders' lives, nor is it a look into the chronology or the history of these icons. Rather, this chapter is an attempt to familiarize ourselves with the inner essence of these great leaders. You could call this inner essence a form of awareness that has shone through the causes and crusades they undertook.

In order to understand the Being Leaders, we must penetrate the mythology and iconography surrounding these individuals. Who better at this than those who have known him best? With that in mind, below I have simply borrowed the words of authors who have spent years studying these leaders.

0. INTRODUCTION

2.1. NELSON MANDELA

Nelson Mandela is best described in the words of Richard Stengel[1], the collaborator on Nelson Mandela's autobiography, *Long Walk to Freedom*.

"A complex man.

We long for heroes, but have too few. Nelson Mandela is perhaps the last pure hero on the planet. He is the smiling symbol of sacrifice and rectitude, revered by millions as a living saint. But this image is one dimensional. He would be the first to tell you that he is far from a saint. And that is not false modesty.

Nelson Mandela is a man of many contradictions. He is thick-skinned, but easily wounded. He is sensitive to how others feel, but often ignores those closest to him. He is generous with money, but counts his pennies when giving a tip. He will not step on a cricket or a spider, but was the first commander of the African National Congress's military wing.

He is a man of the people, but revels in the company of celebrities. He is eager to please, but not afraid to say no. He doesn't like to take credit, but would let you know when he should get it. He shakes the hands of everyone in the kitchen, but doesn't know all his bodyguards' names.

His persona is a mixture of African royalty and British aristocracy. He is a Victorian gentleman in a silk *Tashiki*. His manners are courtly, after all he learned them in colonial British schools from headmasters who read Dickens, when Dickens was still writing.

He is formal, he will bow slightly and hold out his arm for you to go first. But he is not the least bit finicky or prim. He will talk in almost clinical detail about the toilet routine in prison on Robben Island, or how it felt when his foreskin was sliced off in his tribal circumcision ritual at the age of sixteen.

He will use fancy silverware when he is in London or Johannesburg, but when he is in his own home area of the *Transkei*, he enjoys eating with his hands, as is the local custom.

Nelson Mandela is meticulous. He takes tissues from a box and refolds them individually, before placing them in his front pocket. I have seen him remove his shoe to reverse one sock when he notices it is inside out.

In prison, he made a fair copy of every letter he wrote over two decades, and kept a detailed list of every letter he received with the date he got it, and when he replied.

He sleeps on one side of his king size bed, while the other side remains pristine and untouched. He rises before dawn and makes his bed precisely every morning, whether he is at home or in a hotel. I have seen the look of shock on hotel housekeepers' faces when they find him making the bed.

He hates to be late, and regards lack of punctuality as a character flaw.

I've never known a human being who can be as still as Nelson Mandela. When he is sitting or listening, he does not tap his fingers or his foot, or move about. He has no nervous ticks. When I have adjusted his tie, or smoothed his jacket, or fixed a microphone on his lapel, it was like fussing with a statue. When he listens to you, it is as though you are looking at a still photograph of him. You would barely know he was breathing.

He is a power charmer, confident that he will charm you by whatever means possible. He is attentive, courtly, winning, and to use a word that

0. INTRODUCTION

he would hate, seductive. And he works at it. He will learn as much as he can about you before meeting you. When he was first released, he would read journalists' pieces and praise them individually with specific details. And like most great charmers, he himself is easily charmed. And you can accomplish that by letting him see that he has won you over.

The charm is political as well personal. Politics is ultimately about persuasion. And he regards himself not so much as the great communicator, but as the great persuader. He will either get you through logic, or through charm, and usually a combination of the two. He would always rather persuade you to do something than order you to do so. But he will order you to do so, if he has to.

He wants to be liked. He liked to be admired. He hates to disappoint. He wants you to come away from meeting him thinking that he is everything you had ever hoped for. This requires tremendous energy. And he gives it himself to almost everyone he meets.

Almost everyone gets the full Mandela, except when he is tired. Then his eyes droop to half mast and he seems asleep on his feet. But I've never known a man to be so revived by a night's sleep. He can seem a death store at 10pm, but then eight hours later at 6am, he will seem sprightly and twenty years younger.

His charm is in inverse proportion to how well he knows you. He is warm with strangers and cool with intimates. That warm benign smile is bestowed on every new person who comes within his orbit. But the smile is reserved for outsiders.

I saw him often with his son, his daughters, his sisters. And the Nelson Mandela they know often appears to be a stern and unsmiling fellow who is not terribly sympathetic to their problems. He is a Victorian, African father, not a modern one.

When you ask him something that he does not want to talk about, he will fix his face into a frown of displeasure. His mouth becomes an inverted cartoon of his smile. Do not try to force the issue, or he will simply become stony and turn his attention elsewhere. When that happens, it is like a sunny day that has suddenly become overcast.

Mandela is indifferent to almost all material possessions. He does not know or care about the names of cars, couches or watches. But I've seen him despatch a bodyguard to drive an hour to get his favourite pen.

He is generous with his children when it comes to money, but not count on his generosity if you are his waiter. The two of us once had lunch at a fancy hotel restaurant in Johannesburg where he was waited on hand and foot. The bill came to well over one thousand Rand, and I watched as Mandela examined some coins in his hand, and then left a tiny pieces of change. After he had gone, I slipped a one hundred Rand note to the waiter. It was not the only time I ever did so.

Nelson Mandela will always stand up for what he believes is right with a stubbornness that is virtually unbending. I've very often heard him say, "This isn't right." Whether it concerns something mundane or of international importance, his tone was unvarying.

I've heard him say it when a security guard's key would not open his office. And I've heard him say it directly to South African president, F. W. de Klerk, about the constitutional negotiations. He used the phrase for years on Robben Island when talking to a guard or the head of the prison.

'This isn't right'.

In a very basic way, this intolerance of injustice was what goaded him. It was the engine of his discontent. His simple verdict on the basic immorality of Apartheid. He saw something wrong and tried to right it. He saw injustice and tried to fix it."

∞ ☼ ∞ ☼ ∞

2.2. MOHANDAS KARAMCHAND GANDHI

In the words of Dwight Macdonald[11] (March 24, 1906 – December 19, 1982), an American writer, editor, film critic, social critic, philosopher, and political radical:

"Gandhi was the last eminent personage who insisted on dealing directly with people, reasoning with them face to face as individuals, not as crowds roped off, watched by plainclothes-men, sealed safely behind bullet-proof glass. It was a matter of principle with him not to deny anyone access to him, mentally or physically. He refused all police protection. I have heard people say he was a damn fool and got what he might expect to get. They are, of course, right.

Our world is so structured that the 'public man' can survive only by being private, and the most dangerous thing he can do is to meet his public face to face. Gandhi was the last political leader in the world who was a person, not a mask or a radio voice or an institution. The last on a human scale. The last for whom I felt neither fear nor contempt nor indifference, but interest and affection. He was dear to me—I realize it now better than I did when he was alive—for all kinds of reasons. He believed in love, gentleness, persuasion, simplicity of manners, and he came closer to 'living up to' these beliefs than most people I know—let alone most Big Shots, on whom the pressures for the reverse must be very powerful.

(To me, the wonder is not that Gandhi often resorted to sophistry or flatly went back on some of his ideas, but that he was able to put into practice as many of them as he did. I speak from personal experience.) He was dear to me because he had no respect for railroads, assembly-belt production, and other knick-knacks of liberalistic progress, and insisted on examining their human (as against their metaphysical) value. Also because he was clever, humorous, lively, hard-headed, and never made speeches about Fascism, Democracy, the Common Man, or World Government. And because he had a keen nose for the concrete, homely 'details' of living which make the real difference to people but which are usually ignored by everybody except poets. And finally because he was a good man, by which I mean not only 'good' but also 'man'.

Gandhi was not at all unworldly, the Sunday Supplement idea of him to the contrary notwithstanding. He was full of humour, slyness, perversity, and—above all—practicality. Indeed, the very thing which leads people to think of him as unworldly—his ascetic ideas about diet, household economy, and sexual intercourse—seems to me to show his worldliness, or at least his imaginative grasp of The World: how could any one be so concerned about such matters, even though in a negative sense, without a real feeling for their importance in human life, which in turn must come from a deep drive on his part toward gluttony, luxury, and sexual indulgence? That he conquered this drive may be to his credit (though he overdid it, in my opinion) but I think it is clear that he knew what it was all about.

The Marxists, those monks of politics, were shocked by his intimacy with rich Indian men like Birla and Tata, just as the Pharisees, the Trotskyists of their day, were shocked by Christ's sitting at table with bartenders. (The Marxist has a richer intellectual tradition than the pacifist, but his ethical sense is equally simplistic.) It is true that Gandhi "compromised" with the rich, those untouchables of the class struggle, living at their villas (though carrying on there his own ascetic regimen). But he also 'compromised' with the poor, spending at least as much time in the 'untouchables' quarters (he constantly complains of the smells and lack of sanitation) as in the Birla Palace. In short, he practiced tolerance and love to such an extent that he seems to have regarded the capitalist as well as the garbage-man as his social equal."

2.3. Dr. MARTIN LUTHER KING Jr.

One of the world's best known advocates of non-violent social change, Dr. Martin Luther King Jr., embodied ideals drawn from many different cultural traditions. Recent studies of him emphasize the extent to which his ideals were rooted in African-American religious traditions which were further shaped by his education. The image of a social activist and leader was the result of extensive formal education, strong personal values and licit ethics.

Dr. King is not great because he is well-known, he is great because he served as the cause of peace and justice for all humans. He is remembered for his humanity, leadership and his love of his fellow man regardless of skin color. Dr. King had a vision of the truth, the truth that one day his nation would live up to the creed, "all men are created equal". No man contributed more to the great progress of Blacks during the 1950's and 1960's than Dr. King. He was brought up believing "one man can make a difference", and this is just what he did. He believed that America will one-day lead the way in a revolution of values. This revolution will change the way society views itself, shifting from a "thing-orientated" society to a "person-orientated" society. When this occurs, Dr. King believed that racism will be conquered and the American nation will be "Free at last."

Dr. King's unconditional love for all humans was another value that strongly influenced his character and allowed him to have such influence upon others. Dr. King described his meaning of love in one of his many speeches, "A Time to Break Silence", "when I speak of love I am not speaking of some sentimental and weak response. I am speaking of that force which all of the great religions have seen as the supreme unifying principle of life. Love is somehow the key that unlocks the door which leads to ultimate reality." When Dr. King was called an extremist, he replied that it could only be taken as a compliment and he came to the realization that the world was in dire need for more extremists.

Dr. King did not want to be remembered after his death by his Nobel Peace Prize or his many other awards. He wanted people to say "[...] that Martin Luther King, Jr., tried to love somebody [...] And I want you to say that I tried to love and save humanity". Even when his own life and the life of his family was threatened, Dr. King did not react with hatred or violence. He found more strength and courage and told his fellow men, "I want you to love your enemies. Be good to them. Love them and let them know you love them."

Dr. King was asked to be the leader of so many important protest marches and sit-ins due to his allegiance to truth. "He drew people to him from the very first moment by his eloquence, his sincerity, and his moral stature," his mother once noted. Dr. King's followers believed that he would speak nothing but the truth, but in his famous 'Letter from Birmingham Jail' he could only hope that what he had written will be seen as the truth. "If I have said anything in this letter that overstates the truth and indicates an unreasonable impatience, I beg you to forgive me. If I have said anything that understates the truth and indicates my having a patience that allows me to settle for anything less than brotherhood, I beg God to forgive me," he implored.

Dr. King also believed that all people should be treated with equality and fairness and this became the basis of the Civil Rights Movement. "The young people just envisioned a new hope and a new day, and the old folks saw in him a black Jesus. They used to love calling him 'My Boy' or 'My Son'. They worshipped him," said one follower of Dr. King. Dr. King's followers felt this way about him because they had never before been treated with such fairness, they had never anything to equal this in their whole lifetime. He lifted them so high that they could not help but think that he was an act sent to them from God. It is through this caring and inner strength that King has made himself "the unchallenged voice of the Negro people -- and the disquieting conscience of the Whites."

Dr. King unwaveringly believed that one day racial justice will prevail in the United States. "I have a dream that one day even the state of Mississippi, a desert state, sweltering with the heat of injustice and oppression, will be transformed into an oasis of freedom and justice," he proclaimed in his "I Have a Dream" speech. "If you want to say that I was a drum major, say that I was a drum major for justice; say that I was a drum major for peace; I was a drum major for righteousness," he once famously noted. When the Civil Rights Act was signed in 1964 and 1968, Dr. King felt he was one step closer to seeing that his nation can live up to the creed, "all men are created equal". He was an advocate of non-violent means of achieving civil rights reform, which eventually led to the passing of the Civil Rights Act of 1964.

Dr. King had modeled his philosophy on that of M. K. Gandhi, who is one of the world's greatest advocates of non-violent resistance. During his encounter with Gandhi's teachings, Dr. King became more convinced than ever that non-violent resistance was the most powerful weapon for oppressed people in their struggle for freedom. He voiced his beliefs of non-violent resistance in his "I have a dream" speech which has become, for good reason, one of the world's most memorable speeches of our time. He said: "The true meaning of a man is not how he behaves in moments of comfort and convince, but how he stands at times of controversy and challenge. We must not allow our creative protests to degenerate into physical violence. Again and again we must rise to the majestic heights of meeting physical force with soul force". This is why this tactic of active non-violence (sit-ins, protest marches) had put civil-right squarely on the national agenda.

To truly understand Dr. King, you must understand that first and foremost he was a preacher. Dr. King was a man of eloquence, authority and assurance. In choosing to be a preacher, Dr. King found a pulpit from where he could reach all people. One of his childhood goals was realised when he began his ministry and public speaking; that was to speak with eloquence and "big words". He preached a social gospel to fulfil his dream of a just society for all: "[...] the church must incessantly raise its voice in prophetic warning against the social evils in all the institutions of the day. The church must not try to be a state or an economic order, but remaining in its own role as conserver and voice of the state and the economic order. In all its judgements it must avoid even the appearance of being one organisation competing for power and prestige among other organisations. Its peculiar power lies not in self-seeking but in searching for truth and justice and peace for all, in the spirit of Jesus Christ."

Dr. King's stated mission in life was to replace fear with confidence and humiliation with pride. And that meant there had to be desegregation in the southern states. Whites and coloured people should be able to sit anywhere on public transit on a first come first served basis. Blacks should not have to give up their seats to Whites. White and coloured signs should come down from public washrooms and fountains. Blacks should be served at all lunch counters, restaurants and hotels. Other goals included programs for the poor; not just Blacks but all, and work for the unemployed. He insisted that all these goals were to be achieved without violence, by peaceful civil disobedience. He told his followers to meet violence with non-violence.

Dr. King believed that an unjust law is contrary to God's moral law. Therefore, it is not wrong to stand opposed to such laws, or to find oneself in prison for disobeying immoral laws. His aim was not to break the law, but to change it. Dr. King was courteous. As a child he would "turn the other cheek", showing even then that non-violence was the way. In all that he did, Dr. King was not afraid. He did not fear physical harm or what men might say. But injustice angered him. "Justice too long delayed is justice denied", he used to say.

From childhood Dr. King knew his value as a human being made in the image of God. He believed in, "loving oneself, loving one's neighbour, and loving God". Still there was the tension of being Black and knowing he was equal while being treated as a lesser human being. Yet, his faith was in God and he did not fear what men could do to him.

A crucial period in Dr. King's deliberations about his career came during the summer of 1947, when he led religious services for his fellow student workers at a tobacco farm in Simsbury, Connecticut. After several weeks of deliberation, he telephoned his mother to tell her of his intentions to become a minister. Though Dr. King resented religious emotionalism and often questioned literal interpretations of scripture, he always greatly admired Black social gospel proponents such as his father, who always viewed the church as an instrument for improving the lives of African American.

"My call to the ministry was neither dramatic nor spectacular," he wrote in his application to seminary. "It came neither by some miraculous vision nor by some blinding light experience on the road of life. Moreover, it was a response to an inner urge that gradually came upon me. This urge expressed itself in a desire to serve God and humanity, and the feeling that my talent and commitment could best be expressed through the ministry [...]. I came to see that God had placed a responsibility upon my shoulders and the more I tried to escape it the more frustrated I would become."

Even after Dr. King's death, his identity and his beliefs have remained a controversial symbol of the African American civil rights struggle, revered by many for his sacrifice on behalf of non-violence and condemned by others for his revolutionary views. That was to be expected from someone as iconic as Dr. King.[III]

∞ ☼ ∞ ☼ ∞

2.4.   ABRAHAM LINCOLN

He comes to us in the mists of legend as a kind of homespun Socrates, brimming with prairie wit and folk wisdom. There is a counter-legend of Lincoln, one shared ironically enough by many white Southerners and certain Black Americans of our time. Neither of these views, of course, reveals much about the man who really lived; legend and political interpretations seldom do.

As a man, Lincoln was complex, many-sided, and richly human. He was an intense, brooding person, he was plagued with chronic depression most of his life. At the time he even doubted his ability to please or even care about his wife. Lincoln remained a moody, melancholy man, given to long introspection about things like death and mortality. Preoccupied with death, he was also afraid of insanity.

0. INTRODUCTION

Lincoln was a teetotaller because liquor left him "flabby and undone", blurring his mind and threatening his self-control. One side of Lincoln was always supremely logical and analytical, he was intrigued by the clarity of mathematics. As a self-made man, Lincoln felt embarrassed about his log-cabin origins and never liked to talk about them. By the 1850s, Lincoln was one of the most sought after attorney in Illinois, with a reputation as a lawyer's lawyer. Though a man of status and influence, Lincoln was as honest in real life as in legend.

Politically, Lincoln was always a nationalist in outlook, an outlook that began when he was an Indiana farm boy tilling his rather mundane wheat field. Lincoln always maintained that he had always hated human bondage, as much as any abolitionist. He realized how wrong it was that slavery should exist at all in a self-proclaimed free Republic. He opposed slavery, too, because he had witnessed some of its evils firsthand. "What could be done?" Lincoln argued in his early days. To solve the ensuing problem of racial adjustment, Lincoln insisted that the federal government should colonize all Blacks in Africa, an idea he got from his political idol, Whig national leader Henry Clay.

By 1858, Lincoln, like a lot of other Republicans, began to see a grim proslavery conspiracy at work in the United States. The next step in the conspiracy would be to nationalize slavery: the Taney Court[4], Lincoln feared, would hand down another decision, one declaring that states could not prohibit slavery. For Lincoln and his Republican colleagues, it was imperative that the conspiracy be blocked in its initial stage; the expansion of slavery into the West. Lincoln's archrival Stephen A. Douglas fighting for his political life in free-soil Illinois, lashed at Lincoln with unadulterated race-baiting. Exasperated with Douglas and white Negrophobia in general, Lincoln begged American Whites "to

---

[4] Supreme Court Chief Justice Roger B. Taney made the pro-slavery ruling in the 1857 Dred Scot Case that deemed blacks weren't citizens of the United States and hence could be possessed and traded

discard all this quibbling about this man and the other man—this race and that race, and the other race as being inferior."

At the outset of the war, Lincoln strove to be consistent with all that he and his party had said about slavery: his purpose in the struggle was strictly to save the Union. There were other reasons for Lincoln's hands-off policy about slavery. He was also waging a bipartisan war effort, with Northern Democrats and Republicans alike enlisting in his armies to save the Union.

But the pressures and problems of civil war caused Lincoln to change his mind and abandon his hands-off policy about slavery and hurl an executive fist at slavery in the rebel states. Caught in a place of deep inner conflict, he struggled with his choices. He felt sympathy for the slaves, he felt anguish for the soldiers enlisted in the armies, and he felt concern for the future of the Union. In March 1862, in the midst of his struggles with his values, he first proposed a hesitant plan to Congress he thought might work: a gradual, compensated emancipation program to commence in the loyal border states. At the same time, the federal government would sponsor a colonization program, which was to be entirely voluntary. If his gradual state-guided plan were adopted, Lincoln contended that a presidential decree—federally enforced emancipation—would never be necessary. The plan failed. Most of the border men turned him down.

He had given this a lot of grave and painful thought, he said, and had concluded that a presidential declaration of emancipation was the alternative, that it was 'a military necessity absolutely essential to the preservation of the Union.' On July 22, 1862, Lincoln summoned his cabinet members and read them a draft of a preliminary Emancipation Proclamation. Contrary to what many historians have said Lincoln's projected Proclamation went further than anything Congress had done. But he wanted a victory in battle before announcing the Proclamation.

0. INTRODUCTION

In one of the great ironies of the war, Lincoln was presented with the triumph he needed.

Out the Proclamation went to an anxious and dissident nation. As in turned out, the preliminary Proclamation ignited racial discontent in much of the lower North, especially the Midwest. Republican analysts, Lincoln included, conceded that the preliminary Proclamation was a major factor in the Republican losses. Yet, Lincoln's Proclamation was the most revolutionary measure ever to come from an American president up to that time.

As news of the Proclamation went out, more slaves than ever ran away from the Confederate states. The Proclamation also opened the army to the Black volunteers, and the Northern free Blacks and Southern ex-slaves now enlisted as Union soldiers. After the Proclamation Lincoln had to confront the problem of race adjustment, of what to do with all the Blacks liberated in the South. As a consequence, Lincoln had just about concluded that Whites and liberated Blacks must somehow learn to live together in this country. Even so, emancipation remained the most explosive and unpopular act of Lincoln' s presidency.

When Lincoln was re-elected in 1864, Lincoln rejoiced it as a popular mandate for him and his emancipation policy. An elated Lincoln pronounced the 13th amendment "a great moral victory" and "a King's cure" for the evils of slavery. Lincoln conceded that he had not controlled the events of the war, but that the events of the war controlled him instead, that God controlled him.

In the last paragraph of his address, Lincoln said he would bind the nation's wounds "with malice toward none" and "charity for all". He had come a long distance from the young Lincoln who entered politics, quiet on slavery lest he be branded an abolitionist, opposed to Negro political rights lest his political career be jeopardized, convinced that only the future could remove slavery in America. But perhaps it was

Lincoln himself who summed up his journey to the emancipation: his own as well as that of the slaves. "Fellow-citizens, we cannot escape history...The fiery trail through which we pass, will light us down, in honor or dishonor, to the latest generation."[IV]

"Imagination is the extended form of sight," a teacher once told me when I was a child.

"With your sight, you can see the material, because the material has color. But if something has no color, we cannot see it. It becomes invisible to our sight," he added.

"Does that mean that the object becomes non-existent?" I asked.

After a long pause, he said, "No, it does not. When you look at an apple, all you see is its skin. Does that mean it does not have seeds? It has seeds. But we are unable to see it with our sight. That is why need imagination. To see the unseeable."

To gain from the life's lessons of the Being Leaders, I had to remember this truth from the teacher. I had to often look at the Being Leaders with my imagination, not with my sight. When I looked first at them with my eyes, all I saw was the date they were born, the dates they died, the roles they had, the schools they went to and the events they participated in. My eyes did not show me the core essence that lay hidden within them. And it was that essence that fascinated me, what I was after. Imagination helped me see it.

0. INTRODUCTION

Four different leaders with four different personalities, four different settings in four different moments in history, four different set of challenges posed by four different type of adversaries.

They operated in vastly different contexts, and they have all been conditioned in significantly different ways. The challenges they faced and the adversities they overcame were hugely different, but they all possessed the one common leadership trait that I expose in this work.

In the subsequent chapters I expose what I have seen—through the microscope of our collective imagination. I do not take credit for what is presented in the following chapters, but I claim the lessons.

I trust the same of you.

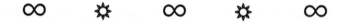

I. DEPARTURE:

Walking through Fire

The Being Leaders went through a three-step rite of passage to claim their higher, masterful selves (see page 14, 'Structure of the Book' for description of the three steps). In the first of these three stages, the DEPARTURE phase, a set of events happened in the lives of the Being Leaders that stripped away all illusions of life and of the self, leaving them naked and confused of life and destiny. All that they knew, everything that they were certain of, all things that seemed to be in their control were taken away from them. Their lives as they knew it were pulled apart and they were left cold and unsure. The roles they had cultivated by virtue of their progeny or skin colour were all disproved.

I call this phase the departure phase.

In this essential first stage towards becoming a Being Leader, your old identity is stripped away by a set of life-crushing events. It is an essential departure that you must make in order to claim your mightiest and serve others from that place of might. The life as you know it must be unfurled and you must be brought back to the bare minimum. The illusion of control that you have sported as part of your persona must be stripped away so that what is left will be free from old associations. As a result of those events, all the power that you or others around you possessed, or any of the hierarchy that existed before must become irrelevant to you. At the end of the departure stage, consider yourself to have left the old, certain shores as you know it.

Departure often contains pain. When you let go of the past that has carried you this far, it is similar to the pain of amputating a part of you. It could involve the foregoing of a relationship, sometimes a spouse or a friend. In many cases, departure involves a farewell from a job you have done for decades, or a country you have lived in all your life. In every case, departure involves divesting your old self. And that can include letting go of patterns, beliefs, habits, values, stories people tell

1. DEPARTURE

themselves in order to cope with their victim hood of life, past conditioning or old identities.

Two types of experiences enabled the Being Leaders to rise to the peak. The first type was a set of painful experiences that moulded the Being Leaders to step into their true being. For the purpose of this work, I will call these experiences the *life-defining experiences*. In the coming two chapters we will examine these experiences in full detail (I call the second type of experiences *synchronous events*. In the ARRIVAL phase, chapter 12, 'BEING' ON PURPOSE, examines *synchronous events*).

Chapter 3, 'ORDEAL OF THE WARRIOR CHILD', traces the wounds that the Being Leaders inherited in their childhood. The chapter 'THE FIERY ORDEAL THROUGH WHICH THE BEING LEADERS PASS' traces the wounds that the Being Leaders inherited as adults.

3. ORDEAL OF THE WARRIOR CHILD

"I think some of it was part of my native structure."
[On not retaliating when a white women slapped an 8-year old Dr. King for allegedly stepping on her foot]

Dr. Martin Luther King Jr.

In the nineteen thirties, a strict system of segregation existed in Atlanta, USA. A black child could not go swimming or play in the public park. By virtue of his skin color, he could not get himself a good education at any so called 'white school'. In many of the stores downtown, a black man could not go to a lunch counter to buy a hamburger or a cup of coffee. He could not attend any of the theatres. There were one or two theatres open to black people, but they played only old movies.

In Dr. Martin Luther King's preschool years, his closest playmate was a white boy whose father owned a store across the street from the Kings home. In September 1935, the two friends entered school—separate schools, the young King noticed. He attended Younge Street Elementary School with Christine, and there was not a single white child there. Then the parents of young King's white friend announced that King could no longer play with their son.

"But why?" he sputtered.

1. DEPARTURE

"Because we are white and you are coloured," he was told.

A deeply distressed young King confided in his parents what had happened, and for the first time his parents told him about "the race problem" in America. They recounted to him the history of slavery in America, told him how it had ended with Abraham Lincoln and the Civil War, and explained how Whites eventually maintained their superiority by segregating "negroes" and making them feel like slaves everyday of their lives.

Yet King's mother counselled him, "You must never feel that you are less than anybody else. You must always feel that you are *somebody*." He did feel that he was somebody. Everyone around him used to note how smart and sensitive he was and praised him for his extraordinary ways. Yes, he had an idea he was somebody. Still, this race trouble was disturbing.

"As my parents discussed some of the tragedies that had resulted from this problem and some of the insults they themselves had confronted on account of it, I was greatly shocked, and from that moment on I was determined to hate every white person," Dr. King noted in his autobiography.

As with other black children of the time, young King's true education was to learn in countless painful ways what it meant to be Black in white America. He found out that he—a preacher's boy—could not buy a Coke or hamburger at the downtown stores. He could not event sit at the lunch counters there. He had to drink from a "coloured" water fountain, relieve himself in a rancid "coloured" restroom, and ride a rickety "coloured" freight elevator. White drugstores and soda fountains, if they served him at all, made him stand at a side window for ice cream, which came to him in a paper cup. White people, of course, got to eat their ice cream out of dishes. If he rode a city bus, he had to sit in the back as though he was contaminated. If he wanted to see a new movie in a downtown theatre, he had to enter through a side door and sit in the "coloured section" in the back balcony. Of course, he could always go to the decrepit "coloured" movie house, with its old films and faded and fluttering screen.

Young Martin Luther King Jr. discovered that Whites referred to Blacks as "boys" and "girls" regardless of age. He saw 'WHITES ONLY' signs staring back at him almost everywhere: in the windows of barber shops and all the good restaurants and hotels, at the YMCA, the city parks, golf courses, and swimming pools, and in the waiting rooms of train and bus stations. Young King found that there were even white and black sections of Atlanta and that he resided in "nigger town".

Somewhere around the same time, young King made a trip to a downtown shoe store with his father. They had sat down in the first empty seats of the front of the store when a young white store clerk came up to them and spoke politely, "I'll be happy to wait on you if you will just move to those seats in the rear," he pointed towards the seats in the back of the shop.

Father King immediately retorted, "There's nothing wrong with these seats. We're quite comfortable here."

"Sorry," said the clerk, "but you will have to move."

We'll either buy shoes sitting here," responded father King, "or we won't buy shoes at all."

Whereupon, father King took the young boy by his hand and walked out of the store. This was the first time that King had seen his dad so furious. This event played a huge role in shaping young King's conscience.

1. DEPARTURE

As they walked down the street, father King muttered, "I don't care how long I have to live with this system, I will never accept it." And he never did.

Segregation caused a tension in young King, a tension between his mother's injunction (remember, you are *somebody*) and a system that demeaned and insulted him every day, saying, "You are less than, you are not equal to."

x   x   x

"IT WAS PART OF MY NATIVE STRUCTURE"

When Dr. King was eight, he was inside a store in downtown Atlanta when suddenly he got slapped on his face. He only remembered hearing somebody scream, "You are that nigger that stepped on my foot." It turned out to be a white lady, who seemed to have believed that young King stepped on her foot. Young King did not retaliate; in fact, he would not have dared to retaliate when a white person was involved.

"It was part of my native structure," is how Dr. King explained it off when he was older. He was never one to hit back, however when his mother learned of what happened, she was deeply upset about what happened to King. She took young King by his hand and immediately left the store. The incident left a deep dent in King's heart that as a civil rights leader he still remembered the event clearly and felt that was an important part of his formative experiences.

At the age of fourteen, King was faced with an experience that made him "the angriest I have ever been" in his own words. During his second year in high school, he won an oratory contest that gave him the opportunity to represent his school in a state-wide contest in Dublin, Georgia. King was starting to show signs of public speaking gifts that would in a few years rouse a whole race across the globe.

On his way back from the Dublin speaking contest, young King experienced firsthand the kind of senseless, painful humiliation against which his father and grandfather and others in his family had been speaking out against for many years. The white bus driver cursed King and his fellow black students for attempting to sit in seats reserved for white passengers. King was ordered by the bus driver to vacate his seat for some white passengers who had just boarded the bus. King was not quick enough to leave his seat to the satisfaction of the driver. A deeply offended King wanted to stay right in his seat, but his speech coach urged him to obey the law and concede his seat to a white man. That night King traveled standing up in the aisle of the bus for ninety minutes. Years later, King was still haunted by the injustice. Much later, in an interview in 1965, King said that it was the night that he was the angriest in his life.[V]

Just before joining college, King took a summer job on a tobacco farm in Simsbury, Connecticut, USA. Until that moment in life, King had never thought that a black man could eat anywhere. In Connecticut, he could eat in the finest restaurants sitting alongside white people.

At the end of that summer, King faced an experience that created in his heart the ideal for his future civil rights struggle. He took a train back to Atlanta. During that trip, he could sit anywhere he wished until he got to Washington. However, in Washington he had move to a segregated car in order to continue the trip to Atlanta. He had to tolerate separate waiting rooms, separate eating places and separate rest rooms.

1. DEPARTURE

"Seated on the other side of a segregated curtain in the same dining car, I felt as if the curtain had been dropped on my selfhood," is what Dr. King wrote in his autobiography referring back to that incident.

Having stood on the very spot in Atlanta where Whites had lynched a Black, and having witnessed night-riding Klu Klux Klansmen beat Blacks in the streets, and having seen "with my own eyes" white cops brutalize Black children, when his parents admonished him to love Whites because it was his Christian duty, a young King asked defiantly: "How can I love a race of people who hate me?" [VI] [VII]

Each one of you is endowed with numerous talents and skills. Yet, your talents and skills are just enablers of your purpose in life. What then truly orients and energizes you towards your Life Purpose? What truly constitutes your Unique Gift that awaken and inspire you towards your Life Purpose?

Your Unique Gift is the set of your *life-defining experiences*. The set of *life-defining experiences* that you have experienced is unique to you among all the seven billion others on this planet. These life-defining experiences are almost always deeply upsetting. Mandela grew up as a persona of African royalty. In his childhood years, he listened to his parents tell him glorious African tales, and listened to his father, Chiefs, and elders recite orally their proud history. He grew up listening to his father's stories of historic battles and heroic Xhosa warriors, and his mother would enchant him with Xhosa legends and fables. These tales usually contained morals of dignity, sacrifice and generosity. Having grown up that way and then being disgraced by the inequality of the 'real' world deeply upset him.

You might not see your *life-defining experiences* as blessings at the moment you are being subject to those experiences. They can appear as traumas, or illnesses, or handicaps of other kinds.

Often your *life-defining experiences* appear not just as experiences, but packages of transformational lessons. The Being Leaders had chosen to seize lessons from each profound experience they went through. They looked at their experiences—even the negative ones—as opportunities to learn and grow. Growing up in his father's farm, Abraham Lincoln was treated as a voiceless slave. Lincoln's father used to beat him around for trivial offences, mentally abuse him and used to treat him like a slave. That experience made him abhor the idea of slavery. In the words of Michael Burlingame, author of "The Inner world of Abraham Lincoln", "One of the main reasons Lincoln hated slavery so much is because he hated the way his father treated him as a boy."

Gandhi's Unique Gift was the experience he had in his early years of persisting against his family's and community's will to follow his own dream, plus the telling experiences he faced in his young years in South Africa. Those *life-defining experiences* outraged him enough to take action against the ruling Afrikaners while in South Africa and later against the ruling British in colonial India.

For Dr. King, the humiliation he had to endure growing up in a segregated world propelled him to mobilise the Civil Rights movement.

All these *life-defining experiences* had a painful impact on the Being Leaders' pure, pristine minds. You could say that in the absence of these experiences, the Being Leaders may not have chosen the paths they eventually undertook. And that is why the *life-defining experiences* are your true Unique Gift.

How you apply your Unique Gift depends entirely upon you. Many of you would simply keep your Unique Gift aside and live a worldly life of

1. DEPARTURE

compliance and certainty. Such individuals simply follow the script that society has written for them. They keep a sharp lookout for jobs that are promising, and accordingly train themselves. In some cases, it brings them significant material and relational success. They smartly navigate through the challenges that come their way, carefully avoiding any landmine that might rock their neatly setup way of life.

Yet, there is a light within them that never gets ignited. The thrill of applying their Unique Gift is lost to them, because they have got caught in the social stream, and they do not seize the opportunities presented to them to express and utilize their Unique Gift.

You do not fully express your Unique Gift unless you take on the challenges that come your way. You may slow down in order to gather your strength, but your sight remains set on that challenge. And once you have mastered that challenge, you Unique Gift shines more. It becomes a part of you.

Summary: The Unique Gift you possess is not your skills or your talents. Standing apart, each of your skills and talents are all commonly found across many people. Even within an organization, you find numerous individuals possessing the same skills. Yes, you can package all your skills and talents together and come away feeling unique. Yet what propels you to make a true difference and leave behind a Noble Legacy[5] is your *life-defining experiences.* Your *life-defining experiences* is your true Unique Gift.

---

[5] Noble Legacy will be dealt with in chap. 13, 'YOU ARE THE SUM OF EVERYTHING YOU HAVE DONE', pg. 223

4. THE FIERY ORDEAL THROUGH WHICH THE BEING LEADERS PASS

"The true measure of a man is not how he behaves in moments of comfort and convenience but how he stands at times of controversy and challenges."

Dr. Martin Luther King Jr.

In 1964, Nelson Mandela and his political comrades were moved to the prison on Robben Island. The conditions that awaited them there were unimaginable. Mandela's cell, like the others in B section, was no more than about seven feet square. A barred window looked out on to a cement courtyard and beyond it to a high wall patrolled by guards. The walls of the cell were damp. There was no bed. Mandela was provided with a sisal mat on which to sleep, three flimsy blankets, a toilet bucket and a plastic bottle of water. In the winter months, his cell was so cold he slept fully dressed in prison garb. When Mandela complained about the dampness of his cell, he was told by a prison official, "The dampness of the cells will eventually be absorbed by your bodies."

"The worst part of imprisonment is being locked up by yourself. You come face to face with time and there is nothing more terrifying than to be alone with sheer time. Then the ghosts come crowding in: they can be sinister, very mischievous, raising a thousand doubts in your mind about the people outside, their loyalty. Was your sacrifice worth the

1. DEPARTURE

trouble? What would your life have been like if you hadn't got involved?" Mandela wrote in a manuscript while in prison.

The crushing effects of the prison system on Robben Island only got Mandela to further doubt his previous choices. The burden to carry was not just constant abuse from warders and hardship at work, but the sheer tedium of prison routine, which was guaranteed to crush the spirit. Prison routine stretched for ever into the distance, week after week, month after month, year after year. Prisoners reporting sick were often turned away by hospital orderlies, castigated for laziness when they were seriously ill; some gained admission to hospital only when it was too late to save them.

For him, the first weeks were particularly difficult. Prisoners in the isolation section of the prison were subjected to rigid control, their every move dictated by a posse of warders ready to pounce on any infringements of the regulations. The routine was deadening. The morning bell rang at 05:30 am. At inspection after breakfast, prisoners were required to doff their cloth caps to warders as they passed by. If the buttons on their canvas jackets were undone or if they failed to doff their caps, they were punished with either loss of meals or solitary confinement.

Nelson Mandela and the other political prisoners were automatically given the lowest classification, category D, according them a minimum of privileges. Category D prisoners were allowed to have only one visitor every six months and to write and receive only one letter during the same period. Sometimes letters were handed over so heavily censored that they made no sense, sometimes they were never handed over at all. With no means of solace, prisoners suffered in anguish and despair.

Mandela and his fellow political prisoners were kept away from all other groups of prisoners, isolating them like lepers. They were made to march each day twenty minutes towards the center of the island into a quarry. The glare from the white lime caused them severe problems. "The reflection from the lime catches the sunlight and throws it back on to you and it can be extremely sharp and scorching," said Mac Maharaj, a political activist who spent twelve years on the island. Mandela and his fellow political prisoners suffered the terrible torment at the lime quarry for thirteen years.

To break the will and resistance of the prisoners, the prison authorities maintained an arbitrary system of dispensing punishments. This caused severe anxiety and resentment among the prisoners. "Except for the brutality of assaults," wrote Neville Alexander, another fellow political prisoner of Mandela, "no other facet of life and experience on Robben Island caused so much bitterness." Some prisoners were sent into solitary confinement, sometimes for periods as long as six months for trivial actions. Cell raids and body searches in the cells became more frequent and more aggressive. Increasingly, rigorous censorship was applied to reading material and to letters. Outgoing letters were confiscated, recreational facilities were drastically curtailed and food rations were cut.

The kitchens on Robben Island were notorious not just for turning out food that was barely edible but also for corruption. They were manned by common-law convicts who ensured that the tastiest foods were kept back for themselves, their friends and the warders who supervised them. The official rations allowed to prisoners were meagre enough, but what emerged from the kitchens was even less adequate. "Lunch and supper, especially the supper of African prisoners, were sometimes so full of sand and miscellaneous kinds of dirt and insects that even the strong stomachs of the most hard-bitten would somersault," said Neville Alexander. "Hungry people would sometimes leave food uneaten."

Around them, the Atlantic winds were so severe sweeping across Robben Island during the winter of 1964 that prisoners working in the

1. DEPARTURE

quarries were numbed to the bone, hardly able to raise their picks; at night they huddled together in groups, desperate for warmth. In cold winter nights, prisoners were kept standing naked for an hour while their cells were searched. "They stripped me and told me to put my hands against the wall," recalled Sisulu, a fellow political prisoner of Mandela. "I was worried because I had flu. I thought that their plan might be that I become ill and eventually die."

What Mandela and his comrades had to face at the hands of the authorities created outrage among human rights champions. Subjected to solitary confinement and prolonged interrogation, allowed no visitors or reading material except the Bible, detainees were constantly taunted with the threat that they could be held in such conditions indefinitely. Their 'cracking point' varied. To hold together their sanity, many on Robben Island relied on the visits of priests on Sundays. However, for the first two years that Mandela was on the island, prisoners were confined to their cells while the priests preached from the head of the corridor.

Writing of her own experience of being held incommunicado for 117 days, Ruth First, a member of the Communist Party's central committee, noted, "Men holding key positions in the political movement, who had years of hard political experience and sacrifice behind them, cracked like eggshells. Others, with quiet, reticent, self-effacing natures, who had been woolly in making decisions and slow to carry them out, emerged from long spells of isolation shaken."

Where interrogation methods failed, torture usually succeeded. "Under torture," said Ben Turok, an anti-Apartheid activist and a member of the African National Congress "many victims found to their regret that they knew too much and that the police knew that they knew".

In prison, occasionally the prison authorities ordered a carry-on—a mass assault—on the prisoners. This was specifically targeted at those who chose to complain or rebel against the prison regime. Prisoners were often severely injured—and sometimes even hospitalized—in the beatings.

"We saw dozens of prisoners running wild or crawling vainly under barbed-wire fences while the batons, staves and pick-handles of the warders fell indiscriminately and mercilessly," a prisoner who had just arrived on Robben Island wrote.

The Afrikaner warders regarded themselves as members of a master race and accordingly required prisoners to adopt a servile manner. They insisted on being addressed as 'baas'—for 'boss'—and referred contemptuously to prisoners as 'kaffirs', 'hotnots' and 'koelies'. Their objective was to destroy the morale of the prisoners, to strip them of dignity and self-respect.

The warders in general were mean and brutal towards Mandela and his fellow political prisoners. One of the warders in particular, van Rensburg, who sported a swastika tattoo on his wrist, enforced much harsher discipline. He stood close to the prisoners, constantly shouting at them to work harder and accusing anyone he considered was not exerting himself of 'malingering'. All this was accompanied by a stream of racial abuse.

On one occasion, Mandela was once caught in his cell reading a newspaper left behind by a guard. He was so engrossed in the paper that he failed to hear the footsteps of an approaching officer. It cost him three days in isolation on a diet of rice water.

Family was one of the most painful thoughts that stole Mandela's sleep while he was in prison. Winnie appeared to Mandela to be under tremendous strain. He had known that his imprisonment would leave her exposed to hardships and hazards with few sources of support.

1. DEPARTURE

Banning orders restricted Winnie's movements severely, and stripped her off her dignity. She was forced to leave her job as a social worker with the Child Welfare Society in Johannesburg. She took a succession of other jobs, working in a furniture shop, a dry-cleaning shop and a shoe repair shop, but at each place she was fired after security police paid a visit to her employers. She was repeatedly charged, often for no more than trivial infringements.

In May 1969, in the middle of the night, the security police arrested Winnie at her home in Orlando, detaining her under the new Terrorism Act, which enabled them to imprison her without charge and without any access to legal representation, in solitary confinement, indefinitely.

Winnie's troubles were only compounded by her impetuous and headstrong nature. "She wouldn't cooperate with anyone. She refused to take advice," recalled Rusty Bernstein, a fellow fighter against Apartheid. "She was an individual piece of militancy, a rogue element." Winnie also had a propensity for becoming involved with shady characters. In Mandela's absence, she maintained a long friendship with Maude Katzellenbogen, the partner of a corrupt Indian businessman. This relationship gave added ammunition to the Afrikaner police to harass her and add more agony for Mandela.

There was nothing that Mandela could do from Robben Island to curb Winnie's wayward conduct. It tore him apart to hear about the trouble created by Winnie, and the trouble it got her into. He blamed himself for being unable to offer her the protection she evidently needed, and his sense of guilt and frustration mounted as the security police instigated a campaign of persecution against Winnie which continued year after year.

Mandela had been tormented by Winnie's imprisonment. He later described it as a desperately distressing experience, more difficult to contend with than anything else he had known in prison. He spent sleepless nights worrying about her plight, worrying too about who was looking after his daughters.

Mandela heard that his two daughters Zeni and Zindzi, aged ten and nine, watched as their mother was taken away. The security police had turned their attention to his two daughters. They had been tossed about in the turmoil of their parents' lives. Both had been deeply affected by the succession of raids, arrests, imprisonments and dark dramas that beset their parents. At the young age of twelve, Mandela's daughter Zindzi wrote to the UN Special Committee on Apartheid in anguish: "Hardly a month goes by without the newspapers reporting some incident concerning Mummy, and her friends and family feel that the public is being conditioned to expect something terrible to happen to her. I know my father, who is imprisoned for life on Robben Island, is extremely concerned about my mother's safety, and has done everything in his power to appeal to the government to give her protection, but without success."

The anguish that Mandela suffered on learning of these events was acute. "To see your family, your children, being persecuted when you are absolutely helpless in jail, that is one of the most bitter experiences, most painful experiences I have had," Mandela recalled.

It did not end there. In 1968, on a day after he had returned from a gruelling day in the lime quarry, a warder, James Gregory, handed him a telegram. It was from Makgatho, Mandela's son, telling him that his mother had died of a heart attack. Mandela sought permission from the authorities to attend her funeral in the Transkei, but was refused. He was torn by the thought how little he has been there for his mother, and his heart wept with the thought of how little he has done for her.

"Her difficulties, her poverty, made me question once again whether I had taken the right path," Mandela wrote in his autobiography. "That

1. DEPARTURE

was always the conundrum: had I made the right choice in putting the people's welfare even before that of my own family?"

An even more painful blow came the following year when another telegram arrived from Makgatho, this time saying that Thembi, his eldest son, had been killed in a car accident. James Gregory, who brought the news to him recalled the moment: "In his eyes I could see the sternness I was to recognize when he struggled to maintain self-control. It was a distancing from me and from others, and in some ways his face receded into a fixed expression, tight lines around his mouth. Those lines always went deeper the more worried, sad or angry he became. At that time, he simply said, 'Thank you, Mr Gregory,' and walked away."

Mandela was devastated by the news. He returned to his cell and stood before the barred window looking out torn and weeping in his heart. He did not emerge for dinner. A night warder later reported that throughout the night he stood before the window, staring out, not moving.

An anguished Mandela wrote the following words to a friend: "I have lost both Thembi and Ma, and I must confess that the order that had reigned in my soul has almost vanished."

Utterly lost in will and suffering from the pain of helplessness, Mandela listlessly digested all the news about his family being harassed and tortured. He dreaded that a horrifying fate, deadlier than his, was awaiting his family.[VIII]

4.1.   ORDEAL OF THE WARRIOR MAN

All your experiences are essential to your awakening. They help you present yourself in unique ways in the lives of those around you. They give you the tools and resources you need to become who you are destined to be. Your experiences are little gems you collect in order to cash in at later stages to become who you are to become. Look at your experiences as feathers in your wings that help you soar out of your future adversities.

Many of these experiences might feel painful at the time you go through it. In the midst of pain, it is difficult to see your experiences for what they really are: lessons. Because of this difficulty, you will act or react upon them in fallible ways. And that in turn will trigger a whole sequence of fallible responses from the world around you. Until eventually the whole interaction will snowball into another overwhelming experience. And you get trapped in it so deep that there seems like there is no escape. Only some life-altering event—like an illness, an unexpected death in the family or marital separation—will get you out of that illusory life. When you refuse to learn the life-lessons from these profound experiences, similar experiences will recur and dominate your life. Seemingly painful experiences will appear and reappear with increased intensity in your life.

Call it good fortune or conscious choice, the Being Leaders embraced the lessons destined for them. Prison gave time for Mandela to reflect on the purpose of pain. It was easy for Mandela to shutout his traumatic experiences in prison and condemn the jail warders. After all, most other prisoners were coping with their challenges by accusing and rebelling against the warders. Yet for Mandela—as well as the other Being Leaders—traumatic experiences were a source of understanding; of the self and others.

1. DEPARTURE

Imagine Mandela's life on Robben island. For most of his years in prison, he believed that his fate was sealed. That he would live the rest of his life in prison and die dreaming of his ideal. Outside, Apartheid was raging. The Afrikaners were increasingly consolidating their network and resources. Their might only seemed to be growing, and they were getting more assured in their suppression of the Blacks.

We attract experiences with life-lessons in them. Sometimes those lessons appear in the form of people who correspond to our thinking. Our character projects, and before we know we find ourselves in the presence of those who mirror us in morals, character and attitude. The Being Leaders have recognized that the best way to attract those with high ideals and fierce passion into their movement was to themselves embody those principles. Thus without any laborious effort, they attracted talented individuals their way.

I have come across several organizations who have set out the noble intention of attracting individuals of specific qualities. Many of these organizations have also themselves put to practice these qualities. When I walked into the office of one such organization that offers remote help service for the elderly, the character of service was instantly visible to me. Their clients were invisible to them, but their attitude of service was no less evident. When I took a seat in the lobby, no less three individuals—two women and one man—passed by enquiring if I am served and if I would like a drink or other refreshment. This example reminds me of their passion for sincere service and how they chose to consciously attract the experiences they desired. This they did by living the values they aimed to attract. Needless to say, the company was coveted by its clients, and they were hugely profitable.

Life endows you with the experiences you need in order to flourish on your purpose. At the time of the experience, it might seem to you as if it was a grave necessity to live through that phase in order to stay afloat or keep your head above water. But the richness of that experience is bound to leave an indelible mark upon you. It might be much later before the time comes for you to dig deep into your quiver of lessons.

In 1970, a very ruthless officer, Colonel Piet Badenhorst, was appointed as the prison officer on Robben Island to enforce a tougher regime and to stamp out all signs of prisoner resistance[6]. Two years of unspeakable brutality later, Colonel Badenhorst was transferred. In a setting like that—bleak with no hope of ever experiencing physical freedom— Mandela was faced with two choices; one was to continue to argue with, revolt against and belittle the prison guards and officers. This he did in his early years in prison. The second choice was to make his peace with where he was in his life. That involved understanding the reality of the life of a prisoner and that of the officers. Instead of seeing Badenhorst as a brute, Mandela believed that "their inhumanity had been put upon them. They behaved like beasts because they were rewarded for such behaviour. They thought it would result in a promotion or advancement." Through all of this practice that cost him years, Mandela started to find forgiveness in his heart for his oppressors (we will study this quality in detail in chap. 20, 'CAPACITY FOR COMPASSION AND FORBEARANCE').

He began taking advantage of his experience in prison by engaging more earnestly with his fellow prisoners. He started to motivate prisoners to learn and earn certifications through distance learning programmes. He taught fellow prisoners. In order to understand the reality of the prison officers, he started to practice Afrikaans, learn Afrikaner history and literature, and understand their culture and passions. He made it a point to understand rugby. Rugby was a collective passion of the prison officers and the Afrikaner race in whole. He studied the history that shaped the hopes and fear of Afrikaners. He forced himself to understand the circumstances that turned the Afrikaners brutal.

---

[6] See chap. 20, 'CAPACITY FOR COMPASSION AND FORBEARANCE', pg. 325

1. DEPARTURE

Today we are able to look back and connect the dots. We can clearly see where Mandela learned the incomparable lessons of building bridges and forging partnerships even with the enemies. From his traumatic experiences in prison, one among the many glorious leadership traits about Mandela that stand out as an inspiration to humanity is his ability to say "I understand why the Afrikaners acted the way they did. Let bygones be bygones."

4.2. "I AM NOT GOOD ENOUGH"

In the face of the tragedies, tears and tumult of dear ones, Dr. King felt himself inadequate to lead a movement as vast and life-transforming as the civil rights movement. "He felt he was not good enough," said Rev. C.T. Vivian, a close friend of Dr. King and a leader of the movement.

On Sunday, September 15th, 1963, a group of white supremacists bombed the Sixteenth Street Baptist church in Birmingham, Alabama. When the bombs went off, walls blew out, stained glass windows shattered, the face of Jesus was blown out and songbooks lay scattered. Four little girls were killed in the blast, deeply shocking the whole nation.

When the news of the bombing reached Dr. King, he was thrown into self-doubt. "Were these sacrifices of innocent lives worth standing against a discriminatory system?" he wondered to his closest associates. He was himself ready to lay down his life for a higher cause, so were his associates. However, four young innocent girls murdered by white supremacists in order to halt the civil rights movement scarred the collective conscience of a concerned nation. There were constant accusations from detractors of the civil rights movement that the fault behind the bombing lay with Dr. King and the activists. They were told on their faces that they have stirred up trouble. Wherever the activists went, people were yelling at them that it was their fault that they were working with this preacher, Dr. King, who was fomenting trouble. Receiving such accusation from the very people who Dr. King was fighting for and making infinite sacrifices for, deeply hurt Dr. King. He asked himself whether he was up for this challenge. "Was all those deaths worth it?" he wondered.

"I shall never forget the grief and bitterness I felt on that terrible September morning. I think of how a woman cried out crunching through broken glass. 'My God, we're not even safe in church!' I think of how that explosion blew that face of Jesus Christ from a stained glass window. I can remember thinking, was it all worth it? Was there any hope?" Dr. King lamented.

Dr. King was chosen to give the eulogy. That Sunday after he gave the eulogy for the four girls with a heavy heart, he was leaning backwards deeply hurt, exhausted, resigned and in tears. He was devastated and he felt as if the whole world had collapsed around him. His heart was deeply wrenched by the heaviness of the responsibility that he had taken upon his shoulders. He was enveloped in a deep sense of hopelessness and wondered if the cause of racial equality was a lost cause. In anguish, he doubted if it was the destiny of the American Blacks to remain condemned as second class citizens in their own country of birth forever.

In the words of his close family friend, a white woman called Deenie Drew, "On the day of the burial (of the four little girls killed in that bombing) he could hardly walk down the church aisle. His back was stiff and leaning backwards."

When Dr. King and fellow activists were headed home later that night, Deenie spoke to Dr. King, "Mikey (a nickname for Dr. King), I thought I'd

1. DEPARTURE

have to come down there and help you. You looked like you were going to fall over backwards!"

"Deenie," Dr. King responded, feeling heavy and in pain, "the way the world was on me, I wondered about my responsibility. Whether or not I'm really right. How could I know?"

In the departure phase, the Being Leaders also went through a time of confusion and self-doubt. This is what you face at the gateway of a life transformation. Life seems gloomy and meaningless and you struggle to hold on to hope. You experience a strong urge to go back to your old ways, even when you have reaffirmed to yourself several times that the old ways do not serve you well anymore. The fear that the uncertainty raises within you urges you to retreat into your old life. Compared to the rolling and pitching of the rough sea of transformation, the solid shore of the old times might seem welcoming.

Self-doubt is a consequence of the battle between something that you love and something you fear. The fear could be the fear of failure, it could be the fear of not living up to the task. In the case of the Being Leaders, at a certain moment, circumstances conspired to strip away everything that they relied on over their entire lives. Despite struggling in the midst of that experience, the Being Leaders carried an intense love and passion for the cause of righting a wrong. This love and passion was countered by a fear about the magnitude of the step they were taking. The obstacles to overcome and the hearts to convert seemed daunting or nearly impossible.

Self-doubt involves darkness and depression that whatever you try is weighed down by a heavy burden. That nothing seem to work out. That all avenues you pursue are either dead ends or turn out to be meaningless. That it feels like all others around you seem to have got it right, and you are the only stupid one without all the answers. This self-doubt will eat away at you. You will go from one teacher or coach to the other. In each case, you will only see the negatives of that individual. Or you will question the source of their knowledge. You might feel that they are either untrained or naive in the ways of the world.

So you will drift again until you reach your next resource. It could be a new book, or a teacher, or a coach, or a new school of wisdom. There again you will encounter the same inner demons. This pattern is characteristic of a leader in departure.

X   X   X

Included at the core of each Being Leader's journey towards inner mastery is the mastery of shame. Shame is an affliction of the 'being'. What blocks you from being your authentic self is shame expressing within you. You feel that you are not worthy of the best, and others will act in response to that belief. Thus your inner belief of your unworthiness will shape events in your life, and these events in turn will further reinforce your notion of self unworthiness. Unchecked, this vicious cycle would continue expressing forever in the form of self-doubt.

Throughout the early stages of their activism, the Being Leaders have carried the unconscious or conscious belief that there is something wrong with them. Circumstances often worked to reinforce this notion. Dr. King sometimes expressed that he was not good enough. Gandhi noted that he was inadequate by any normal social standard. Lincoln famously spoke of himself as "a piece of driftwood" that had drifted into his role.

1. DEPARTURE

In my work with leaders I have found that those who have mastered their shame are the ones who would eventually elevate themselves to become transformational leaders. Shame is a demon that they must slay in order to reclaim the immense power of their true being. And once achieved, it leads to an unparalleled level of mastery that is within reach for each human. It involves having to go beyond their past conditioning and reclaiming their self-worth. It involves learning to love oneself again and believing again in their own immense power.

When I first met Todd (name changed), he was a mid-level leader in a provincial party in Canada. What struck me most about him was the self-defeated energy he carried about himself. He was seeing a coach, and he told me that he was resigned about his development process. Beneath his strong facade, there was a visible streak of vulnerability when he spoke about himself.

For the past four years, he had been stuck at his current level of contribution and position. Any amount of effort or training was not helping him create new impact in his personal or professional spheres. The previous two years, he found himself orienting more of his attention and effort to volunteering and philanthropy, finding greater meaning in contributing his extensive experience and exceptional talents to small-scale organizations seeking to stay relevant.

After spending twelve years within the same organization, Todd had lost trust in his ability to lift himself out of his disillusionment and his strength to reinvent himself. When he first started within this leading political organization, he was quickly labelled one of the promising stars of the future. He came with an optimism of making a huge impact within the organization. Seven years later, he was relegated into a lonely corner within the organization, thoroughly disillusioned with the course of the party.

The Fiery Ordeal

"We were filled with a post-war generation of men who were more consumed with themselves and their move up than with the core purpose of the organization. In my early days I was appalled by how little they were concerned about the citizenry, and their planning was limited to elections. They were least concerned with the real social concerns of the time. For an organization that was about people, there was limited defence for humanitarian policies. It frustrated me," Todd lamented.

After years of attempting several new roles within the same hierarchy, he and his organization had given up on his prospect for growth. First he was entrusted with the role of partnerships with coalition partners. Eighteen months later he was moved into community organizing, primarily responsible for protecting citizens' property rights against corporate encroachment. For a while, he was involved in Native welfare. He also spent time growing the party within certain regions.

Having failed to make any significant impact, Todd was a thoroughly defeated man, devoid of any zest for life and with no prospects of a new career. His allegiance still lay with the political ideologies of his party, and he could not see himself in a different field. His relationship with his wife was seriously fractured, and twice he had ridden himself into debts gambling. Within his organization, he was twice sanctioned for being involved in relational breakdowns, once with a friendly labour union representative and another time with a group of donors.

A week before we first met, his organization had asked him to hand in his resignation and seek a new job outside the organization within sixty days. No amount of effort could make Todd conceal his emotions behind a mask. On our first appointment, he did not succeed in disguising his unconscious signs of anger, bitterness, loneliness or despair. He built around himself a mask of self-discipline, steeling himself to face whatever ordeal his resignation would bring. He distrusted emotion, prizing cold reason and logic as a coping mechanism. Time and again, he tried to hold back his anguish when he spoke with me.

"It requires all my self-discipline not to lose my mind and do something drastic," he sighed.

Every single awakened leader I have met has found himself in such a deflated place at some point of his journey of reclaiming his true being.

4.3.   BATTLE OF THE SELVES

Lincoln's greatest fear about not being re-elected as president—not because his legacy would be hurt, nor his livelihood threatened—was that his arch nemesis McClellan would arrive at a truce with the South that will split the Union and take the Blacks back into slavery.

On the one hand, Lincoln wanted to see the slaves free, but on the other hand he felt that putting the Whites and Blacks together would lead to them slitting each others throats. Upon him was vested the great powers to hold the Union together while there was a majority of his friends and party men from the North who did not want anything to do with the freed Blacks. He sunk into deep inner turmoil confronted by the choices of his heart and his fellowmen, those very close to him and his essential allies. He remained wrenched by his noble principles and his lowly existential concerns.

In the midst of the civil rights movement, Dr. King went through severe inner conflict. His doctrines of equality, justice and non-violence in life were over and over again tested.

The Fiery Ordeal

Dr. King felt that beyond the race question, America had to deal with the question of violence. "We could not solve problems in America or in the world through violence. We had to find ways to resolve conflicts without destroying persons or property," Dr. King reminded America.

In Canton, Mississippi, Dr. King and a group of civil rights activists had gathered for a peaceful meeting in a school yard to talk to all the people who had joined for the march. Among others, Dr. King was also scheduled to speak. As the gathering got stronger, singing and chanting, state troopers started to line up in full battle gear and tear gas masks, carrying a mass of weapons.

Without any provocation the police starting tear gas. Everyone was humiliated, running for shelter in every direction. They tried to find protection in poor people's homes and churches. One journalist on the scene shared his observation about the police, "They came stomping in behind the gas, gun-butting and kicking the men, women, and children."

An indignant Dr. King declared, "this is one of the best expressions that I have ever seen of the fact that this is a police state. Mississippi is still evil. It is still the lowest and worst state in our Union. And we are again gonna make it clear that we ain't gonna be stopped."

Deeply frustrated, he thought at that moment that the country was not the country that he thought it was. The good America which would hear him, that there were darker parts of the country. He was wrestling with that.

The evening again he deeply doubted himself and his values. A part of him was seriously challenging his own belief, his bedrock of non-violence. He doubted if he could ever successfully counter violence with non-violence. That was a moment where he came close to embracing a path of violence to counter all the violence around him.

1. DEPARTURE

In 1893, during his first year in South Africa, Gandhi, aged 24, was travelling inland across the state of Natal by railway. European settlers in South Africa always travelled first class. Indians in South Africa were expected to travel third class, but Gandhi's employer had reserved a first-class seat for Gandhi.

On the day of his travel, Gandhi settled into the compartment comfortably and traveled alone until he reached the high mountain town of Maritzburg in the evening. There another passenger, a European, entered the compartment. He took one look at the dark-complexioned man seated in his compartment and left, only to return with the railway officials.

"You will have to leave here," one of them told Gandhi pointedly. "Go to the third-class car."

"But I have a ticket for this compartment," Gandhi objected.

"That doesn't matter. You must leave or I'll bring the police to put you out," the official responded.

"You may," Gandhi agreed heatedly. "But I have every right to stay here, and I refuse to get out voluntarily."

So the police arrived and Gandhi was pushed out of the train and left to spend the night sitting in the deserted, unlit railway station of Maritzburg. His overcoat and luggage had disappeared with the officials. It was bitter cold. He sat there alone, shivering in the darkness, struggling furiously to understand how anyone could find pleasure or satisfaction in causing suffering to others. It was not his own injury or humiliation that infuriated him; it was the much deeper cancer of man's inhumanity to man, the persecution of whole races because of differences in skin color or belief.

The Fiery Ordeal

By morning Gandhi had decided that to return to India would be cowardice. He would have to stay; there could be no turning back. He was compelled to act. The man who had been unable to talk in court to enhance his own career would find within himself the resource to speak and write and organize effectively to relieve the distress of others.

Much later, when someone asked Gandhi what was the most creative incident in his life, Gandhi told the story of this night in Maritzburg station. Over the years, he had to undergo many trials, suffer abuse and even physical attacks, but that long night in the Natal mountains he made the decision never to yield to force and never to use force to win a cause.[IX]

That long night in the empty train station in Maritzburg, Gandhi was torn between thoughts of violet retaliation and the ideal of peaceful mastery of the darkness that reigned in the hearts of the Afrikaner rulers of South Africa. The events that night made him look beyond himself for the first time, beyond his narrow interpretations and his private needs, and into the heart of the terrible suffering of his impoverished and exploited countrymen.

He doubted if there was any space for his noble ideals, and strongly felt that it would take brutal force to combat a much larger enemy.

x   x   x

Each of the Being Leaders went through a formative phase where they faced a prolonged inner battle between the noble ideals of his *unconditioned self* and the self-preserving emotions of his *conditioned self* (see chap. 7, 'LOOK IN THE MIRROR: SEE THE TWO SELVES', pg. 80 for detailed description of the *conditioned self* and the *unconditioned self*).

1. DEPARTURE

A young Mandela succumbed to the roar of his *conditioned self* and set out to bomb installations. This landed him in jail. It is when their paths forward seems dark and hopeless that the Being Leaders questioned their higher ideals.

Inner turmoil originates out of the conflicting voice between your *unconditioned self* and your *conditioned self*. The *unconditioned self* speaks through love and compassion, even for your enemies. Gandhi and Dr. King staunchly preached and practiced conquering their hate-filled enemies with love. This is the nature of the *unconditioned self*. The *unconditioned self* aspires for the collective good, and it aims to uphold the dignity of humans and others. It is motivated by its calling to make a difference and shape a Noble Legacy. This self and its attributes are constant to each of us.

The *conditioned self* speaks through fear and doubt. Self-preservation is its motive. Lincoln knew that many of his constituents and party members were not pleased with the prospect of co-existing in community with the freed slaves. That posed a real threat of the Union splintering if Lincoln would advance his ideals of racial equality. Due to this, Lincoln was highly tempted to overlook the whole idea of seeking freedom for the slaves.

The *conditioned self* is motivated by the prospect of achieving power and prestige. It propels you through fear, guilt and shame.

Those who are not well rooted in their higher ideals will find themselves caught in an inner turmoil of these two differing voices. Yet, the pathway to find that anchor is one of inner turmoil, as seen in the departure phase of the Being Leaders' lives.

4.4.   COPING WITH THE THROES OF DEPARTURE

The Being Leaders found various ways of coping with their inner pain. Lincoln relied heavily on humour. Lincoln was famed for his storytelling capabilities. When he ran a store in Springfield, Illinois, his store was a popular hangout for men in town. Lincoln was famed for his endless reservoir of stories, and he could trade, maintain accounts and tell stories at the same time. The other coping approach for Lincoln was reading poetry. He was renowned for staying up late into night reciting poetry to others, often many of them gloomy in nature.

Lincoln was also known to fall into "a sad terribly gloomy state—pick up a pen—sit down by the table and write a moment or two and then become abstracted." Whether due to his domestic unhappiness or due to the setbacks in his political career or due to his chronic worry that his opponent Stephen Douglas would legalize slavery in the north, or due to the severe setback that slavery would have on the free market system in Illinois, Lincoln would slip into depression. Herndon, Lincoln's law partner, would pull the curtain across the glass panel in the office and leave, locking the door behind him to protect the privacy of "this unfortunate and miserable man."

Gandhi went deeper and deeper into his spiritual practice as a means of coping with his inner crisis. His reading and his pursuit of the epics was another way for him to make sense out of an imbalanced world.

Having no one up close to support him, Gandhi dabbled in various religious beliefs all at once. He found himself spiritually uncommitted yet a serious and eclectic spiritual seeker. He got involved with Evangelicals to experience its merits and power. He spent a lot of his time with his White Evangelical friends and spent time attending daily prayers. He also got involved with the Esoteric Christian Union, which he called "a synthesizing school of beliefs that sought to reconcile all religions by showing that each represents the same eternal truths."

1. DEPARTURE

Gandhi also called himself an agent for the London Vegetarian Society. He also deeply delved into the wisdom of the Islamic practice.

Mandela's own vegetable garden on Robben Island—and later in Pollsmoor Prison—was his private space to connect with his own pain and confront his crisis. He carefully nurtured that space and used it to remain connected with himself in the midst of all the adversities in his life. No one was invited into that space, it was a time for him to reflect and find himself. That space helped him deal with his pain and crisis within.

In the midst of his deepest agony, Dr. King would go into prayer and reading. Prayer for him was his opening into his heart and accessing his deepest wounds. In his pain he saw the sacrifice of many before him and the noble intentions of many—both Blacks and Whites—who felt that the nation would never look equal in the eyes of God. In the life example of Jesus he found consolation for the sufferings that he and his fellow activists endured. During long hours, he would also talk extensively about his self-doubts and share his pain with his friends.

At different stages of their lives, when the Being Leaders started to realize the hardships of their paths, they sunk into a void where they were unreachable by those around them. They found different ways to console and comfort themselves, and deal with the uncertainties of life. This was a crucial phase for them. This time was not only a phase of silence, rather it was a time of inner dialogue and a time of reflection. It was a time of self-examination and confronting self-doubt.

II. PASSAGE:

The Practice and Preparation

"'Passage' is the arc of your process of integrating life's lessons." The teacher spoke to us, looking introspective. "It starts with understanding and end with apprenticing."

As I sat across the teacher, I could not contain the excitement of learning the various steps of initiation from an accomplished master.

This teacher had a reputation for having supported many renowned business and political leaders through their initiation. He carefully chose his protégés, and when he was not travelling supporting leaders, he led the life of a recluse.

This day I was there to learn about what the 'passage' phase entailed.

"Passage is a time of integration," he elaborated looking into the distance. "It is a time for understanding what the Universe is trying to tell you. Once you have departed from the old self, you are in a passage of sculpting the new, authentic you. In this phase, you become more aware of yourself and your core values."

"You have left the old shore and you are on your voyage. Sometimes the voyage would be on rough seas. There would be rolling and pitching. You will get thrown around and you might feel lost and unsettled." After a long pause he continued. "And that is OK. Continue with the learning. Don't seek the destination. Make the passage itself meaningful. The destination will unfold itself. You will know when you have reached the end of your 'passage'."

One of my fellow participants wanted to know if she could hold on to the past and still embrace the new.

"To usher in the new, you must make space in your lives," the teacher responded. "The old must be removed so that you can make room for

2. PASSAGE

the new. It is like the clearing an attic or basement. The clutter of the past must be eliminated so that we can welcome in the future."

To illustrate his point, he extended his right hand to receive her donation. As she dug out some cash and a bead chain as donation, he opened his palm. Just as she was about to place her donation on his palm, he swiftly with his left hand placed an apple on his extended palm. That confused her. There was no more space in his open palm for her donation.

He smiled comfortingly at her confusion. She got the message that he was trying to make. "The old must be removed so that you can make room for the new," the teacher repeated his previous statement again.

After a short break, we reconvened for a deeper understanding of the 'passage' phase. "Passage is also a time of apprenticing in life's lessons. This is the time to sharpen your teeth. You may have learned a few things, you still have to make those part of your new habit."

later, as we she stood up to leave, he shared the following quote attributed to MK Gandhi: "Watch your thoughts, they become words. Watch your words, they become actions. Watch your actions, they become habits. Watch your habits, they become your character. Watch your character, it becomes your destiny."

"This is your motive during the 'passage' phase," he stated as he slowly limped out of the room. "Take your time...take a whole lifetime if you need."

x   x   x

In this section of the book, we will look at some of the key lessons and practices that the Being Leaders embraced while in 'passage'.

There is an ancient Indian fable that tells the story of how the Gods arrived at a place to hide the Greatest Truth. Only those special souls who have truly earned it should find it, the Gods felt. So they asked suggestions from the various Gods. One God suggested that they hide it among the clouds, so that only those who are willing to rise up above the worldly realm could find it. Another God suggested that they bury it very deep in the earth so that it could be found only by those who have dug deep and got their hands dirty. Then a sagely God came up with a brilliant idea. He suggested that they hide the Greatest Truth inside man. That way the truth can be so close and feel so natural that man would not think of looking there to find it.

To claim a new you means to remain open to the new. Yet what you encounter in your passage is as old as time can be. You have already experienced your new truths in your olden days. Those truths are so natural that they are not just a part of you, they are you.

The chapters in the 'passage' section advocate a sort of reverse journey. You must reclaim the innocence you had as a child and release any inhibitions you may have acquired since being a child. That is when you throw open your heart to experimentation. The Being Leaders looked at life as a constant journey of experimentation. Each of their encounters exposed them to something sacred about human consciousness. What they learned, they also apprenticed on. In the chapter, 'Sharpening the teeth', you will see examples of how the Being Leaders used life as an apprenticeship towards something great.

In the 'passage' phase—and in the whole of life—perhaps the greatest elevation in their consciousness was their understanding of the self. Knowing the dual nature of the self, including the *conditioned* and the *unconditioned* natures, altered how they approached their life's calling. This we will study in chapter 7, 'LOOK IN THE MIRROR: SEE THE TWO SELVES'. The Being Leaders also developed the ability to have faith and

2. PASSAGE

operate in acceptance of a higher power. Internally, that meant knowing their true measure. Two chapters in this section examine these topics.

Mastering the idea of death awakens you to aliveness in life. Overcoming the fear of death, but also readying to the time of their passing was the last evident step of the Being Leaders' apprenticing that is examined in this section.

5. THE LABYRINTH BEING LEADERS WALKED

"Gandhi was a pioneer in these new realms of consciousness. Everything he did was an experiment in expanding the human being's capacity to love, and as his capacity grew, the demands on his love grew more and more severe, as if to test what limits a human being can bear. But Gandhi had learned to find a fierce joy in these storms and trials . . . By the end of his life he was aflame with love."

Eknath Easwaran (author of 'Gandhi, the Man')

His concern for racial and economic justice already high in college, Dr. Martin Luther King studied "On Civil Disobedience", an essay by Henry David Thoreau. This was his first encounter with the principle of non-violent resistance. This essay was a courageous refusal of a New Englander to pay taxes and instead go to jail than support a war that would spread slavery into Mexico. Deeply touched by the idea of non-cooperation with an evil system, Dr. King became convinced that non-cooperation with evil was as much a moral obligation as was cooperation with good.

Years later, the teachings of Thoreau came alive in the civil rights movement led by Dr. King. Whether expressed in a sit-in at lunch counters, a freedom ride into Mississippi, a peaceful protest in Albany, Georgia, or a bus boycott in Montgomery, Alabama, evil was resisted through non-cooperation.

2. PASSAGE

Later in 1948, when Dr. King entered the Crozer Theological Seminary in Chester, Pennsylvania, he started a serious study of the likes of Plato, Aristotle and Rousseau. All these masters stimulated Dr. King's thinking, and he learned a great deal from their works. He also found things to question in each of them.

Walter Rauschenbusch's Christianity and the Social Crisis gave Dr. King a theological basis to work against the social evils of the time. Rauschenbusch's teachings propounded that the gospel deals with the whole man—not only his soul but his body; not only his spiritual well-being but also his material well-being. At the same time, Dr. King struggled with Rauschenbusch's "cult of inevitable progress" and his identification of the Kingdom of God with social or economic systems.

In 1949, Dr. King spent his Christmas holidays studying Karl Marx and the principles of Communism. He carefully scrutinized *Das Kapital* and *The Communist Manifesto*. He also studied some interpretive works on the thinking of Marx and Lenin. He was drawn to the Communist ideals of an equal society and the upliftment of the less privileged. He noted that Communism grew as a protest against the hardships of the underprivileged. Communism in theory emphasized a classless society and a concern for social justice.

At the same time, Communism—avowedly secularist and materialistic—has no place for God. This Dr. King could not accept, for he believed that there was a creative power in this Universe who is the essence of all reality. All of humanity and history is ultimately guided by that Spirit. The absence of immutable principles and an absolute moral order within communist thinking, and the restrictions on personal expression also made it difficult for Dr. King to see Communism as a path towards racial justice and equality.

During that period in his life, Dr. King started to doubt the power of love in solving social problems. He felt that the ethic of love was only applicable to personal relationships. His faith in love was shaken by the philosophy of Nietzsche. He read parts of "The Genealogy of Morals" and the whole of "The Will to Power", and felt that Nietzsche minimized ordinary mortals. Any virtues of piety and humility, the otherworldliness of Christian morality, and the Christian attitude towards suffering seemed to Nietzsche as a glorification of weakness, as making virtues out of necessity and impotence.

Having grown up in strict fundamentalist tradition of Christianity, Dr. King was occasionally taken aback by the liberal interpretations of religion. However, the liberal interpretations gave him an intellectual satisfaction that he never found in fundamentalist practice of Christianity.

This inner dispute between the values of fundamentalism and liberalism took Dr. King through a state of transition in his belief. His upbringing was tainted by some of the vicious race problems that he faced as a child, and this experience was mixed with the orthodoxy of his practice. Liberalism, while being foreign to him, urged him to believe in the natural goodness of man and the natural power of human reason. However, his personal scars made it difficult for him to embrace such a belief. Dr. King noted in his autobiography, "the more I observed the tragedies of history and man's shameful inclination to choose the low road, the more I came to see the depths and strength of sin. Liberalism's superficial optimism concerning human nature caused it to overlook the fact that reason is darkened by sin."

Historically, liberalism had been all too sentimental about human nature. Dr. King was also part liberal. And that liberal in him made him see some noble possibilities in human nature and made him optimistic about human nature. Liberalism's devotion to the search for truth and its insistence on an open and analytical mind and its refusal to abandon the best light of reason attracted him to it. But he could never see pure fundamentalism or pure liberal as his doctrine in life.

2. PASSAGE

The pacifist position advocated by Dr. A.J. Muste seemed too idealistic and far from practical as a tool against evils. A young Dr. King felt that while war could never be a positive or absolute good, it could serve as a negative good in the sense of preventing the spread and growth of an evil force. He felt that war might still be preferable to surrender to a totalitarian regime like the Nazis or Fascists. This feeling was only reinforced when he for the first time came in touch with the works of Reinhold Niebuhr.

Niebuhr had been the national chairman of the Fellowship of Reconciliation, a pacifist organization, before he became a critique of the pacifist position. He argued that there was no intrinsic moral difference between violent and non-violent resistance. Niebuhr emphasized the irresponsibility of relying on non-violent resistance when there was no ground for believing that it would be successful in preventing the spread of totalitarian tyranny. It could only be successful if the groups against whom the resistance was taking place had some degree of moral conscience.

Then one afternoon Dr. King heard a sermon when for the first time in his life he came in touch with the life and teachings of M.K. Gandhi. Dr. King was electrified by Gandhi's message and soon became deeply fascinated by Gandhi's campaigns of non-violent resistance. He was particularly moved by Gandhi's Salt March to the sea and his numerous fasts. The whole concept of *Satyagraha*[7] was profoundly significant to Dr. King. As he delved deeper into the philosophy of Gandhi, his scepticism concerning the power of love gradually diminished, and he came to see its potency in the area of social reform.

Until then, Dr. King had always assumed that the ethics of Jesus were only effective in individual relationships; when racial groups and

---

[7] Gandhi coined the term Satyagraha—a Sanskrit word meant as 'Desire for truth'—for his non-violent resistance

nations were in conflict a more realistic approach seemed necessary. But after reading about Gandhi and the power of love, he felt that Gandhi was the first person to lift the love ethic of Jesus above mere interaction between individuals to a powerful and effective social force. In the Gandhian emphasis on love and non-violence, Dr. King found the method for social reform that he had been seeking all his life. Such pacifism was not non-resistance to evil, but non-violent resistance to evil. He saw with clarity and conviction that there was a world of difference between the two. Gandhi resisted evil with as much vigour and power as the violent resister, but he resisted with love instead of hate. True pacifism was not unrealistic submission to evil power, rather it was a courageous confrontation of evil, but using the power of love.

In 1954, when Dr. King ended his formal training in Boston University, he found himself risen in clarity. During his training, he had developed a conviction—in the depth of his soul—that non-violent resistance was one of the most potent weapons available to oppressed people in their quest for social justice. It was a conviction that permeated his being with a resounding conviction of his power. As he walked away from college in Boston, he knew what road he would take, but he knew not where the road would lead him. But that lack of knowing did not deter him. He was just in the midst of an experiment.

To embrace another's truth takes surrendering what you think you know. It involves relinquishing the illusion of power and stepping into innocence. You must become open to whatever comes your way. Give it a try. Then your inner self will tell you if it is something for you or not. It will tell you if what you have experienced resonates with your core.

2. PASSAGE

Innocence is at the core of experimenting. To walk the labyrinth of life takes faith in the unknown. You do not know what is awaiting you at the next turn, but that is OK. Be in anticipation. Be open to whatever will unfold because powerful resources await you. When you make a conscious choice to experiment, you release your inhibitions. Remember, you are just trying out. You have no fear of what people think or how badly the outcome will affect you. You are studying whether what comes out of your experiment speaks to your core or not.

Some carry the illusion that at the end of an experiment they will arrive at clarity. They feel that they may have found the answer, the holy grail. And once they feel that they have achieved some level of clarity, they settle into it permanently. That is because clarity is comforting. It brings certainty to their lives.

The Being Leaders looked at life as a constant journey of experimentation. They remained open to learn and relearn. That did not mean that they did not have clarity. At the peak of their lives, they had perfect clarity of the life lessons we examine here. Also clear to them was that all of life is in constant evolution. We can only apply force to slowdown this evolution. Once you realize that, you will start treating your life as one long experiment, or a series of short experiments.

Through the course of his life, Gandhi dabbled in various religious beliefs. As an Indian, he showed substantial interest in the epics of the Hindu religion. He also got involved with Evangelicals to experience its merits and power. He spent a lot of his time with his White Evangelical friends and spent time attending daily prayers. He also got involved with the Esoteric Christian Union, which he called "a synthesizing school of beliefs that sought to reconcile all religions by showing that each represents the same eternal truths." He also deeply delved into the wisdom of the Islamic practice. Each of these encounters exposed him to something sacred about human consciousness. As a result, different set of beliefs came together to form the foundation of his philosophy of non-violent resistance.

Another virtue that supports experimentation is humility; humility to accept that there are things you can learn (we will study humility in greater detail in chapter 9, 'HAVE A TRUE MEASURE OF THE SELF', pg. 147). There are others who possess resources that can accelerate your growth. Be willing to accept their abundance and be willing to give their wisdom a study.

Mandela's experiment with South African democracy was woven in humility. His early experiment—that landed him in jail—was one of trying to get majority power for the black South Africans. During the years in jail, the nature of his experiment changed. He came to the realization that South Africa has been home for white settlers from Europe for centuries, and there was nowhere to send them to. Thereafter, his experiment in democracy recognized that the white South Africans had as much a place in South Africa as the black South Africans. His grand ambition was not anymore to enforce black supremacy, instead he felt the humility to learn and adopt past experiments in democracy.

You will progress further on the path of the Being Leader when you believe in impermanence. Nothing is constant, and nothing is permanent. As quickly as something has come your way, will it go as well. What you learn at this moment is what you have been given to serve your cause at this moment. As soon as you have learned and applied that lesson, a new lessons awaits you. Once you believe in impermanence, your life becomes open for experimentation. Your relationships, your way of working, your eating habits, your work schedule, the way you manage people, everything becomes a source of play. Yet, limiting your experiments to the mundane level is to forego the opportunity to lift yourself into an inspirational soul. As effortlessly

2. PASSAGE

as you experiment with mundane things, you can also experiment with your values and your moral fabric.

Gandhi conducted unique and bold experiments throughout his life. He experimented with diets including unpolished cereals, vegetables and fruits. He also laid great emphasis on proper mastication of foods. He initiated the cult of drinking goat's milk. Once, while advocating raw food, he lived largely on peanuts for four months. He tried cooked food as a way of destroying some of the inhibitors present in food that prevent it from being digested completely by the body. Gandhi experimented with many unorthodox treatments relying on naturopathy. He tried out treatments with wet sheet packs and orange juice and water diets. Once, he even cured his wife's anaemia, when she was critically ill and in grave danger, with limejuice and a salt-free diet.

Yet, his experiments—like with the other Being Leaders—were not limited to the mundane. His experiments were one long moral quest. During the second world war, he committed to support the British. He urged Indians to join the British Army to fight for their cause. He believed that India had a moral obligation to support the British in their hour of need. Later, when the ruling British were not very morally inclined to reciprocate the Indian gesture and sacrifice, he turned against the British. Being Leaders looked at their experiments as an essential part of elevating the self and shaping human consciousness.

When you embrace all of life as an experiment, you see all of life as a spiritual practice. Each passage brings a certain clarity, but is never an end in itself. As time goes by, life will present the answers to the greater questions in life. That is the role of the 'passage' phase. The experiments may reduce in numbers and intensity, but will never stop. Never let them stop.

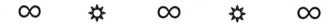

6. SHARPENING THE TEETH

"Every step toward the goal of justice requires sacrifice, suffering, and struggle; the tireless exertions and passionate concern of dedicated individuals."

Dr. Martin Luther King, Jr.

In 1831, Abraham Lincoln had just left home and it was not clear to him what career he might ultimately follow. He had a strong body, a great presence of mind and a willingness to try. In the next ten years, he worked as a riverboat man, store clerk, soldier, merchant, postmaster, surveyor, lawyer and politician.

As a riverboat man, Lincoln's ethos of hard work was at full display, so was his resourcefulness and ingenuity. In April 1831, the whole village of New Salem, Illinois watched as Lincoln worked at saving his grounded boat and cargo with his "boots off, hat, coat and vest off. Pants rolled up to his knees and shirt wet with sweat and combing his fuzzy hair with his fingers as he pounded away on the boat." Unable to budge the boat, he bore a hole in the bow and unloaded enough barrels of cargo so that the stern rose up. When the water poured out through the hole, the whole boat lifted and floated.

New Salem, Illinois, was a place for which young Lincoln was well suited. He was hardworking and accommodating, and he was ever available to lend a hand to any others. As a store clerk, not only did he manage business, there he first practiced the art of pulling people towards him. Lincoln turned his store into the watering hole where everyone exchanged news and gossip. His jokes were riveting and were known to all village folks, men and women.

Village folks welcomed Lincoln because he had an inexhaustible store of anecdotes and stories. One concerned an Indiana Baptist preacher who, dressed in old-fashioned baggy pantaloons and a shirt fastened only at the collar, announced his text: "I am the Christ, who I shall represent today." Then a little blue lizard ran up his leg, and the preacher, unable to slap it away and unwilling to stop his sermon, loosened his pants and kicked them off. But the lizard proceeded up the minister's back, and this time, without missing a word, he opened his collar button and swept off his shirt too. The congregation looked dazed, but one old lady rose up and shouted: "If you represent Christ then I'm done with the bible."

Once when he was chided by the Clary's Grove gang[8] to a wrestling bout, he accepted it. He was not considered a match for their wrestling champion, Jack Armstrong. But that did not faze him. A vigorous wrestling match ensued, and more than the outcome, it was Lincoln's enterprising nature that registered with the New Salem residents. His courage to accept the invitation won the admiration of the Clary's Grove gang, who became Lincoln's most loyal and enthusiastic supporters through his later political career.

"He was among the best clerks I ever saw," schoolmaster Graham recalled. "He was attentive to his business—was kind and considerate to his customers and friends and always treated them with great tenderness—kindness and honesty."

---

[8] The Clary's Grove boys lived near New Salem, US. They had a reputation for being a loud, reckless, frontier crowd who enjoyed fighting and drinking. They boasted they could wrestle better and hit harder than any other group throughout Illinois. At times they could also be generous and good-natured.

In 1832, at the age of twenty-three, Lincoln declared himself as a candidate for the Illinois General Assembly. He lost the race but got nearly every vote in his precinct, which, said another candidate, was "mainly due to his personal popularity". The same year Lincoln volunteered for a state militia campaign against a band of Native Americans under Chief Black Hawk, a part of the bloody Black Hawk war, where his company elected him captain.

John Todd Stuart, a U.S. Representative from Illinois and an acquaintance of Lincoln, noted that during Lincoln's Black Hawk war service he stood out for his great strength and athletic ability, as well as his kind manner and as a story teller. Many sources have described his command ability as capable and spoke of him as a popular leader.

"One popularly repeated story from Lincoln's Black Hawk war service illustrates Lincoln's qualities of honesty, and courageous, competent leadership. It involved a Potawotami who wandered into Captain Lincoln's camp and Lincoln's men assumed him a spy and wanted to kill him. The story goes that Lincoln threw himself between the Native American and the men's muskets, knocking their weapons upward. The militia men backed down after a few heated seconds."[X]

Lincoln's lessons from the Black Hawk war were mixed. Among the green officers unable to maintain discipline in his company was a pock-faced, stoop-shouldered, slab-sided assistant storekeeper from New Salem, a two-rut, hilltop settlement near Springfield, Illinois. The first order Captain Abraham Lincoln ever gave to his men received the retort: "Go to the devil, Sir!" Some of his men later confessed that they elected Lincoln as their commander, rather than his rival, William Kirkpatrick, because "they would be able to do as they liked under Abe."[XI]

Lincoln's service in the militia during the Black Hawk war gave him his first understanding of military life and his first experience as a leader of men. Nearly three decades later, Lincoln wrote that his election as militia captain was "a success which gave me more pleasure than any I have had since."

In May 1833, Abraham Lincoln was appointed as the village postmaster in New Salem, Illinois. It was in that role that he first put to practice his signature approach to public duty. Lincoln carried the unusual notion that a public servant's first duty is to help people, rather than to follow bureaucratic regulations. If a resident of the village did not pick up her mail at the post office, he would walk miles to deliver them in person. And if a resident forgot to have his letter stamped, Lincoln would simply frank the letter for him instead of imposing a fine of $10.

Such behaviour confused some in small town New Salem, while friends were not surprised as this seemed typical of the Lincoln they knew.

It was in this job as the village postmaster that he first learned and perfected his ability to maintain public office administration. He kept detailed financial records and resented the idea of any irregularities. More than a year after he left his job as postmaster and moved to Springfield, Illinois, he made a payment of the exact balance of $248.63 to the Post Office Department. This was what he owed the government. In later years in office, he had such mastery of government accounts that he could match treasury secretary Salmon P. Chase on what it cost to wage a war and run a country.

In the fall of 1833, Abraham Lincoln picked up the job as a land surveyor. A job as a land surveyor might seem mechanical to the casual eye, but his job had a strong interpersonal component. In his role as a surveyor, he was often called on to settle boundary disputes.

It is known that in Petersburg, Illinois, he once laid out one street crooked. Running it straight and regular, it would have put the house of one Jemima Elmore and her family into the street. Lincoln knew her to be working a small farm with her children and she was the widow of Private Travice Elmore, honourable in service in Lincoln's company in the Black Hawk War. As a resident of Athens, Illinois, recalled: "Mr Lincoln had the monopoly of finding the lines, and when any dispute arose among the settlers, Mr Lincoln's compass and chain always settled the matter satisfactorily." Interestingly, it was not as a lawyer in his later life but as a land surveyor that Lincoln for the first time acted as an arbiter of men.

During Lincoln's rise as a state politician in the late 1830s, the country's economy was booming, and nowhere more than in Illinois. To support that growth, a bill was passed to create an extensive system of rails, roads and canals. Lincoln was a true believer of these "internal improvement" projects. But in 1837, the United States fell into one of its worst financial crises. Across the country banks failed, unemployment rose and fortunes crumpled. Erstwhile champions of the "internal improvement" projects abandoned their support, however Lincoln fought to expand those. When the canals and roads were finished, he argued, the state would reap the rewards, so it ought to endure the short-term pain.

But as money dried out, there was a search for scapegoats, and questions were raised about Lincoln's role in promoting such a harebrained and disastrous scheme. Such criticism was unfair. Firstly, though Lincoln favoured and supported the "internal improvement" projects, he was not the lead man. Secondly, had the projects continued, they might have done as much for the prosperity of Illinois as other projects have done for other U. S. states.

When those accusations failed to yield the kind of damage opponents sought to inflict upon Lincoln's career, he was later criticized that the only reason why he supported the "internal improvement" schemes was to secure, in return, the relocation of the Illinois state capital to Springfield.

2. PASSAGE

By any standard, Lincoln was unfit for the mudslinging found in U.S. politics even as far back as 1836. This was as true during his presidency as it was during his first state legislative role. As a result, as early as 1836, many observers had ruled out Lincoln's viability as a career politician.

What Lincoln lacked in his ability to play petty politics, he more than made up with legislative astuteness. Springfield, after all, was a better choice as a capital. Vandalia, the then capital, was too small, too inaccessible, and most importantly, was far too south in a state where the central and northern regions were growing most rapidly.

Springfield, however, was far less sympathetic to slave holding and slave trading. Hence many proponents of slavery were opposed to the choice of Springfield as the new capital of Illinois. These opponents tried to whittle down the influence of supportive delegations in the legislature by splitting their counties. That attempt failed when the committee chaired by Lincoln counter-proposed a new redistricting plan that was certain to fail in the state senate.

When the attempt to reduce the influence of supportive delegations failed, a key proponent of slavery threatened to investigate the Illinois State Bank, located in Springfield, which would probably put that institution out of business and at the same time deliver a severe blow to Springfield's chance to become the capital. To pre-empt any such attempt, Lincoln took to the floor to make his first extended speech in the state legislature.

"The demand for an investigation (of the Illinois State Bank) was exclusively the work of politicians," Lincoln claimed, "a set of men who have interests aside from the interest of the people."

Such effort, Lincoln claimed would lead "to the ultimate overthrow of every institution, or even moral principle, in which persons and property have hitherto found security."

Later when a resolution was passed condemning abolitionist societies and affirming that slavery was guaranteed by the Constitution, Lincoln voted against the resolution, albeit quietly to prevent damage to the prospects of shifting the capital to Springfield.

After overcoming all efforts to prevent moving the state capital of Illinois to Springfield, Lincoln and other team members shepherded through the legislature the bill to move the capital. The task required a delicate touch, and Lincoln's political and legislative astuteness were repeatedly tested. Several times it seemed that the bill would meet certain defeat. Each time, Lincoln added amendments, made changes to the bill, lobbied doubtful members, designed clauses to eliminate competing towns, made concessions, defended the virtues or Springfield as the capital of Illinois, and inspired those around him to follow his lead. In 1837, the capital of Illinois was moved to Springfield.[XII]

Precious little is spoken in history books about Lincoln's pre-president days. But it is crucial to take a look at the path that Lincoln took to finally arrive at the White House.

Lincoln, like all the other Being Leaders examined in this work, had a life workshop where he sharpened his teeth. When you look into the years before he became president, you can connect the dots between the traits he displayed during his presidency and the life lessons that went into shaping those traits.

2. PASSAGE

Over a span of 30 years, Lincoln developed his faculties and his people management abilities. On each occasion, Lincoln never entertained the thought of compromising his deep held ideals, but saw defeat as an opportunity for renewal and reassessment of self. He held an awareness of each individual's self-motivation and carried an undying belief that within the confines of self-motivation there was sufficient space to find solutions that advanced the common good.

In his later years as president, Lincoln demonstrated great dexterity in handling—and in many cases even pre-empting—political manoeuvrings from those opposed to him. It could be said that the lessons that Abraham Lincoln acquired from his earlier jobs as a riverboat man, store clerk, soldier, merchant, postmaster, surveyor, lawyer and politician were preparing him to for the momentous four years as a wartime president and the author of the now famous Emancipation Proclamation liberating slaves in America.

Whether serendipity or by choice, preceding glory were years of toil. These years were an essential phase, a phase where the Being Leaders learned the art of living and polished their trade. They were exposed to life and the vagaries that life threw at them. Thirstily, they accepted the opportunity to learn. They did not curse life because they had been dealt a—seemingly—bad hand. Instead, they approached their lessons with gusto and humility. They did not challenge the meaning of the lessons they were receiving, nor did they condemn the path they were on.

Look at this process as follows: The pathway to mould yourself into instruments of a grander design is similar to a blacksmith's workshop where a tool is shaped one piece at a time. Each component of the whole needs to be sculpted carefully and artfully. That might take years, sometimes decades.

Sharpening the Teeth

In 1893, at the young age of twenty four, Gandhi arrived in South Africa to work as a legal representative for the Muslim Indian traders based in the city of Pretoria. This is where he developed his political views, ethics and political leadership skills.

In South Africa, Gandhi faced the discrimination directed at all coloured people. These events shaped his social activism and awakened him to social injustice. Gandhi began to question his place in society and his people's standing in the British empire. This inner reflection led him, in 1894, to help found the Natal Indian Congress, and through this organisation, he moulded the Indian community of South Africa into a unified political force.

In 1906, Gandhi put to practice his still evolving (now legendary) methodology of *Satyagraha*[9], or non-violent protest, for the first time. At a mass protest meeting held in Johannesburg on 11 September that year, he urged Indians to defy the discriminatory laws and to suffer the punishments for doing so. The community adopted this plan, and during the ensuing seven-year struggle, thousands of Indians were jailed, flogged, or shot for striking, refusing to register, for burning their registration cards or engaging in other forms of non-violent resistance. The government successfully repressed the Indian protesters, but the public outcry over the harsh treatment of peaceful Indian protesters by the South African government forced the South African government to negotiate a compromise with the Indians in South Africa. Patiently, over a period of 21 years Gandhi perfected the weapon of *Satyagraha*, the full might of which was at display in his subsequent struggle against the colonial powers ruling India.[XIII]

Looking forward we cannot see the synchronicity between the past experiences and their future relevance, we can only connect the dots

---

[9] Gandhi coined the term Satyagraha—a Sanskrit word meant as 'Desire for truth'—for his non-violent resistance

2. PASSAGE

looking backwards. If you read the autobiographies of the Being Leaders, you can see this evidence of the dots connecting. Where you are right now is where you are meant to be. Learn the lesson. Do not seek shortcuts to the apprenticeship of life. Shortcuts will only lead to other shortcuts. And before you know, life would have flowed by, and you would have reached a peak in your life without having lived your true purpose or shaped your Noble Legacy. You would fail to have made a meaningful difference to humanity or the world at large.

x   x   x

Often years go by in the process of 'sharpening your teeth'. In most cases it takes years, sometimes it may take decades to put yourself through all the relevant experiences and learning. You might not be aware of your passage when you are on it. You might not notice your apprenticeship as you are going through it. In fact, at this very moment even as you are applying the strengths that you mastered in your yesteryears, it is entirely possible that you are also apprenticing on a different set of strengths that are destined to take you further on your purpose.

The best of leaders amongst you have already recognized the above truth. You clearly see the passage you are on because you are learning. You cannot yet point out the endpoint of this passage you are on or the value of the learning you are undertaking. But you can feel deep within that everything that you are undergoing is a build up towards something greater, something grander.

If you are on your 'passage', you are already seeing your life as an everlasting, ongoing, fulfilling apprenticeship.

7. LOOK IN THE MIRROR: SEE THE TWO SELVES

"If we could change ourselves, the tendencies in the world would also change. As a man changes his own nature, so does the attitude of the world change towards him. ... We need not wait to see what others do."

M.K. Gandhi

∞ ☼ ∞ ☼ ∞

From a letter from Nelson Mandela to Winnie Mandela while being confined to the Kroonstad Prison in South Africa, Dated February 1st 1975:

"Incidentally, you may find that the cell is an ideal place to learn to know yourself, to search realistically and regularly the process of your own mind and feelings. In judging our progress as individuals we tend to concentrate on external factors such as one's social position, influence and popularity, wealth and standard of education. These are, of course, important in measuring one's success in material matters and it is perfectly understandable if many people exert themselves mainly to achieve all these. But internal factors may be even more crucial in assessing one's development as a human being. Honesty, sincerity, simplicity, humility, pure generosity, absence of vanity, readiness to serve others – qualities which are within easy reach of every soul – are the foundation of one's spiritual life. Development in matters of this nature is inconceivable without serious introspection, without knowing yourself, your weaknesses and mistakes. At least, if for nothing else, the cell gives you the opportunity to look daily into your entire conduct, to overcome the bad and develop whatever is good in you. Regular meditation, say about

2. PASSAGE

15 minutes a day before you turn in, can be very fruitful in this regard. You may find it difficult at first to pinpoint the negative features in your life, but the 10th attempt may yield rich rewards. Never forget that the saint is a sinner who keeps on trying."

Imagine you have been a hermit for fifteen years starting at the age of ten. You have no reference for what it means to be a teenager in the normal worldly setting. Thus, all the experience of asserting your independence as a teenager will be missing. You will not go through the challenges of contrasting yourself against your parents and other elders. As a consequence, a big part of the experiences that define a normal youngster at the age of twenty-five will be absent in you.

Now assume that at the age of twenty-five you decide to rejoin society. The way you relate to others will vastly differ from the way other twenty-five year olds do. You will possess an identity that varies from that of other twenty-five year olds. This identity would have been different had you been subject to a different set of experiences in those fifteen years you otherwise chose to live as a hermit.

This should demonstrate to you that your identity is shaped—to a large part—by your experiences. Each new event in life is constantly reorganizing and reframing this identity. Each experience is adding or subtracting from this identity. Thus, your identity is in constant flux, evolving and adapting according to the constant input it receives.

You are born into this world with a certain inclinations and talents[10]. At birth, you carry into this world an intelligence, a certain consciousness,

---

[10] More on talents under chapter 'ORDEAL OF THE WARRIOR CHILD', pg. 51

that helps you relate to the world you are born into. Birds and animals are born with an intelligence to fly, to breed and to nest. No one taught them how to do it. Birds can navigate across the globe, fishes can swim thousands of kilometres to spawn, turtles can return years later to the very same spot where they were hatched.

Similarly, humans are endowed with a subtle intelligence that helps us navigate through the realm of human existence. Call it an innate tendency. This tendency is a quality of our *unconditioned* nature, the soul nature if you prefer to call it. This nature is pure and expresses itself in non-local, timeless ways. It has none of the references that the grownup *conditioned self* carries. The *conditioned self* is nurtured through the experiences of life. **Understanding the duality of the *unconditioned self* and the *conditioned self* is the first step to understanding yourself.**

The *unconditioned self* is immense in its potential. It is infinitely creative, it has the ability to intuit and tune into others' thoughts, it can effortlessly go between the past and future, it can rise above cravings and aversions, it is selfless and unified with all. That self is a pure, childlike nature.

Unlike the *unconditioned self,* as adults we carry a narrow experience of time and space, an experience which is absent in a newborn. Adults experience time as a linear phenomenon constructed in units. We let ourselves be led by time constraints. We are self-conscious, and how we relate to the world around us is shaped by the conditioning we acquire through life's experiences. This is typical of the *conditioned self.*

The paradoxical nature of this *conditioned self* is that the more you try to reinforce this identity, the more insecure you become. Away from the objects or situations you identify with, you become more unsure of yourself. Moreover, in the absence of those who give you that sense of

2. PASSAGE

identity, you feel incomplete. It is this incompleteness that drives you to crave for relationships.

Self-identity and self-preservation are core to the *conditioned self*. The *conditioned self* sees itself as separate from those around you, and yearns to belong, and to be recognized and respected. The habit of seeing yourself or viewing yourself as somebody important is very set in your *conditioned self*.

In its extreme form, the *conditioned self* is territorial and self-centered. This happens when you are conditioned through the wounds, the rejections and the dejections of your childhood. When that happens, you might see the world as your enemy. Events around you trigger fear or one of the lower emotions. You become self-consumed. Survival becomes your motto. Self-preservation turns into a constant battle. You will exert force as a means of taking control. It does not matter to your *conditioned self* if you lie or cheat, it just needs to win and be proven right. You feel the need to subdue those around you as a way of staying in control. When you get rejected, you might turn narcissistic. When you are ignored, you feel belittled, and in turn, you become cold and indifferent. Military means become a 'natural' for those amongst us who operate from their *conditioned self*. Many corporate leaders can be found operating from such a place. Many nations are in the above consciousness.

Your interests, history, quirks, skills, achievements, background, likes and dislikes, successes and failures, they all have elements of conditioning in it. If you had remained unconditioned since birth, clean and pure, some of these aspects of your life would be different, and—in some cases—even not-existent. It is important to recognize this truth since these inclinations drive your actions in life.

Your stories, your roles, your possessions, your labels, your titles, all are manifestations of your *conditioned self*. The first two, your stories and the various roles you play, are important to examine in this work since they form perhaps the most important manifestation of your conditioning. They also profoundly drive the core of your leadership in all aspects of life.

7.1. YOUR STORIES

As a young adult, Dr. King wanted the world around him to believe that he was not a subject of discrimination and a victim of prejudices. He took it upon himself to not be seen in places that were segregated so that no one would notice him as different from the privileged class. Abraham Lincoln felt embarrassed about his log-cabin origins and never liked to talk about them. He did not want others to know that he grew up as an Indiana farm boy tilling his rather mundane wheat field.

All your stories are powered by your *conditioned self*. You have many stories that you are not aware of, the one you are not even aware you are telling yourself. Some of them you made up to explain the behaviour of your parents, or the lack of control over your circumstances, or how some things outside your control happened to you, or the tough educational choices you made to get where you are.

Then there are those stories you deliberately tell yourself and others. You tell stories about who you are and stories about who others are. You regard the stories as facts, as how things are. In fact, in your world of stories facts do not matter. That is the power of stories. All that matters to you is how well the story props you up. They define your identity within group settings. Your stories give you comfort and presents you in an agreeable light among those around you. They help you belong within groups, they draw attention to you, and they become your hooks for approval and appreciation from those around you.

So you create stories, sometimes consciously, other times unconsciously. Either ways, your stories are always evolving with time and according to the circumstances. They take on new dimensions, new actors appear in these stories, new roles are played, and new endings are created. As time goes by and your experiences evolve, you refine your current stories, and even create new ones, not only to cope with the demands of the world you live in, but also to navigate the waters of society. These are all simply expressions of your *conditioned self.*

7.2. YOUR ROLES

Gandhi was punished by his eldest son, Harilal, for transcending the narrow confines of his role as a father. Through most of Harilal's adult life, he had a fractious relationship with Gandhi. In 1911, Harilal departed their settlement in Phoenix, South Africa, without telling his father. The son left a letter behind reproaching his father for 'being a deficient father' and announcing that he, Harilal, was breaking all ties with his parents. Soon after, during a whole night of talks between father and son, Harilal accused a compassionate father that he favoured the other kids on the settlement over his sons, was hard-hearted towards Harilal, and was unconcerned about the son's future.

A major element in Harilal's resentment was Gandhi's decision in 1910 to send another youngster from their settlement rather than Harilal to study law in England with a scholarship provided by a well-wishing benefactor. While Harilal saw himself as entitled to a special privilege, Gandhi saw Harilal as one ward among many special ones on the settlement. Gandhi saw his family as a part of a magical experiment involving all races and class, all wards of the settlement needing the special care, love and attention that his family deserved. Harilal, unable to lift himself from his conditioning, sought his father's partiality to place him ahead of others even though he was undeserving of that privilege.

An unconditioned soul sees beyond roles and embraces the wellbeing of all. He is naturally inclined towards creating value for the collective and is less inspired to operate in the zero sum realm. Gandhi was consumed with shaping a new dignified reality for all the Indians living in South Africa, not just his own or his family's. He was not confined to the narrow role of a father, but could lift himself beyond a role that defined him. As part of that vision, all beings—including his sons—expressed their humanity through the humanity of all.[XIV]

Your roles are situation-specific and are driven by your *conditioned self.* A role can be defined only in connection with others or other things. In the absence of that context, the role ceases to exist.

Imagine you are receiving a call from a superior insensitively giving you orders. You might notice that your energy is more closed, you might even feel subdued or controlled, you might notice your chest is contracted and your voice milder.

Imagine now that you are on a phone call where you are the one giving orders. You might sound assertive, your voice might be louder, your chest might feel more expanded and your posture might also be more authoritative.

To some you are known as a salesperson. And these are usually people who come into your store. Others know you as a neighbour. Through the lens of the role assigned to you, others determine if you have fulfilled the requirements of that role. If you have fulfilled the requirements of that role, you are considered good and vice versa. From the moment you wake up until the time you go to sleep, you play hundreds of roles depending upon the persons you interact with or the scene you are placed in.

Amongst the strongest of all conditioning is that of your family roles. Imagine yourself as a child every time you are in the presence of parents or elders. However grownup you are, most of you will sink into the same roles that you donned decades back. Or the role as a parent. However grownup your children are, in the presence of your children you will regress back into that role you played as a parent.

How you behave in different moments depends on your role in any given situation. We tend to behave one way when we are giving orders, another way when we are receiving them. We have one personality when we are commanding and another personality when we are following. Who we are, whether in the professional setting or at home, seems to change according to our role. Conclude that you don various roles and you are many different people every day.

In your 'passage' phase, you become aware of the stories and roles that carry you through life. You learn who are being in different situations, and to what extent you are attached to your roles. This awareness is powerful. It sets the way for you to step out of your conditioning and step into your true self.

7.3. THE ILLUSION OF IDENTIFICATION

In 1964, when Mandela was moved to Robben Island, the island prison in South Africa, he was placed with other political prisoners of warring factions. They were all placed in an isolated section in the prison compound for fear that the political prisoners would have a negative influence on the rest of the prisoners.

There was often intense rivalry among the prisoners from the various political factions. Mandela himself was allied to the militant wing of the African National Congress (ANC), while he considered Walter Sisulu, a member of the ANC, his mentor. Govan Mbeki, Andrew Mlangeni, Raymond Mhlaba and Ahmed Kathrada, all convicted to life imprisonment together with Mandela were moderate in their views towards the struggle against Apartheid. Mandela was lodged with George Peake, a white man and one of the founders of the South African Coloured People's Organization. Another white man and a coloured political activist, Dennis Brutus, was imprisoned alongside Mandela for violating his bans. Billy Nair, a coloured man of Indian origin and a long-time member of the Natal Indian Congress, stayed in a cell next to Mandela's. Neville Alexander, a prominent coloured intellectual and member of the Non-European Unity Movement had formed a radical organization called the Yu Chi Chan Club in Cape Town, and Fikile Bam, a member of this competing organization believed that they had a better path forward to end Apartheid compared to Mandela's. Zephania Mothopeng, a member of the Pan African Congress National Executive, a competing faction to ANC was also in prison alongside Mandela.

Many prisoners preferred to spend their days among their own party members and comrades. They would cluster together during the day and talked only to the ones whose beliefs agreed with theirs. During meals,

2. PASSAGE

they would be seen eating together. Mandela knew some of them and he had heard of some others. He agreed with the doctrines and philosophies of some and he disagreed with others. But for Mandela the various political factions were bound together with a common cause; upholding the dignity of all races living in South Africa. Unlike most others around him in prison, Mandela was not tied up in his ideology. Instead he saw the commonalities and felt inclusive towards those who differed from him.

In 1965, when Mandela started working at the quarry, they were joined by a number of other prominent political prisoners. Some of them were from the militant group Mandela used to be a part of, while others like Mac Maharaj and Eddie Daniels were individuals of a different race and different factions who were often at odds with the beliefs and charter of ANC. Not only did Mandela succeed in integrating them into a common world bound by common ideals, some of them even became close friends of Mandela in the years to come.

At around the same time, Mandela's conditioning was test in a severe way. In order to counterbalance the high numbers of political activists in Robben Island, the prison authorities also put a handful of common-law convicts in the prison section where Mandela was housed. These men were hardened criminals, convicted of rape, murder or armed robbery. They were brawny and surly, their faces bore the scars of the knife fights that were common amongst such criminals and they were used to terrorize other prisoners. These criminals would regularly attempt to push the political prisoners around and take their food.

While many of Mandela's comrades looked at the common-law criminals as condemned souls worthy of the gallows, Mandela did not identify with any such ideology. Stepping above any judgment, Mandela objectively saw the common-law criminals as raw material to be converted into valuable soldiers for the anti-Apartheid cause.

One day a common-law criminal approached Mandela in the corridor and asked for his help. This criminal had been savagely beaten by a warder at the quarry. His face was cut and badly bruised. Overlooking the labels attached to such ruthless common-law criminals, Mandela agreed to take up the case. His action only endeared Mandela, the ANC and its cause among the common-law criminals. As a result, some of these criminals proved invaluable to Mandela and the ANC during Mandela's prison years.

On weekends, the political prisoners were permitted to visit the football field to watch the other prisoners play. Whenever Mandela used to walk to the football field on Robben Island, he would be seen walking to the field with an Indian or a person of another race. He wanted to show that he was not in favour of groups or cliques, for him that was separateness.

x   x   x

In prison, Nelson Mandela took special care to present himself as being above any kind of identification. Doing so felt unusual and took practice in the beginning. Yet he believed that he was a leader for all, and classifying folks based on stereotypes and labels went against his grain. He wanted to represent all races—including the white Afrikaners—and classes of prisoners on Robben Island, and in doing so, he wanted to be seen as an agent of all humanity. This practice was part of his passage.

There is a powerful lesson for you from the passage of the Being Leaders. Stop identifying yourself with the things you DO, or the things you HAVE. Do not lean on your labels to pad up your identity. Once that label is taken away from you, you will feel empty.

People have known me by many titles. Let me pull out two simple examples. In college, I was a Cinema Club facilitator. In business school I was President of the Students' Society. In the former title, I had a say on how my fellow students entertained themselves during their leisure

2. PASSAGE

hours. In my latter title, I had power to decide what extracurricular and entertainment activities were offered to my fellow students, and how the funds available for such activities were spent. I was being two totally different individuals in both settings, and even within those settings, I played countless roles depending on who I was interacting with. If the same person carried two different titles in their interactions with me, they saw two different me. If my counterpart was one of the sponsors, I would behave more humble, service-oriented and pleasing. If, on the other hand, the same individual was a supplier of movies and for the Cinema Club, I would be more customer-like and demanding.

None of these roles were the real I. I know now that they were simply different expressions of the real I.

x   x   x

In 2007, I had a fascinating meeting with an entertainment mogul in Europe. He carried a well-known family name that was renowned in the reality TV industry. I met with him together with a friend who was a founding partner of a little known company with plans for a big step in the 'infotainment' market. This friend felt that a tie up with the entertainment mogul could be valuable to his plans.

"Rest assured," Mr. Burns (name changed), the entertainment mogul stated confidently. "That deal will be yours. We are the partner of choice for any player in the entertainment industry."

Not able to contain my curiosity, I asked the entertainment mogul what made him feel so confident that he could seal the deal.

"Because we are the standard for reality TV in Europe, perhaps even across the whole world," he asserted. Not impressed by his reasoning, I asked what he brought to the table that makes his enterprise valuable to my friend's little known company.

"My name," he blurted in response. He looked offended that I questioned his equity. "Nobody says no to Burns," he stated confidently.

Several weeks later, after carefully studying the fit of his company with Mr. Burns' company, my friend concluded that a partnership with Mr. Burns was not the right step for his little known company. My friend had chosen for a competitor of Mr. Burns' firm to partner with.

I later came to hear that Mr. Burns was incensed by my friend's decision. The thought of a little known company choosing against his mighty enterprise was too much for him to handle. Mr. Burns threatened my friend that his initiative was bound to fail in the face of the challenge offered by the mighty enterprise of the entertainment mogul. Not used to not having things his way in the entertainment industry of that nation, Mr. Burns took the rejection personal. He went to great lengths to conceal from the media the news of not being selected, and when that failed, he resorted to a long campaign of misinformation against my friend's company. He relented only after my friend came on the news and announced that his company hopes one day to become eligible to partner with the prestigious company of Mr. Burns.

Mr. Burns suffered from a sense of identification. He identified with the role and reputation he had in a small world where he saw himself as king. His self-identification with his role influenced the way he interpreted the world. He saw others in relation to his role, and the recognition others gave him determined how he treated them. His conditioning as an entertainment mogul added a value to things not visible to others. It blurred his objectivity, preventing him from understanding the rationale of my friend's decision to not partner with the mogul. And Mr. Burns could not see my friend for who he really was.

I have a friend who is quick to correct anyone who mispronounces her name. She is so attached to that identity that how others pronounce her name determined how she felt about them. Recognize this: when we speak of identity, we often mean identification. This identification is with the *conditioned self,* a role or a label we have acquired as a result of years of upbringing.

For identity to exist, there must be something against which you define yourself. Without a child, there is no mother. Without an employee, there is no employer. The absence of the employee makes the employer non-existent. Yet, the person does not become non-existent when that identification is stripped away, only the role does.

To begin to see yourself irrespective of your environment begins with dis-identification. A big challenge in dis-identification that I have faced both in my personal practice and in my support of leaders in politics and business has involved dis-identifying with family. Yet another step in dis-identification is the mastery of death. This step we will study in great depth in chapter 10, 'HUMAN ELEVATION NEEDS A MARTYR'.

7.4.   THE PRACTICE OF DIS-IDENTIFICATION

Dissolving your identification starts with self-awareness. A small part of the iceberg is visible above water. Similarly, there is a small part of you that most of you are aware of. And this part that you are aware of, you can dis-identify with. As you continue to expand your awareness, there is more of your conditioning that you can free yourself from.

For example, you could catch yourself being pessimistic and say, "I'll stop being pessimistic and be OK with whatever the outcome is." That is a simple start to the practice of dis-identification.

Look in the Mirror

As the big part of the iceberg is submerged under water, so is a huge part of your identity submerged in your unconscious. The fact that a huge part of your conditioning is submerged in your unconscious does not mean that it is not operational. It is alive and in action. When you are unaware, you are simply acting out the habits that you have conditioned within you. You might be an expert at typing, and you could type out your name without using any awareness. In the presence of unexpected bad news, some managers are prone to automatically consider their self-preservation or safeguard their self-interest. These are conditioned patterns expressing from your unconscious.

During a retreat that I was facilitating, I had a participant ask, "How do I practice dis-identifying myself from my stories and roles?"

"Simply start by observing yourself," I shared. "Observe yourself in all settings. Notice who you are being while you are alone or with others."

"What should I look out for?" She asked.

To answer her question, I reached for the velvet-bound pocket diary I always carried with me to my talks and retreats. From the diary I read out to her a piece I had noted. "Firstly, listen to those others around you. Their responses are a response to who you are being. They reflect and respond to your thoughts, words and deeds are finding expression through them. Many are unconscious of the answers they are giving to you about who you really are being in interpersonal settings. Yet they offer valuable insights what you identify with and the roles you play. Though their responses are coloured by their own emotions and conditioning, in their moments of awareness they can gift you a profound awareness of who you really are being."

"Secondly, notice the outcomes you are creating in your life. What you are manifesting in your life is a direct consequence of who you are being. The type of relationships you have in your life, or the kind of energy that exists between you and your colleagues are all examples of what you have shaped. Stop blaming others for their part in those stories and dramas and see it all as a reflection of your own inner state.

By simply observing yourself, your sensations, your sensorial experiences, your breath, your feelings and your thoughts and fantasies you transcend the conditioning of that identity. You cease to act from habits and old patterns. Your leadership is no more some absentminded behaviour, instead you become choiceful in your thoughts, words and actions."

"Lastly, look inwards and listen to your inner voice. There is a part of you constantly speaking to you through thoughts and through your feelings. Your thoughts sometimes can be just a whisper—difficult to decipher, and other times very loud. But the patterns and nature of your thoughts tell you a lot about who you are being and what you identify with. If you are a person who generally has positive or optimistic thoughts, you are bound to see the abundance around you. You tend to inspire others, and give them hope and purpose.

Perhaps the clearest voice from within that you can connect to and work with is your feelings. For instance, if you feel threatened by the expectations the organization have for you or the demands it places upon you, you identify with the organization in a victim role. You will relate to the organization through fear. This is a most noticed pattern among managers active in the corporate setting.

Your words and actions also speak of your identity. Many words and actions arise from your unconscious. They express outside your direct choice, and looking back at them can be very insightful about who you are being."

x   x   x

Let me summarize. In the 'passage' phase, a very crucial learning that you can achieve is in understanding the self. This can be a life long process, yet this is a step that all the Being Leaders found essential to their passage. Even at the peak of their lives, the Being Leaders continued with this spiritual practice of self-realization.

In this section, we looked into some of the patterns of the *conditioned self*, including how the *conditioned self* expresses itself in your stories and roles. We looked at how leaders' sense of identification can distract them from being the greatest they can. We also examined some simple practices available to develop awareness of the *conditioned self*. In the follow-up Being Leader Workbook, more detailed and descriptive practices are included for your ongoing practice.

In the next section, we will look at the nature of the *unconditioned self*.

7.5.   THE UNCONDITIONED SELF

Operating as the *unconditioned self* may seem impractical in the worldly realm.

During the early years of his movement, Dr. King pondered whether non-violent resistance was indeed effective in the face of brutality. There was a part of him deep within that had the realization that he could conquer his adversaries through love. Yet the practical world was populated with more examples of those who have had to embark on righteous wars to win their cause. There were too few examples of causes won through love and non-violence.

2. PASSAGE

That left him with many doubts and unresolved questions. For example, how would the practice of non-violence help against a violent force all bent on annihilating you? Or how could you practice compassion with white supremacists who do not hesitate to torch you or bomb your home? At certain times in his life, it felt impractical for Dr. King to practice compassion against a force to whom the same principles did not apply.

What made Dr. King unique compared to other leaders of his generation was that he persisted with his relentless application of the *unconditioned self*. That inner practice was his larger movement, more so than the national struggle for social justice. This practice is a reverse journey. After decades of conditioning, the Being Leaders had chosen to come a full circle to where their life began; back to that selfless and sharing self. They started to become aware that they were imperishable and their cause would survive even after their bodily demise. They saw themselves as a part of a grander design, a product of an inexplicable cosmic conspiracy. They repeated to those around them that the core values of their opponents or detractors were the same as theirs. That evil and selfish gain only exist at the conditioned level. Hence Dr. King called on his fellowmen to resist from annihilating the enemy through hatred, rather converting them through love.

x   x   x

To get to the *unconditioned self* is a journey of removing the decades of conditioning that we carry. It is a process of subtracting the patterns and habits that you have acquired. When you start peeling all the layers of the various identities, it can seem chaotic and confusing. You have left behind the certainty and solidity of the old shores and started a voyage on the rough seas. There is bound to be rolling and pitching, and the turbulence of losing old comforts and the false sense of security that came with your old stories, roles and labels would have gone. You might experience vulnerability. Faced with chaos and confusion, many quickly shift back to their old selves and refuse to examine who they are, or try to figure out what they are doing wrong. Do not turn back.

Your stories are not facts. They are only ideas and projections arising in the moment. Your stories distract you from what you are actually experiencing. To stop the projections, you must drop the stories about who you are and how you are meant to be. Drop everything and open to what you actually experience, the play of physical and sensory sensations, emotions and feelings, and thoughts and ideas. Open up to the whole mess until you can rest in the clear empty awareness from which the whole mess arises. And when you touch it, you will know what to do with it and how to deal with it.[XV]

Do not expect your whole identity to reveal itself through any one practice, one exchange or any one interaction with your environment. One aspect of you or several aspects of you become available through each exchange. Receive it with love and joy. Let that revelation enthral you. Rejoice that awareness.

And then relinquish that identity. Then you allow the next revelation to appear. It is a slow, tedious process, and there are no shortcuts. In the fast, quick fix culture of the current times, we are looking for huge leaps. Many leaders who step into the path of claiming their leader nature come with the expectations of taking huge leaps. They expect that a few huge leaps later, they would have scaled the summit and then they can sit back and reap the rewards. That is seldom the case. Enjoy the journey rather than shorten the road.

Many believe that the recipe to be a better being is to embrace a new identity; a new, better, more likeable identity. Many organizational development programmes are designed to shape individuals according to a prescribed mould. Studies have shown that certain behavioural traits are more effective or efficient within organizations, and hence aspiring leaders are encouraged to emulate those traits. That can be effective to a certain extent. But once leaders have reached the peak of their performance through emulating such behavioural traits, a fraction of them turn to a deeper examination of the self. That is when the real impact of dis-identification becomes visible.

Dis-identification has been the way of the Being Leaders. When we look at the lives of the Being Leaders, we see instances of them transcending any narrowly defined roles. Dr. King was seen leading rallies linking hands with Whites, those who carried the same outrage for segregation as did the Blacks. This often confused many, including some older Blacks who grew up with the wounds of segregation inflicted by the Whites. Many older Blacks felt that racial equality was a fight for the Blacks and ought to be fought by the Blacks.

7.6. THE VIRTUES OF SELF-AWARENESS

"Why is understanding the self so fundamental to advanced leadership?" A young emerging leader raised her hand as she asked.

This lady, she looked to be in her mid thirties and seemed an intense person. She sat on the front row and I noticed that she was deeply absorbed in the topic we were discussing. As part of the leadership development programme within one of the leading banks in The Netherlands, the bank invites speakers on leadership and management every Spring and Fall. I was invited to speak in the Fall of 2012.

The audience comprised of men and women who operated in the lower-middle and middle managerial levels within the bank. During the talk I invited them to identify some of the attributes exhibited by the leaders who inspired them. I asked them specifically not to identify the attributes that inspired them, rather present the attributes that these leaders demonstrated that made them legends. Many attributes came up: Humility, vision, contagious passion, eternal positivism, resolve, delivering on commitment, seeing the big picture, etc. ... but the attribute that topped the list was 'self-awareness'.

Next I invited the participants to elaborate what self-awareness meant to them. I compiled their definition for self-awareness, which turned out for them to be "an unparalleled knowing of who I am, beneath all my roles and stories".

Thus arose the question from the young emerging leader: "Why is understanding the self so fundamental to advanced leadership?" I acknowledged the depth of her thinking. She was attempting to draw a connection between knowledge of the self and its role in leadership. I reached again for my velvet-bound pocket diary. I got to the page where, in 2008, I had noted my teacher's words of wisdom on the virtues of self-awareness. From the diary, I read out to her:

"The window through which you can truly see others is your self-awareness. When you become aware of yourself, you have become aware of all others. You understand yourself and you have understood others. You connect with yourself and you can connect effortlessly with others. You relate to yourself and you can relate to all others intuitively. When you can gain visibility into your own vanity and silliness, you can get a clear view into the same within those around you. You can understand it when others are exhibiting it. Your self-awareness gives you the ability to shrug it off instead of letting it get to you. When you become aware of the roles you play, the masks you wear, the stories you tell, you understand them when you see those in others.

When you respect yourself, you find yourself automatically respecting others. After all, your roles with others is a reflection of your relationship with yourself. You have your values, your weaknesses, your idiosyncrasies, your quirkiness. Those make each individual unique as much as the mix of your attributes make you unique. You carry certain hopes, dreams, fears and aspirations that propel you through life. Others may not carry the same hopes, dreams, fears and aspirations, but they carry some. They hold those as precious as you hold yours. They toil through life in order to fulfill those hopes and dreams. They relate to their fears with the same worry with which you relate to yours.

You treat yourself with patience and you will notice that you treat others with patience. When you truly enjoy the company of yourself you will truly enjoy the company of others.

When you can become aware of your own fears, you can empathize with your opponents fears. Your fear gives you a frame of reference for others. You start becoming aware that all fear is legitimate to the one who fears. We can stand on the fence and minimize other's fear, labelling it as illegitimate or irrelevant. But when you can understand the consuming nature of your fear, you start to understand the enormity of others' fears, even your enemy's."

Dr. King did not feel fear or awe for Birmingham's police chief, Eugene 'Bull' Connor. Connor was the Commissioner of Public Safety for the city of Birmingham, Alabama, during the American Civil Rights Movement. Connor was a fierce man. During the Civil Rights demonstration, he infamously directed the use of fire hoses and police attack dogs against peaceful demonstrators, including children. Most Blacks feared him.

Yet, Dr. King felt compassion for Connor. Dr. King saw Connor as a desperate man, fearful of losing his way of life and his grip on power. Dr. King's compassion came from his observation that the chief's actions did not seem like that of a bold and courageous man. Instead they seemed like the actions of a desperate man. That explained why Dr. King did not feel any hatred for the chief.

Look in the Mirror

When you have a deep awareness of yourself, you recognize that you live in honour of the deepest longing of your *heart* more than the rational demands of the *head*. After all, it is their emotional wounds that set the Being Leaders on their paths, not a calculated agenda that included a path to profit or fame.

To make that reverse passage to your *unconditioned self,* self-knowing is everything. I have understood that it is that simple. The more you can hold that awareness of your highest self in your life, the more you can transcend the bondages of your conditioning. Then you assume your fullest. You become infinitely creative. A study has shown that children are six times more inventive than adults. They are naturally inclined to make free associations. The filters that come with conditioning are absent among children. This allows creativity in children to flow more freely. Because children do not evaluate ideas or stop to think about why ideas would not work—all features of the conditioning that you go through—they are naturally more non-judgmental and access solutions more effortlessly than adults. They are open-minded, curious, expressive and hands on. Children—being mostly unconditioned—exhibit the ability to intuit and tune into others' thoughts and emotions. They are known to effortlessly move between the past and future, and be fully alive and absorbed in the experience of the present. Given the right motive, children can effortlessly rise above cravings and aversions. They exhibit spontaneous selflessness and union with others.

There are certain characteristics associated with the *unconditioned self,* it is constant and irreducible. This *unconditioned self* is immense in its potential. It has the capacity to operate with love and compassion towards all, whether friend or foe. This you notice in the lives of the Being Leaders. At the peak of their lives, they were aflame with compassion for all.

In the state of the *unconditioned self,* you also become filled with infinite possibilities. When you combine the unlimited nature of the

2. PASSAGE

unconditioned self with the advanced intellect of the adult, you develop the capacity to access your awesome power. You exhibit the potential to accomplish all your faculties. Just a simple thought mobilises the masses around you. Like the Being Leaders, you become noticed as ideal-centric and principled, expressing you Unique Gifts, soaring in your mission, and not trapped in your attachments.

This chapter was a brief look into the duality that you carry. Gaining visibility into all aspects of your life, including your stories and your roles, as well as your creative and unlimited selves, is perhaps the greatest step that you can take in your 'passage'. It may take you years, if not decades, to undertake that journey of growing in self-awareness and still come away feeling a starter. The level of fulfillment you receive in life and the level of greatness you achieve in life is directly proportional to the extent of the passage that you have undertaken.

The more you peel the layers of your conditioning, the more you revert back to the *unconditioned self*. This state of 'being' was what Eknath Easwaran, the author of 'Gandhi, The Man', was referring to when he noted of Gandhi, "[...] by the end of his life he was aflame with love."

From the forbearance and compassion that the Being Leaders had achieved by the end of their lives[11], we can surmise that through their passage, they had accessed the state of 'being'.

---

[11] We will study the Being Leaders' quality of forbearance and compassion in detail in chap. 20, 'CAPACITY FOR COMPASSION AND FORBEARANCE', pg. 325

8. PART OF A GREATER SEA

"There is something unfolding in the universe whether one speaks of it as an unconscious process, or whether one speaks of it as some unmoved mover, or whether someone speaks of it as a personal God. There is something in the universe that unfolds."

Dr. Martin Luther King Jr.

Abraham Lincoln, the great giver of liberty, the emancipator of millions and the re-builder of a floundering republic was also a "fatalist", someone who believed that there was no thing called freewill. Fatalism, for Lincoln, was the idea that all future events have a pattern that is pre-established and unchangeable. While he believed in the capacity of individuals to improve themselves via a free-labour system that "gives hope to all, and energy, and progress, and improvement of condition to all", he also believed that human actions were decided by powers beyond human control.

"I have all my life been a fatalist," Lincoln informed his Illinois congressional ally, Isaac Arnold. "Mr. Lincoln was a fatalist," remembered Henry Clay Whitney, one of his Springfield law clerks, "he believed [...] that the universe is governed by one uniform, unbroken, primordial law." His Springfield law partner Herndon likewise remembered that Lincoln "believed in predestination, foreordination, that all things were fixed, doomed one way or the other, from which there was no appeal." Even Mary Todd Lincoln, Abraham

2. PASSAGE

Lincoln's wife, acknowledged that her husband had been guided by the conviction that "what is to be will be, and no cares of ours can arrest nor reverse the decree."

Clearly, Lincoln believed that "there was no freedom of the will". Human's destiny was scripted by a higher power over which they had no control; fate settled things and laws ruled the universe of matter and mind. When it came to matters of destiny, man was just a simple tool, a mere cog in the wheel. Even as president, Lincoln often described himself as "but an accidental instrument, temporary, and to serve but for a limited time." He compared himself over the years to "a piece of floating driftwood". Even at the height of the Civil War in 1864, he told Canadian journalist Josiah Blackburn that he had "drifted into the very apex of this great event".

According to Joseph Gillespie, a long time political ally of Lincoln, Lincoln believed that he was an instrument foreordained to lead the American Civil War, put down the rebellion and free the slaves. Orville Browning, Lincoln's friend, recalled Lincoln's certainty in the 1850s that he had before him "what he considered some important predestined labour or work [...] nobler than he was for the time engaged in."

Lincoln's denial of freewill presented a contrasting picture for the early Americans who valued human liberty and personal sovereignty. To see the man who urged "work, work, work" as the formula for professional success, who lauded the Declaration of Independence as his political inspiration, and who gave political freedom to millions through the Emancipation Proclamation—to see this man disavow any belief in the individual's freedom to choose gives the impression of a man with a divided heart. Yet, Lincoln believed in people's ability to work towards their liberty and personal sovereignty.

Though Lincoln passionately believed in that higher power that preordained for things to happen, how and when we reach that destiny was well within each individual's control. Through sheer hard work one could attract the grace of the higher power.

But who or what, then, is this higher power? During his presidency, Lincoln frequently spoke of "an all-wise Providence" or "the Divine Being who determines the destinies of nations" as the intelligent and self-conscious controller of destiny. Lincoln could be seen often discussing this higher power with Herndon, Lincoln's law partner, in the years Lincoln and Herndon shared their Springfield law office.

Lincoln provided another large piece of evidence of his belief in a higher power. During his 1846 campaign for an Illinois, US, Congressional seat, Lincoln had experienced considerable anxiety. He was running against Peter Cartwright who was questioning Lincoln's spiritual beliefs. Worried by rumours of Cartwright's "whispering campaign" against Lincoln's spiritual beliefs, Lincoln promptly drew up a formal statement to be printed in several central Illinois newspapers. In this "handbill" Lincoln stated "that the human mind is impelled to action, or held in rest by some power, over which the mind itself has no control." Lincoln held the notion that all human conduct is the forced result of natural laws, with the possible implication that Lincoln believed that there was no such thing as right or wrong human action, only action compelled by some unseen force.

Lincoln believed that human choice is caused by the mind being compelled—without any power of its own—to cooperate with a higher power. This belief originated from Lincoln's childhood; "his early Baptist training" may have come from Thomas Lincoln, Abraham Lincoln's father. Thomas and Nancy Lincoln (Abraham Lincoln's biological mother) were members in Kentucky of the Little Mount Separate Baptist Church, a congregation that believed that a higher power existed. Lincoln's foster mother Sarah Bush Lincoln, and sister Sarah, were members of the 'Separates' who believed that God had already determined who are His children and who not. Add to this the

2. PASSAGE

fact that Thomas Lincoln was "one of the five or six most important men" among the Indiana Separates, and it becomes clear that Abraham Lincoln was brought up in Indiana in an atmosphere that believed in the presence of a greater power that conspired to shape each human's destiny.

There is also evidence that Lincoln had significant access to formal intellectual resources in theology, metaphysics and law wherefrom he may have embraced his beliefs. Lincoln was also known to have an inclination to philology wherefrom his belief in a higher power may have grown.

There is further evidence of Lincoln's deep held belief in a higher power. In 1851, Lincoln composed a farewell letter to his stepbrother John D. Johnston for his dying father, assuring Thomas Lincoln that "He who notes the fall of the sparrow, and numbers the hairs of our heads [...] will not forget the dying man, who puts his Trust in him." A year later, Lincoln eulogized Henry Clay as "a man the times have demanded, and such, in the providence of God was given us." And it is well known that during his embattled presidency, Lincoln often alluded to "the Divine Being who determines the destinies of nations," and to "an all-wise Providence," and to "Divine assistance" without which "all must fail". He repeatedly described himself as nothing more than "a humble instrument in the hands of the Almighty" and expanded that on at least one occasion to claim that "we are all agents and instruments of Divine Providence". In Providence Lincoln could find an answer to all events unseen and beyond his control.

Lincoln's belief in a higher power seems too real to be only political window dressing. On those occasions when Lincoln derived some measure of confidence from his belief in that higher power, he chided those of little faith, like Congressman James Wilson and his Iowa delegation in 1862, with the assertion that "my faith is greater than yours". And when the war news turned disastrous, he frequently surrendered to a sense of helplessness in the face of an inscrutable cosmic will. In a private memorandum during the dark September of 1862, Lincoln admitted that "the will of God prevails," but that God's purpose in doing so was deeply puzzling. In 1864, he pointed out that "now at the end of three years' struggle the nation's condition is not what either party, or any man devised, or expected" and that "God alone can claim it". More dramatically, he "moaned and groaned in anguish" to Pennsylvania governor Andrew Curtin saying over and over again. "What has God put me in this place for?"

What is clear is that Lincoln remained gripped throughout his life by the same sense of a universe whose order transcended human control.[XVI]

"In the universe there was a power that worked for righteousness as it seemed to us," Lincoln once said.

In the passage phase, the Being Leaders developed a strong sense of fate, not as a force that slows us down and let things happen to us. They recognized that they were parts of a much larger whole that has its own inscrutable origins and ends. They learned to accept that other factors, beyond their control, often shaped their paths in unexpected ways. They understood that this fate was a higher power that—when followed—takes us towards our destiny. That is an important education we notice in the lives of the Being Leaders.

If you can accept fate, you can focus better on acting and thinking in the here-and-now without illusions or bitterness or regret. The more you act in coherence with that fate, the faster you arrive at your destiny.

Andrew Young, social activist and friend of Dr. King, remembered of Dr. King that "he always understood that this was not a course that he charted. It in

2. PASSAGE

some way—almost mystical way—had been charted for him. He understood that forces had come together and coalesced and pit their hand on his shoulder. But it wasn't what he sought."[XVIII]

How did the Being Leaders' belief in a higher power reflect upon their lives?

The Being Leaders were leaders who saw effort as the formula for success in life. Along their passage, they acquired the belief that they could not control the outcome, all they could do was to focus on the effort, and all else would follow. Gandhi famously said, "full effort is full victory". He meant that you have control only over your actions and not over the outcomes of those actions. Neither can you be attached to the fruits of your labour. Each outcome has many factors contributing to it, several of them unknown to the limited human mind. Hence, a pure motive would be to conduct actions selflessly and with the aim of making a difference. When conducting actions in such a manner, the righteous power of the higher power would work beneficially towards the outcome.

To conduct yourself this way takes acceptance of faith, faith in a power that is non-local and omnipresent in nature. Faith is a large component that drove these leaders to their destination. Their faith did not grow out of their naiveté. Neither was it forced upon them by their parents or institutions. It came from their realization of the righteous nature of this higher power.

This is where faith differs from sight. With the support of sight, you believe in what is visible. What is here around you at this very moment becomes real to you. You can experience and understand it with your limited mind, and that gives you the conviction that it is real.

Faith on the other hand is believing without the virtue of sight. Whereas what you can see is limited, what you can experience through belief is infinite. Through faith, everything that is beyond your vicinity and beyond the current time becomes real. Faith is letting go of the familiar and allowing the new to appear. Faith is what helps you step beyond the known into the world of the seemingly unknown. Faith is learning to let go of your limited selves in order to find your immensely potent grander selves.

Faith is not a foreign experience to you. As children you have practiced faith. It was essential because—as children—you were dependent upon others or other things for your survival. That kind of faith is instinctive to you. Ironically, what you relied on as children for survival—faith—is precisely what you stop relying on as adults.

As adults, you long to bring certainty to life by taking control of circumstances. You refuse to leave anything to chance, let alone to others. You insist on seeing things and touching them before accepting them as real. This is the reality of your survival instinct. Faith, on the other hand, gives you the strength to lay aside the survival agenda and stand for a greater agenda. It helps you to take advantage of all resources available in the universe instead of relying solely on your physical might. It gives you the power to actualize life fully and make a magic out of each day. That is when you make a difference.

As adults, faith must be a chosen quality. With such a choiceful faith, life opens up in infinite possibilities. Life does not remain confined to the immediate and the present moment. Your potential does not remain limited to your physical faculties. Instead faith expands beyond the immediate and the present to encompass the collective and beyond. This the Being Leaders knew. They did not believe that their real strength was limited to their physical self, instead whole of humanity—and beyond—was their resource as much as they were an integral part of that whole.

"I am quite aware of the fact that there are persons who believe firmly in non-violence who do not believe in a personal God, but I think every person who believes in non-violent resistance believes somehow that the universe in some form is on the side of justice." This was Dr. King's stand on faith. "That there is something unfolding in the universe whether one speaks of it as an unconscious process, or whether one speaks of it as some unmoved mover, or whether someone speaks of it as a personal God. There is something in the universe that

2. PASSAGE

unfolds for justice and so in Montgomery[12] we felt somehow that as we struggled we had cosmic companionship. And this was one of the things that kept the people together, the belief that the universe is on the side of justice.[XVIII]

8.1. BRANCHES OF THE SAME TREE

In the words of Nelson Mandela, "In the old days when we were young, a traveller through a country would stop at a village, and he didn't have to ask for food or for water. Once he stops, people will give him food, entertain him. That is one aspect of *Ubuntu.*"

Ubuntu does not mean that people should not care for themselves. A question therefore is, 'Are you going to do so in order to enable the community around you and to be able to improve?' These are the important things in life. And if one can do that, you have done something very important, which will be appreciated."

Ubuntu comes from a Zulu proverb. Its essence is that we all are part of a greater whole, and each individual has a role and a proper place in this infinite whole. Our energy energizes or de-energizes others. We are subject to forces that are not limited to us. That through humble service, we enrich the lives of others, and in that process enrich ourselves.

---

[12] The Montgomery Bus Boycott, a seminal event in the U.S. civil rights movement, was a political and social protest campaign against the policy of racial segregation on the public transit system of Montgomery, Alabama. The campaign lasted from December 1, 1955, when Rosa Parks, an African American woman, was arrested for refusing to surrender her seat to a white person, to December 20, 1956, when a federal ruling took effect, and led to a United States Supreme Court decision that declared the Alabama and Montgomery laws requiring segregated buses to be unconstitutional

Part of a Greater Sea

As the aphorism goes, "A rising tide lifts all the boats." That defines the role of each individual in the collective whole. A person is a person through other people. We do nothing entirely on our own. We all are part of an infinitely complex web of other human beings. We are all bound with one another. We are all branches of the same family tree.[XIX]

x   x   x

In parts of the Western world defined by individualism and personal sovereignty, *Ubuntu* cannot be easily understood. Leaders in such cultures are so busy trying to assert themselves that the ability to see what binds all of us into a synergistic whole is lost to them. They rush to associate collectivism with socialism, communism or redistribution. Such expression has created a strong force against our collective expression of ideas and building the magic and miracle that comes from togetherness. We have effectively stifled synergies as a consequence. I have met leadership aspirants who have financed political campaigns to keep the values of individualism as the defining character of their organizations and nations.

For such men and women, achievement and accomplishment is a distinguishing factor, not a unifying code. They believe that they stand on their own and they perish alone. Many of them are driven by fear, for unconsciously they believe that if they do not possess as much wealth as possible and accrue the greatest share of exhaustible resources, their survival is threatened. I have found that these individuals compensate for their inner scarcity with external opulence. That I call the drive for self-sufficiency, not the pursuit of greatness.

During their passage, the four Being Leaders examined in this work learned that they were not isolated entities in a collection of individual living beings. They clearly recognized themselves to be interlinked to and influenced by each other. More than that, they believed that their fates were interlinked with forces external to them. All these legendary leaders believed in a power that consisted of a force field of all the living beings coexisting in a collective space.

2. PASSAGE

Whether it was the abeyance to the constitution, as was the case with Lincoln; or to the power of god, as was the case with Gandhi; or to the goodness of humanity, as was the case with Dr. King; or to the collective strength of community, as was the case with Mandela, the Being Leaders learned to see themselves as part of a whole that included many distinguished men and women who have led before them in noble ways. They understood that their efforts were existent only in the context of all others. That if there were not those who saw society as naturally unequal, there was not a need to defend justice. That in the absence of the defenders of inequality, there was no room for a leader who could lead the way and take a stand for equality.

The Being Leaders also developed the ability to operate and excel within the rules, whether from corporations, religion or the constitution. This takes self-awareness. It involves knowing how effective you will be when operating under a set of principles that govern all fellow beings. Mandela was at his effective best not when he was operating as a radical, rather when he could master all his faculties and bring it under the umbrella of his noblest values. That is when he became unstoppable.

Therein lies the paradox. How can one be outside the 'system' in ones unlimited thinking while at the same time be a defender of a set of rules or principles? It is this unwavering reliance on his set of higher principles that led Lincoln to seemingly supersede the constitution and use wartime powers, including shutting down newspapers and putting away agitators who championed principles that did not benefit the collective good. Yet he was operating within the rules albeit a different set of rules. Who except one who had massive self-awareness could transcend procedural limitations and shine in his might?

The Being Leaders learned that the principles of spirit are so all-encompassing that when a person operated in alignment with those principles, he automatically transcended the limitations of a set of rules established by the limited mind. This step-up could be achieved even while operating within a framework of values.

Part of a Greater Sea

A retired community organizer from the United States once wisely pointed out to me, "look at those leaders who are threatening the governments to deregulate, do they give society a comforting feeling that they will self-govern themselves?" His voice was shaky but his face was illuminated by a smile as he shared his thoughts.

"Regulations appear only in lands where self-regulation is non-existent," he declared philosophically looking into the distance. "That is the reason why I admire how the Swiss conduct themselves on the road. There doesn't seem to be a need for traffic police or traffic light or dividers or even markers. There seems to be a level of self-responsibility among the people there."

"I don't see a need for any further regulations for the Swiss streets. Why?" He asked me a question for which the answer was obvious.

9. HAVE A TRUE MEASURE OF THE SELF

"The seeker after truth should be humbler than the dust. The world crushes the dust under its feet, but the seeker after truth should so humble himself that even the dust could crush him. Only then, and not till then, will he have a glimpse of the truth."

M.K. Gandhi

On March 1ˢᵗ 1971, Nelson Mandela wrote to Fatima Meer, his authorized biographer, expressing his reservations about writing an autobiography;

"I shall stick to our vow: never, never under any circumstances, to say anything unbecoming of the other [...]. The trouble, of course, is that most successful men are prone to some form of vanity. There comes a stage in their lives when they consider permissible to be egoistic and to brag to the public at large about their unique achievements. What a sweet euphemism for self praise the English language has evolved! Autobiography, they chose to call it, where the shortcomings of others are frequently exploited to highlight the praiseworthy accomplishments of the author.

I am doubtful if I will ever sit down to scribble my background. I have neither the achievements of which I could boast nor the skills to do it. If I lived on cane spirit every day of my life, I still would not have had the courage to attempt it. I sometimes believe that through me Creation

2. PASSAGE

intended to give the world the example of a mediocre man in the proper sense of the term. Nothing could tempt me to advertise myself.

Had I been in a position to write an autobiography, its publication would have been delayed until my bones had been laid, and perhaps I might have dropped hints not compatible with my vow. The dead have no worries, and if the truth and nothing but the whole truth about them emerge, and the image I have helped to maintain through my perpetual silence was ruined, that would be the affair of posterity, not ours [...] I'm one of those who possess scraps of superficial information on a variety of subjects, but who lacks depth and expert knowledge on the one thing in which I ought to have specialized, namely the history of my country and people."

Building a true measure of the self is one of the core steps taken by the Being Leaders in their apprenticeship of life. Before building a true measure of the self, the Being Leaders attempted to assert themselves against their opponents by force. They had an illusion that they could match force with force and overcome their adversaries. Only when the Being Leaders were subdued by their opponents did they get a true measure of their military might and a clear estimate of their limitations in the game of life. That got them into the practice of humility.

Humility is the ability to make a right estimation of one's self[13]. It is the quality of being modest. Humility, in various interpretations, is connected with notions of transcendence, other-worldliness or the utmost unity with the universe or the divine, and living without ego. There is no ego, pride or arrogance attached to humility.

---

[13] Sendjaya, 2005

Have a True Measure of the Self

In the *Bhagavad-Gita*[14], it is said that "the war within, the struggle for self-mastery that every human being must wage if he or she is to emerge from life victorious" and "the language of battle is often found in the scriptures, for it conveys the strenuous, long, drawn-out campaign we must wage to free ourselves from the tyranny of the ego, the cause of all our suffering and sorrow."

In KCP Low's work, 'Gandhi and His Value of Humility'[15], the understanding of humility is well captured: "If one is not self-effacing or humble and goes around with one's ego, one may not be detached; attachment or ego-nurturing may follow. This means that one may not listen to others, and whatever one behaves or does things, one's mindset is self-centered; only thinking of himself/herself, but not of others. This is, in fact, contradictory to the purpose of being a leader, which is to serve or assist others. In this regard, a leader has to behave egoless and selfless."

When you have a true measure of the self, you would not want for yourself and instead would want to do more for others. That is what makes the Being Leader altruistic and caring. The Being Leaders were serving because they were not in the control of their ego; in other words, they were selfless, serving and are, most beautiful of all—like loving parents, willing to make sacrifices for their children.

You are humble before the world even when you are sure you are on the right path. That confidence makes you not arrogant, instead you willingly suffer the world's punishment and bow to its judgment. That is humility.

The greatest trap of humility is indifference. In the urge to practice humility, leaders I have met have resorted to being detached from their

---

[14] A treatise on life from ancient India
[15] Low KCP, Ang SL and Robertson, RW (2012) 'Gandhi and His Value Of Humility', 'Gandhi and His Value Of Humility', Leadership & Organizational Management Journal, ISSN 2152-8675. Volume 2012 Issue 3, p. 105 – 116

2. PASSAGE

true worth. They stop being themselves, instead pretending to be someone there are not. They lose touch with their core essence, and disconnect from their own aspirations and intentions.

In 'Gandhi and His Value Of Humility', Low, Ang and Robertson gives leaders valuable cautionary advice: "Humility must not be taken overboard or used as the slightest excuse to do things less well, or worse, not to do anything at all. Some tend to confuse humility with passiveness or lack of courage. I have met leaders who have also—at times—used humility to assume "zero responsibility and no accountability", and hide behind "anonymity and pseudonyms". Yet others may have nothing, yet they may act as if they have everything. Then there are those who have been foolishly proud and extravagant, seeming like an empty shell or sounding like a noisy vessel."

Gandhi made a habit of wearing what the common man wore. He spun his own clothes. Lincoln even received guests in bare feet. He was known to have woken up each morning to find a newsboy to buy a newspaper for himself. Lincoln's whole Whitehouse staff consisted of two men in their twenties. That is hard for us to imagine when the measure of a leader's success these days is the size of the corner office they hold, the type of vehicle they drive, and the corporate jet and the other perks that have become a measure of a leader's stature.

When you have a true measure of yourself, you let the wonderment of the child within takeover. In that child-like state, all judgments are suspended and it gets replaced by wonderment. Nothing is worthy of judgment, and everything is worthy of experiencing. Fully.

When you judge a situation, you judge it against something. That something is your conditioning. As a child, you were unconditioned to a large extent. Hence there was little to judge any experience or event against. As a result, each experience felt new and filled you with wonder. There was no frantic effort to find a place for that experience and make sense out of it. You simply surrendered into that moment, free from any agenda to understand it.

To force yourself to understand the events and experiences around you is to take control of it. You take control of situations not only by controlling the events and experiences happening in your lives, but also by judging those external experiences against your conditioned selves. By relating those experiences to your conditioning—through your judgment—you say, "now I get it" or "now I understand it".

As a result of your judgment, how you see the world around you is not how the world really is. You could look at a man in his workplace and perceive him to be ruthless, or see a woman in her worldly setting and judge her to be manipulative. You can recognize this effect of your conditioned self by observing how you relate to the world around you. You might interact with others in distrust or even resentment. When you see someone in a position of power and authority, you unconsciously adore them if you are conditioned in hierarchical cultures. Or you could react in resentment, defiance, contempt or indifference if you were conditioned in a non-hierarchical home. This is all a consequence of your judgment.

The opposite of judgement is the practice of surrender. In surrender you are fully experiencing the experience rather than striving to understand it. And as you let that experience continue to infiltrate your senses, it will awaken a deeper knowing within you. You start to understand the deeper truth of the experience and you start to see the real color of the actors in the experience. You comprehend the un-stated motivations of those you engage with, motivations which are often unknown even to themselves.

Having a true measure of themselves helped the Being Leaders surrender their judgment. The Being Leaders did not see themselves judge and jury, rather their movements were against self-anointed

2. PASSAGE

judges of society. Free from judgment, the Being Leaders naturally related to their allies and opponents with love. At moments when they felt their hearts close and their understanding blocked, they set the practice of suspending judgment as a standard in their lives, or as a duty unto themselves. This is what made the Being Leaders dangerous to their opponents. They could not be overcome because they could not be trapped in their judgments.

Dr. King refused to judge the white Southerners as evil. This endlessly confused his opponents, those who fought to maintain their current way of life. Dr. King insisted to his fellowmen that their non-violent struggle sought to attack the evil system rather than individuals who happen to be caught up in the system. He always asserted that the struggle in the South is "not so much the tension between white people and Negro people". The struggle is rather between justice and injustice, between the forces of light and the forces of darkness. "And if there is a victory it will not be a victory merely for fifty thousand Negroes. But it will be a victory for justice, a victory for good will, a victory for democracy," His idea was not to humiliate the opponent and score a win, but to win the opponent over. And that, Dr. King believed, they could not achieve from a place of judgment.

At the center of the civil rights movement stood the philosophy of love. The only way to ultimately convert the white people in the South was to keep love at the center of each life. People have asked Dr. King what he meant by love and how is it that he could insist that they love those persons who seek to defeat them and stand against them; how could anyone love such persons who have created only wounds in their lives? Dr. King responded by making it clear that one must love for the act of loving, as you must undertake your actions for the pure act of doing. And if you could not accomplish that in your life, you recognize it as your duty towards humanity, or because you have established that action as a standard in your life. Dr. King felt that it is the love of God working in the minds of men. It was an overflowing love which sought nothing in return. And when you come to love on this level you are no more the judge.

Opponents with batons and fire hoses did not know how to respond to such a movement. They were used to subdue those who acted in violence. They had the might and the means to throw rioters and vandals in prison. Their weapons were designed to overpower miscreants who broke the law, or ambushed innocents in the dark. But they were at a loss of idea on how to defeat a movement that walked towards them with outstretched hands and love in their hearts.[XX]

A true measure of the self worked as the inexhaustible source of love that rode the Being Leaders into the path of legend-hood. The more the Being Leaders understood their measure, the more naturally surrender came to them. That, in turn, helped them let go of any need for judging their adversaries.

9.1. MAKE YOURSELF SMALL

Gandhi's living takes inspiration from many sages and mystics, both from within India and beyond. In his practice of humility, he found enormous strength from the words of *Bhagavad-Gita*[16]. In it, he found the conviction to open up and surrender into a higher power that went beyond the self.

Gandhi also gained enormous inspiration from the life of Jesus Christ. Such was the impact

---

[16] A treatise on life from ancient India

that the life and teachings of Jesus had on Gandhi that he even considered becoming a Christian for a while, until—it is told—he actually visited a church in South Africa and was refused entrance by a white usher due to his brown skin. Until his very end, Gandhi practiced his humble living along the lives of Jesus and the various sages who saw themselves as part of a greater sea.

What truly strikes anyone about Gandhi was the way he led others. He led people both by becoming radically open to what he was called upon to do and by inviting others to follow their highest calling.

It is noted that in the meetings in which Gandhi participated, he would unhesitatingly take the tea set and serve the participants. Such action was discomforting for many participants who hailed from the higher castes in India and were used to being served by someone who was socio-economically inferior. They would feel embarrassed, and on many occasions urged to Gandhi that they could serve themselves.

Gandhi serving tea to others was also awkward for the orderlies and servants originally assigned to such tasks. They were accustomed to receiving orders from the likes of Gandhi and serving accordingly. However, Gandhi doing such 'menial' tasks made many orderlies conclude that the reason why Gandhi served tea was because they were not doing it right. Gandhi had to console them that he was only doing it because it needed to be done and he could do it right as well. It is told that with some orderlies, it took years of convincing before they saw that it was Gandhi's openness to spirit that made him see no difference between tasks, big or small. For Gandhi, serving tea to others was simply an act of leading others by serving them.

In another demonstration of humility, Gandhi was visiting a city to give a lecture to an organization he supported. Yet none of them knew what he looked like, so when he arrived, no one recognized him. He entered their building, and amidst the last minute chaos of people preparing for the event, he noticed that a certain area of the floor needed sweeping. So he found a broom and began sweeping. And when they finally realized who he was, they asked him, dumbfounded, "Why are you doing such a menial task?"

Gandhi replied, "Because it needed to be done."

What was most astonishing about Gandhi was his willingness to suffer on behalf of others. While the leaders of most movements try to insulate themselves from suffering, Gandhi embraced it. He was always willing to put himself on the front line to receive beatings from his enemies. Like all the other Being Leaders, he was not a high and mighty general who led his lowly troops from a distant command centre. In South Africa, as a leader in the struggle for suffrage for those of Indian descent, Gandhi was willing to take terrible beatings from the constables, beatings that left him severely injured. He did so to demonstrate to other Indian expatriates that while their bodies could be broken, their spirit could not be killed. He may have been a meagre man, but he was part of an indestructible whole. In South Africa, Gandhi led his fellow Indians into a peaceful rebellion in order to secure voting rights for all Indian immigrants.

x   x   x

Gandhi led from a strength rooted in humility. The Being Leaders teach us that there is strength in humility, and that humble leadership exposes self-interest and selfishness in both enemies and friends alike, as it simultaneously purifies motives. When we lead from a sense of humility, willingly putting aside our own motivations and desires in favor of a greater cause, we create the context in which people are more willing to put aside their self-interest.

One of the everyday refrains we hear is that our leaders are out of touch with average people. Organizational leaders are accused of being out of

2. PASSAGE

tune with the rest of the organization. Political leaders are accused of being out of touch with the masses. So their everyday concerns seem alien to contemporary leaders. These leaders have lost the ability to think at the meagre level at which most of the world think and experience the world.

The Being Leaders teach us that whatever we are doing, humility allows us to step into the truth of others. That opens up the path to greater creativity and possibility in whatever we are doing. Gandhi demonstrated, time and time again, how humility enabled him to discern creative solutions. His solutions to apparent problems and obstacles were ingeniously creative—and creativity made his non-violent path toward Indian independence a powerful force. The British colonialists could never anticipate what he was going to do.

For instance, at one point the Indian independence movement was stalling. There was tremendous pressure for Gandhi to do something, anything, to get the movement back on track. Gandhi did something, but it was not what his followers expected. They wanted quick, decisive action. Instead, Gandhi spent eight months at his *ashram*[17] in prayer and contemplation despite pleas from millions for action. Suddenly one day, he received a personal opening. He told his followers to pack a few belongings, and he and his supporters began to walk. Day after day they walked through towns and villages, and as news of his march spread, many of the villagers joined the procession. With thousands of followers now behind him and many British soldiers surrounding him, Gandhi walked calmly to the edge of the sea where a large chunk of salt had been formed by the evaporation of the sea water in the hot Indian sun. He picked up the salt, walked over to a British soldier, and said, "I have manufactured salt. You must arrest me!"[18]

---

[17] Monastery

[18] Under British rule, Indians were prohibited from making their own salt. Gandhi broke the law with this march, now famously called the Dandi March of 1930.

Why was this so important? It was important because Gandhi, with his ability to be small, opened a door into an everyday concern of the Indian masses. In a small chunk of salt Gandhi had found a symbol of Indian freedom. A few years earlier, in an attempt to maintain power over the Indian economy, the colonialists had made it illegal for Indians to manufacture this essential element. Only the British could manufacture salt. In a simple gesture, Gandhi had shown the absurdity of British law in India by presenting the British with a dilemma. If they arrested him, they would reveal the oppressiveness of their laws to the Indian people, the British population, and to the world. If they did not arrest him, they would give implicit permission to the whole Indian population to defy the British in this and every other economic concern. They arrested Gandhi, but his imprisonment ended up giving freedom to the Indians as millions made their own salt by pouring seawater into pans and letting it evaporate on their rooftops.

In his life practice, Gandhi discovered how powerful humility was, and how leaders grounded in humility could transform hearts, minds, souls, and nations when they were willing to become humble leaders. Gandhi learned how dangerous humility could be to others. It could expose the falseness and hypocrisy of the world's ways. Humble leaders can show people how to experience and follow their inner voice in ways they never expected; a pilgrimage that transforms them in ways that they may not anticipate or always welcome. At the same time, humble leadership can be personally challenging to those of you who seek this humble way. It exposes you to your own weakness, powerlessness, fear, and anxiety. It is impossible to be a humble leader and not grapple with these forces.

The way of humility invites you to recognize that you are all part of a larger whole which includes all other people and other beings. It asks you to sometimes surrender to that higher power, a path that potentially leads to failure—the failure to achieve your ambitions through brute force in a world that worships power. When you lead

153

through humility, you are choosing a path that emphasizes gentleness, leaving you open and vulnerable to the manipulations of those devoted to wielding power. If you are to become humble leaders, you have to develop a different kind of strength. This strength is a strength of character that few are willing to form, a strength of the Spirit.

There is yet another powerful lesson of humility to learn from the lives of the Being Leaders. You discover that when you surrender into the wisdom of the universe—instead of showing haste to take control—you keep out of the way of the universe. This way of the universe you can call nature. Nature takes its own course when you do not meddle with it with your false impression of power. This course of nature is ultimately the ideal course for all of us collectively. It is strongly corrective in nature, and it is always balancing the conflicting forces that operate in nature. For instance, when you intervene in the natural food chain, certain species go extinct. One very real threat that we are facing today is that due to the constant use of harmful chemical substances on plants, there is a real threat of bees becoming extinct. If bees were to become extinct, it is calculated that two-thirds of the worlds food crops that depend on bees for crosspollination will soon disappear. That will harm our continued existence. By aligning your will with that of this power of nature, you invite the universe's power to flow through you and into whatever organization or party you are leading.

It is not uncommon for business leaders today to talk about wielding political and even military power as a step up. How often do you come across contemporary leaders self-righteously declare their position as "the correct" position and all opposing positions as wrongheaded or ignorant? Humility in leadership today seems to be in short supply.

Many in our culture assume that cultivating a humble life gets in the way of leading an organization towards its full potential. But the Being Leaders teach us that humility does not mean becoming feeble. Instead, it means having a fierce openness to spirit and bringing that servantship into our leadership. They demonstrated that to be humble actually means to be strong in your giving and then to have the courage to lead others into giving despite the resistance and outright opposition by those who want us to hold on to the old, obsolete ways of the business culture. Humble leaders recognize that they are part of a greater sea and they guided people to follow their noble paths.

At the peak of their powers, the Being Leaders always were humble; for it is out of their humility that they found ways to inspire and motivate those they lead, and unify those who opposed. That was a passage based on first surrendering into spirit's calling and then on leading others toward their spirit's voice. Your passage, after all, awakens others and attracts others to step into theirs.

Conventional leaders mostly carry no coherent vision for their lives. Coherence of vision comes from self-examination, a practice that does not come from business schools or corporate apprenticeship. The most advanced among the conventional leaders carry a coherent vision in their lives. Such leaders motivate people to follow the leader's vision. The Being Leaders, on the other hand, motivated people to follow their own vision, a vision higher than the limited self.

As the Being Leaders grew on their path, they learned to voluntarily give up pride, arrogance, ego, and selfishness to become open to the guidance of a higher voice. They had a strength of character, conviction, vision, and faith that was awe-inspiring to those around him, yet it never led them to become prideful, arrogant, manipulative, or dismissive of others, especially of those who disagreed with them. They stayed small throughout their passage—and beyond—and steeped their leadership in the understanding that they were a minute part of a larger whole. They saw their lives as being in service of that whole.[XXI]

9.2. MINIMIZE THE SELF

In 1994, Mandela became the first president of post-Apartheid South Africa. Over the years—before and after being elected as president—Mandela strove to heal the divide that existed between the white rulers and the black oppressed. "There was a need to free the Blacks from bondage as there was a need to free the white Afrikaners from fear," Mandela claimed.

There is nothing more subtle and abstract than freeing someone from fear. Yet, Mandela took the effort to come more than half way when he had no reason to move an inch. Afrikaners noticed the effort that Mandela made and felt open towards him, and he won them over.

In the 1995 Rugby World Cup in South Africa, un-fancied hosts South Africa won a nail-biting final against favourites New Zealand. And President Nelson Mandela—who had been imprisoned for 27 years by the brutal Apartheid regime who adored rugby and saw rugby as a symbol of Afrikaner supremacy—presented the trophy to white captain Francois Pienaar, while wearing the player's spare No. 6 shirt and a Springbok cap.

Former South Africa winger Chester Williams said: "When Nelson Mandela walked into the changing room wearing that Springbok rugby jersey, it was done. We had to win that game.

"Everybody expected him to wear a suit and tie. It changed the attitude and spirit of the team—and it changed the whole mindset of the nation."

It created a historic and unprecedented moment in South Africa's race struggle. It was a symbol of unity which helped to heal the bitter wounds of racial division in the nation. The Afrikaners who saw Mandela as a threat to their way of life and viewed his rise with apprehension trusted him and saw him as their president.

"And when you have won over them, never gloat," Mandela stated referring back to that moment in history. "The time of your greatest triumph is the time when you should be most merciful. Do not humiliate them under any circumstances. Let them in fact save face. And then you will have made your enemies your friend."

x   x   x

In their apprenticeship of life, the Being Leaders learned that their truth was not greater than that of others, or that they were exceptional beings with special powers to handle truth. They have felt that what they were capable of, others were too. They discovered that their truth was not out of this world, rather even children could embrace it.

The Being Leaders were well aware of the legacy that they were shaping. But they all felt that they were living an unremarkable life in the service of the greater good. They always insisted that there were better individuals to have undertaken the tasks that they themselves undertook. Mandela stated that Walter Sizulu, his mentor, would have been a more capable anti-Apartheid leader for South Africa. Lincoln felt Henry Clay, his role model, was a better person to meet the challenges faced by the American Union.

In the aftermath of the seven debates against Stephen A. Douglas, Lincoln's archrival, that propelled Lincoln into the national spotlight, people and reporters were asking him if he planned to run for presidency. "I must in candour say I do not see myself fit for the presidency," Lincoln shot the idea down when an eager newspaper editor raised the question of running for presidency with him. "Just think of a sucker as me as president," he joked to another.

2. PASSAGE

Gandhi liked to say to his visitors that others in the Indian National Congress would have led the freedom struggle of India better.

There is a story of a man traveling by train on the same bench as Gandhi. However, the man did not know that the old man on his bench was Gandhi. So, all night long this man lay down on the seat, occupying the entire bench, pushing Gandhi, putting his feet on him, and leaving Gandhi with barely enough room to sit upright. However, Gandhi did not complain. He simply let the man use as much of the seat as he desired. As the train pulled into their destination, the man mentioned that he was going to see the famous Gandhi. Gandhi still remained silent. He felt no need to proudly proclaim his identity. As Gandhi descended from the train, a crowd of thousands roared in welcome. The man was deeply embarrassed and sought Gandhi's forgiveness. Gandhi only smiled and reminded the man that he should be more respectful of others, regardless of who they were.[XXII]

This episode contrasts again the nature of some business and political leaders who I have met. I am often astonished by how much many leaders and emerging leaders rely on their titles. Often their names are a long string of titles, and mostly these individuals are unaware of their own motivation for adding titles to their names. It has become a collective conditioning in the organizational setting, especially in North America, to always be associated with their titles.

While I was seated in the office of one of my clients during the early days of our mutual acquaintance, he had a call from a reporter asking for information about a situation that has affected the campus where his office was. From his expression, I knew that he knew nothing of the situation and could not give her any assistance. When he hung up the phone, I could sense a grain of irritation brewing within him. As I observed his emotions, he rang his secretary and curtly asked: "Why didn't anyone warn me?"

His secretary responded back noting that it was not an important matter, and the issue has already been taken care of as soon as it appeared...and listen to this, "it was not our problem, so we were not informed."

In his "I am so important thinking", he forgot that others are important and competent too. But, because he had a tendency to look at every situation as 'life and death', he got caught up in his belief that if he did not know the answers, it will be a setback. Nope. If he was not kept informed, it simply meant that someone else has taken care of it, away from his involvement.

Taking oneself too seriously is assuming one is more important than he or she really is. It results in our expecting more respect and attention than is warranted. We begin feeling that we, more than anyone else, should be notified the moment God has new plans for His church—and, of course, these plans should include us.

We operate in a corporate and political culture where individuals who inflate themselves are disproportionately rewarded. Substance gets overlooked. This has created a greater incentive to 'show-off' oneself as being better than the rest. The pot of gold is limited, and it needs to be divided among the staff. To claim a larger portion means to expand the ego and capture the imagination of those who hold the purse string.

There is a major downside to this. Instead of being engaging, connecting, evolving, being and synergizing, some leaders today are groomed to be self-inflating, controlling, one-up manning and claiming.

An important lesson for the Being Leaders was to keep the locus of their actions within themselves. Yet, they were seldom self-consumed. There was a greater cause to focus upon, and the beneficiaries of their actions were others. As we will see in the next section, ARRIVAL: Being in Mastery, this quality will have a huge impact upon themselves and humanity as a whole.

9.3. HISTORY MAKES MEN

In 1906, when Gandhi was thirty-seven, he found himself placed in a moment created by history. Gandhi had just returned from his ambulance duty during the Zulu "rebellion" in South Africa, fresh from his decision to devote his life completely to community service. But the kind of community service that he was destined to offer was dictated to him by fate.

The white government of the Transvaal—a South African province—had just introduced new legislation to deprive South African Indians of what civil rights they still retained under the law. If the 'Black Act' was passed it would mean the end of the dignity of the Indian communities in South Africa.

On Gandhi's call, a great crowd of Indians gathered in Johannesburg to decide on a course of resistance. Gandhi had not come prepared with any plan; he only knew that it was "better to die than to submit to such a law." Most Indians were reticent and resigned to the course of their destiny. They had too often seen the futility of resistance, and accepted that they had no choice than to accept the draconian and humiliating laws brought out by the Afrikaner government of South Africa. To resist would be to further infuriate the government, which meant further harassment to them and their families. To them, it was their destiny to be marginalized and degraded.

It turned out during the meeting that a second passionate group of opponents to the 'Black Act' wanted to call for violent action. They felt that they had the numbers, means and the passion to counter the administration. Right was on their side and the wrong doers – the brutal regime of the Afrikaner government – must be taught a lesson in a language that they understood. And that language was violence.

In the midst of the two polar groups which advocated alternate ideologies, the inspiration came to Gandhi to offer an even higher challenge to the Afrikaner government; to refuse to obey such degrading legislation and accept the consequences without violent retaliation but without yielding an inch in their demand for fair and equal treatment under the law. This course of action seemed at that moment as the oddest choice, but it was the *Third Way*[19] for him. He clearly felt that the *Third Way* will not only condone the past, it will also script a noble future.

With persuasion, every man and woman present in the gathering rose to meet the challenge and pledged non-violent resistance even to the point of death.

"Up to the year 1906 I simply relied on appeal to reason. I was a very industrious reformer [...] But I found that reason failed to produce an impression when the critical moment arrived in South Africa." This is what Gandhi had to say about that moment.

"My people were excited; even a worm will and does turn—and there was talk of wreaking vengeance. I had then to choose between allaying myself to violence or finding out some other method of meeting the crisis and stopping the rot; and it came to me that we should refuse to obey the legislation that was degrading and let them put us in jail if they

---

[19] One of the gifts of the Being Leaders was the ability to unfold unconventional solutions. I call such solutions Third Ways. We will examine the Third Way in chapter 16, 'THREE SIDES OF A COIN'

2. PASSAGE

liked," Gandhi wrote triumphantly. "Thus came into being the moral equivalent of war [...]"

The movement spread swiftly through South Africa. What Gandhi proposed was an entirely new method of fighting. Instead of fanning hatred with hatred and violence with violence, he argued that exploitation could be overcome simply by returning love for hatred and respect for contempt, in a strong, determined refusal to yield to injustice. It was a style of resistance which demanded the highest courage and such depth of commitment that every temporary setback only strengthened the resisters' determination more. Thousands of men, women and children courted jail sentences in open but disciplined defiance of South African exploitation. Eventually, in 1914 the laws most offensive to the Indians in South Africa were repealed and basic civil rights voted into law.

Many say that Gandhi—by his courage, by his determination, by his refusal to take unfair advantage, but especially by his endless capacity to "stick it out" without yielding and without retaliation—chose to be in that moment in history and wrote that script. Yet for himself, he was in a moment where he was a victim of events outside his making. If not him, then another would have one day stepped up and led the Indians against such indignity.[XXIII]

The Being Leaders are larger than life figures for all of us. They have inspired humanity and made history. Seemingly impossible situations have been turned around by them in ways never ever seen by humanity before. They have led masses to create outcomes unprecedented for the human imagination.

Yet, to themselves they were ordinary individuals in trial, attempting an extraordinary task. They felt as if they had been thrust into a role too big for them. They often claimed that circumstances conspired to place them in that time in history in that place that called for redemption. Lincoln considered himself to have accidentally been elected as president. Referring to the civil war, he spoke of himself "as a piece of driftwood that had drifted into the very apex of this great event." In 1864, Lincoln confessed to Albert G. Hodges, editor of the journal *Commonwealth*, that "I claim not to have controlled events, but confess plainly that events have controlled me."

"Circumstances placed me here in this role," Mandela claimed with modesty. The Being Leaders assumed that they just happened to be there where they found themselves in the midst of their battles, and things were thrust upon them more than they physically shaping things.

It is inspiring to note how the Being Leaders saw themselves as little beings upon whose shoulders had been thrust this unwanted, painful exercise that others shied away from. They claimed [...] history has made them, not the other way around.

That thinking says plenty about the Being Leaders that they believed that history makes men. It not only showed their humility, it was also evidence of their belief in some greater power that conspires to shape things for them. "I've done nothing special. Any man who finds himself in such indignity would have acted the same way I did," stated Gandhi.

2. PASSAGE

9.4. LEARNING TO HUMANIZE ONESELF

The sit-ins started on February 1st 1960, when four black students from North Carolina A&T College sat down at a Woolworth lunch counter in downtown Greensboro, North Carolina. The students—Joseph McNeil, Izell Blair, Franklin McCain, and David Richmond—purchased several items in the store before sitting at the counter reserved for white customers. When a waitress asked them to leave, they politely refused; to their surprise, they were not arrested. The four students  remained seated for almost an hour until the store closed.

The following morning about two dozen students arrived at Woolworth's and sat at the lunch counter. The next day there were sixty-three students sitting-in, occupying nearly every seat at the lunch counter. By the end of the month, sit-ins had taken place at more than 30 locations in seven states, and by the end of April over 50,000 students had participated.

Dr. Martin Luther King encouraged this "revolt against the apathy and complacency of adults in the Negro community, against Negroes in the middle class who indulge in buying cars and homes instead of taking on the great cause that will really solve their problems." The endorsement for their movement from the great Dr. King was a huge boost in legitimacy and morale for the rallying students. To many it felt as if no greater recognition for their efforts could come than the blessings and encouragement they received from Dr. King.

Non-violence was a central component of the student-led demonstrations. Dr. King wrote: "The key significance of the student movement lies in the fact that from its inception, everywhere, it has combined direct action with non-violence. This quality has given it the extraordinary power and discipline which every thinking person observes."

In a statement prior to the opening of the conference, Dr. King emphasized the "need for some type of continuing organization" and expressed his belief that "the youth must take the freedom struggle into every community in the South."

In October 1960 Atlanta student leaders convinced Dr. King to participate in a sit-in at a local department store. That was a big step for them to invite such a revered personality as Dr. King to their sit-in. He was, after all, the conscience of the "Black liberation" movement and the one dealing directly with the U.S. President and the Congress.

Though reluctant about being arrested due to legal troubles stemming from his activities in Alabama, Dr. King participated in the sit-in with the students. He sat with them, ate as the students did, and conducted himself as one of them. He permitted himself to be hauled off to jail with around 300 students. In solidarity with those following the "Jail-No-Bail" strategy, he refused to post bond and remained imprisoned. He had the means and the support of eminent lawyers, many white, to be released, instead he remained in jail with the students. Later the students were released, but Dr. King remained in jail while officials from the U.S. state of Georgia determined whether his sit-in arrest violated parole conditions Dr. King had received earlier.[XXIV]

x   x   x

Dr. King did not see himself as a messiah even as many around him saw him as one. He saw himself as a normal human being dealing with the personal wounds inflicted by a racially divided nation. In spite of the power he held over a whole race, he was open with everyone about his fears and self-doubts. He did not see himself inaccessible from those

2. PASSAGE

who he was fighting for, nor did he believe that a different set of rules applied to him. He saw himself as equal to all others.

As the Being Leaders grew in awareness of who they were and what drove them, they noticed their massive presence in the lives and imagination of those around them and their opponents. Such presence can corrupt the minds of normal individuals, but the Being Leaders took special care to humanize themselves.

In one amusing episode narrated about Gandhi, one day a mother came to Gandhi with her little boy for help. She asked Gandhi, "Please Bapu[20], will you tell my little boy to stop eating sugar? He simply eats too much sugar and will not stop." Gandhi told the mother to leave and come back with the boy in a week.

The woman left puzzled but returned a week later, dutifully following Gandhi's instructions. "We have come back as you asked," she told Gandhi. Gandhi turned to the boy and said, "Young boy, stop eating sweets. They are not good for you."

Then he joked for a while with the boy, hugged him, and sent him on his way. But the mother, unable to contain her curiosity, lingered behind to ask, "Bapu, why didn't you say this last week when we visit you? Why did you make us come back again?"

"Last week," Gandhi smiled as he spoke, "I too was eating sugar."

This episode is a great demonstration of how the Being Leaders saw themselves as human like those around them. This view has conferred upon them great honours for leading revolutions that liberated the soul

---

[20] Bapu is a Hindi word for "father", as Gandhi used to reverentially be addressed by others

of nations and upholding human dignity. Yet, the Being Leaders viewed themselves as plain humans who were instruments of some grand design.

Finding the right measure of the self is a crucial training to undergo for any leader. Leaders with low self-worth see themselves as inferior to others. Such leaders are consumed with an ever present need to prove themselves and gain validation from others. Leaders who self-inflate their own worth see the world as being at their service and are driven by a false sense of entitlement. They become blinded towards the needs and concerns of others and are unable to see themselves as instruments of a greater good. Here is where having a measure of the self helps. Knowing that measure holds them in self-love while endearing themselves to the world around.

10. HUMAN ELEVATION NEEDS A MARTYR

"The art of dying follows as a corollary from the art of living."

M. K. Gandhi

During the month of January 1948, there was an ever-present death threat hanging over Gandhi's life and all those close to him were in a constant state of anxiety. There has already been one recent violent murder attempt on his life during an evening prayer meeting. He narrowly escaped an explosion meant to end his life.

There were some elements of estranged Muslim communities who wanted to see Gandhi dead, as there were some from the partitioned Punjab region who disapproved of him. Punjab had just a few months back been partitioned to create the new nation of Pakistan.

But the greatest threat came from Hindu fanatics who abhorred Gandhi for preaching the message of non-violence and reconciliation with Muslims. During and after the partition of pre-independent India, Gandhi had been a vocal critic of fundamentalist plans to turn India into a Hindu nation. Until the day of his assassination, Gandhi sported the unwavering faith that he could reunify India and Pakistan into one nation where Hindus and Muslims lived once again in harmony.

All those around Gandhi—his family, friends, well-wishers and followers—were aware of a conspiracy against his life and were in a constant state of worry. Yet Gandhi remained indifferent to the prospect of death.

In the words of Robert Payne, biographer of Gandhi and the author of "The Life and Death of Mahatma Gandhi":

"He held meetings with the cabinet, continued his lessons in Bengali, sat over his spinning wheel, addressed prayer meetings in the garden, and he did all these things as though he had twenty years to live, as though the air was not electric with violence, and at the same time he was aware that at any moment there would be another explosion of guncotton or the burst of a hand grenade.

Although he firmly believed that he was under God's protection, he also believed that God might very well have ordered his death, and this death would crown his life."

Exactly a week before his assassination, Gandhi had a vision of his beloved grandniece, Manu, present at his death, comforting him and blessing him.

Two days before his assassination, Gandhi shared with a local princess: "If I am to die by the bullet of a madman, I must do so smilingly. There must be no anger within me. God must be in my heart and on my lips."

Just like any other day, punctually at 03.30am on Friday, January 30th, 1948, Mahatma Gandhi awoke to greet the last morning he would ever see. Unlike any other day, this day Gandhi had a closer realization of impending death. It seems Gandhi could feel that this was his last day.

Since September 9th, Gandhi was staying in the tense atmosphere of Delhi, the strife-torn capital of newly independent India. He had arrived in Delhi from Kolkota[21], where he had just performed a miracle of peace-making. And it was 12 days since the successful end of his fast to bring about a reunion of hearts in Delhi.

That morning, a female member of Gandhi's care giving staff had failed to rise in time for prayers. This disturbed Gandhi. He mused whether she should leave him, and concluded by saying, "I do not like these signs. I hope God does not keep me here very long to witness these things."

Also a consequence of his recent fast, Gandhi suffered from a bad cough. To treat it he would take herbal medication including powdered cloves. But by this morning the clove powder had finished. Instead of joining him in his morning walk, a stroll up and down the room, Manu, Gandhi's grandniece, sat down to prepare some more. "I shall join you presently," she said to Gandhi. "Otherwise there will be nothing at hand at night when it is needed." Gandhi replied, "Who knows what is going to happen before nightfall or even whether I shall be alive. If at night I am still alive you can easily prepare some then."

At 07:00am, Gandhi handed Pyarelal, his personal secretary, his draft submission for the new Indian National Congress[22] constitution, written for the forthcoming Congress Working Committee meeting. Gandhi asked him to go through it carefully. "Fill any gaps that you may find in my thinking," he instructed. "I have prepared it under heavy strain." Gandhi felt the need to have it finalized soon. After receiving a massage Gandhi asked Pyarelal whether he had finished the revision. The urgency to finish it was visible to Pyarelal.

Manu then gave Gandhi his bath. During this he asked her whether she was doing the hand exercises he had prescribed. Manu told him that she did not like the exercises, then listened to a long but gentle rebuke from

---

[21] Erstwhile Calcutta
[22] The main political party of the Indian freedom movement in colonial India

2. PASSAGE

Gandhi, who told her of the responsibility he had taken for her health and moral development. He also reminded her that in his absence she must take care of herself.

Gandhi and Pyarelal then talked at length about the volatile situation at Noakhali, a district in Bangladesh were looting and massacres took place months ago. He told Pyarelal also of his plans to visit Pakistan, to discourage violence and to persuade Pakistanis to reunite with India. He asked Pyarelal to go back to Noakhali, but to wait until he had returned to Sevagram, his home in Gujarat. Pyarelal was surprised at this request, for it was unusual for Gandhi to delay anyone returning to their post.

Morning had given way to afternoon. Soon Gandhi was visited by a delegation of Delhi Muslim leaders who were calling daily. Communal tensions and the refugee crisis still darkened the atmosphere in the capital. Gandhi sought the permission of these leaders to leave Delhi for a few days. "I do expect to be back here by the 14th. But if Providence has decreed otherwise, that is a different matter. I am not, however, sure whether I shall be able to leave here even on the day after tomorrow. It is all in God's hands."

When two village elders visited Gandhi just before prayer time, he instructed his secretary to ask them to wait. "Tell them that I will, but only after the prayer meeting, and that too if I am still living. We shall then talk things over." Yet again, Gandhi had spoken of his possible imminent demise, and on this occasion in front of the men with prime responsibility for his safety.

Then Gandhi got up, put on his slippers, and stepped out for the group prayers through the side door of the room into the twilight. He wore a shawl for warmth. As usual he leaned gently on his two "walking sticks". Manu was on his right and Abha, the wife of Gandhi's grandnephew, on his left. Strangely, on that day two attendants who would walk with him to prayer each day was not there, neither was the recently assigned plainclothes policeman.

Thus Mahatma Gandhi set out on his final 200 yard journey, his final trek, his final march. He had come from Porbandar, to Rajkot, to the Inner Temple, to Bombay, to Durban, to Pietermaritzburg, to Johannesburg, to Phoenix Settlement, to Tolstoy Farm, to Champaran, to Sabarmati, to Yeravda, to Dandi, to Kingsley Hall, to St James Palace, to Sevagram, to the Age Khan Palace, to Noakhali, to Calcutta, to Delhi. And now, his final steps to eternity.

As the shots were fired Gandhi was still standing, his palms still joined. There was no sign of fight, no resort to violence, no scream for help, no begging for mercy. The only words he chanted were "Oh Lord, Oh Lord". Then he slowly sank to the ground, palms joined still, possibly in a final ultimate act of *Ahimsa*[23]. The Mahatma was slumped on the ground, his head resting in the laps of both girls. His face turned pale, his white shawl of Australian wool was turning crimson with blood. Within seconds Mahatma Gandhi was dead. It was 05:17pm.

The night before Gandhi was assassinated, foreseeing the manner of his death he told Manu: "If I were to die of a lingering disease, or even from a pimple, then you must shout from the housetops to the whole world that I was a false Mahatma. Then my soul, wherever it might be, will rest in peace. If I die of an illness, you must declare me to be a false or hypocritical Mahatma, even at the risk of people cursing you. And if an explosion takes place, as it did last week, or if someone shot at me and I received a bullet in my bare chest without a sigh and with Ram's name on my lips, only then should you say that I was a true Mahatma."[XXV] [XXVI]

---

[23] Non-violence

2. PASSAGE

Death was not a faraway idea for the Being Leaders. They have seen life sink to the deepest penury ever imaginable that the idea of death did not feel abhorrent. Attempts have been made on their lives and death threats have been many. Even alive, they were subjected to immense suffering and they had to endure severe disgrace. They have seen deaths around them, also among their near and dear ones. All of these experiences were the life lessons that the Being Leaders encountered in their 'passage'. Through their passage, they had learned to accept the idea of death. As a result, at the summit of their lives, the idea of death was a natural corollary to the idea of life.

On a Saturday afternoon in 1958, as Dr. King sat in a Harlem book store signing copies of his book, he was stabbed with a letter opener by a mentally imbalanced woman. As Dr. King was being taken to the hospital, the razor tip of the weapon was touching Dr. King's aorta. If the knife had been a fraction closer to the heart, his aorta would have been punctured and he would have drowned in his own blood.

As he was recuperating from the attack, he wrote, "If I demonstrated unusual calm during the recent attempt on my life, it was certainly not due to any extraordinary powers that I possess. Rather, it was due to the power of God working through me. Throughout this struggle for racial justice I have constantly asked God to remove all bitterness from my heart and to give me strength and courage to face any disaster that came my way. This constant prayer life and feeling of dependence on God have given me the feeling that I have divine companionship in the struggle. I know no other way to explain it. It is the fact that in the midst of external tension, God can give an inner peace."[XXVII]

x   x   x

There is one thing that the assassinated Being Leaders had in common. They all seemed to have a conscious or unconscious awareness of the arrival of their time to leave. Consequently, they demonstrated tremendous grace as is evident from a glimpse into the last day in the lives of the assassinated leaders. "If physical death is the price that I must pay to free my white brothers and sisters from a permanent death of the spirit, then nothing can be more redemptive," Dr. King famously declared.

It is only when death is treated as a foreign concept, to be battled and kept away, that death becomes an enemy. When you deeply reflect on death and experience its omnipresence, and when you have entertained the thought of death in your mind you truly recognize the inevitability of death. Often times this happens because the idea of death has appeared unexpectedly at your doorstep. Someone close to you met with death, or you or a dear one met with serious illness. In rare cases, without a death in the family, some integrate the inevitability of death. Then instead of battling the idea of death, desperately trying to stay afloat on the back of medical advancements, you start choosing for each day to be spent on purpose.

In April 1865, the Union Army[24] had taken the Confederate[25] capital of Richmond, US. Richmond was the target of numerous attempts by the Union Army to seize possession of the capital, finally falling to the Federals in April 1865. Not only was Richmond the seat of political power for the Confederacy, it served as a vital source of munitions, armament, weapons, supplies, and manpower for the Confederate Army, and as such would have been defended by the Confederate Army at all costs regardless of its political status. Soon after its capture, Lincoln visited Richmond in spite of death threats.

When someone cautioned Lincoln on his choice, he casually replied, "If someone wants to kill me", he said, "no amount of vigilance can stop them. I must remain accessible to the people," he added.

---

[24] The Union Army was the Federal army that fought for the Union during the American Civil War
[25] The rebel Confederate States of America

2. PASSAGE

Clearly, the Being Leaders welcomed death as much as they revered life. Their Life Purpose was always more important to them than their life. For them, laying down their lives for their cause was as effortless and easy a choice as giving away a spoon. This made them indomitable foes for their opponents.

The Being Leaders are remembered for tempting fate. Gandhi tempted fate by choosing to visit Pakistan soon after the partition of independent India. When emotions were running high between Hindus and Muslims immediately after India and Pakistan attained independence from the British colonial rule, Gandhi announced: "I am simply going to prove to Hindus here and Muslims there that the only devils in the world are those running around in our own hearts. And that is where all our battles ought to be fought."

The consequence of such belief is that we see the Being Leaders as infinitely more meritorious and glorious after death than they were seen when they were alive.

10.1. OVERCOMING THE DEMON OF FEAR OF DEATH

"I learned that courage was not the absence of fear, but the triumph over it. The brave man is not he who does not feel afraid, but he who conquers that fear."

Nelson Mandela

x   x   x

Though the Being Leaders were at peace with the idea of their own deaths, it did not mean that they did not have fear. They often feared for their family, and they feared for the plight of the world were they to die leaving behind a job half-done.

On January 30th, 1956, Dr. King was speaking at a mass meeting when he heard the terrifying news that his house had been bombed. He immediately told the audience what happened, left the church and rushed home filled with dread for the physical and emotional wellbeing of Coretta, his wife, and his ten-week-old baby.

Nearing his house, Dr. King saw Blacks brandishing guns and knives, and a barricade of white policemen. A worried Dr. King went inside and pushed through the crowd in his house to the back room to make sure that his wife and child were okay. He had the cold realization that—should he choose to continue with his cause—he could not keep his cause and his dear ones apart.

Having been assured of their safety, he calmly stepped outside his house and addressed the crowd. He politely asked them to cleanse themselves of hatred. He once again reminded them to replace hatred and resentment with love. "Go home to your family, pray for them and go to bed," he urged the crowd. That night the black town folks and the white policemen witnessed true courage.

Courage is preventing fear from guiding your choices. When you let fear choose, you are guided towards choices that preserve you. You become consumed with your sole wellbeing. Fear narrows your vision to the self. To not be guided by fear, you must not be intimidated by fear. Death is not the end of things. Remember: Your legacy outlives your life.

x   x   x

Arthur Peuchen, at 52, was one of the few men to survive the sinking of Titanic. As the ship was sinking, men, women and children rushed to the

2. PASSAGE

lifeboats. Even as some women refused to enter the boat and save themselves, because they wanted to be with their husbands, Peuchen saved himself by allegedly forcing the second officer to let him into one of the lifeboats under the pretext that he could man the boat.

Peuchen claimed later he did not realize Titanic was going to founder until he saw it from the lifeboat. Peuchen was also accused of exaggerating his own efforts in helping in the lifeboat. It was reported that Peuchen had even complained of tiredness and refused to row until goaded by ladies in the boat.

Critics later noted that Peuchen was at great pains to discredit Captain Smith and the crew of Titanic. "They seemed to be short of sailors around the lifeboats," he testified, "I imagine this crew is what we would call in yachting terms as scratch crew, brought from different vessels. They might be the best, but they were not accustomed to working together."

Upon his return back to Canada, Peuchen was deemed a coward largely because of his self-serving behaviour. The Toronto Mail wrote: "He put himself in the position of a man who had to defend himself before the necessity for the defence was apparent." One taunt about him that circulated was "He said he was a yachtsman so he could get off the Titanic, and if there had been a fire, he would have said he was a fireman."[XXVIII]

Unlike the Being Leaders, most of you are not faced with life and death situations in your lives. Yet as leaders in various domains, many remain guided by existential fears, an irony to the cozy, comfortable lives we live. Put to the test, many of us will turn out to be of the mould of Arthur Peuchen than of a Being Leader. We value surviving long over living deep.

When you consciously tell yourself not to be guided by fear, you stop choosing solely for yourself. You stop being obsessed by wanting to insure yourself against death. There is no insurance against death. There is a valorous path though; embrace physical death as an inconsequential part of the continuum of life.

It is not that the Being Leaders did not have fear, the Being Leaders simply chose not to be led by their fears. As you persist with the mastery of fear, fear subdues. Things that used to fill you with fear, doubt, uncertainty, etc. cease to affect you anymore. Management decisions refuse to be a matter of life and death.

In their passage. this was a crucial scholarship for the Being Leaders. At the peak of their lives, the Being Leaders had attained the state of liberation from the bondage of fear. They noticed their fears, they acknowledged their fears, but they did not let themselves be led by their fears. For if they had been following their fears, they would not have followed their missions. They would not follow their legacy work which was fraught with danger.

10.2. TIMING DEATH TO PERFECTION

"When a man has done what he considers to be his duty to his people and his country, he can rest in peace."

Nelson Mandela

x   x   x

Carefully looking at the long arc of history, you can see the perfection of the Being Leaders' death. The uncanny coincidence of their death was only surpassed by the amazing glory of their lives. They could not

2. PASSAGE

have died sooner, not could they have lived longer. To have died sooner would have been to leave what they began half done. To die later would have been to unjustifiably expect more from them of what is beckoned upon the rest of us to do.

Even in the passing of Mandela at a late age of 95, we see that his presence was still needed to hold the South African nation to the rule of law, and for him to be seen as the guardian of the idea of the rainbow nation. He could not have died sooner, because his successors had to live up to Mandela's creed in his very own presence. He could not have died later because that would have not have given a democratic nation the time and space to grow up to the measure of the Highest Ideal that Mandela has set for them.

In the rousing words of Revered Jeffery R., offered as eulogy for Abraham Lincoln, we can gain a true picture of the perfect timing of great leaders' passing:

"Men have regretfully wondered why Abraham Lincoln was not spared to finish the work he had undertaken. They forget themselves. He had finished it. Attempts to assassinate him had been made before; but they had failed. His hour had not come; his work was not completed. It was decreed that the 14th of April, 1865, should be an era in the annals of history, an epoch in the cycles of time, the Good Friday of American redemption. Four years before, on that very day, rebellion committed its first overt act. It fired on the American flag that floated over Fort Sumter. Four years had elapsed; years of carnage, of cruelties, of hopes and fears; but all this time what moral changes were going on! The genius of the American nationality was developing itself. Republicanism was proving its vitality. A race of slaves was being made free, and a nation of freemen was being brought up to the measure of their high vocation, in deeds of unexampled sacrifices, wondrous charities, valiant courage and enlightened justice. God permitted the rebellion to be strong enough and blind enough, to last long enough, to exhaust itself and die. So that just at the end of four years to the very day, the flag that was shot down from Fort Sumter was restored to its place, the proud symbol of a restored, disenthralled and victorious nationality.

This done, and the mission of Abraham Lincoln was accomplished. And strange, marvellous coincidence! On that very day, not in the morning before the Stars and Stripes had been raised over Sumter, but in the evening, after the glorious deed was done, Abraham Lincoln received his summons to resign his trust. He had done his work. He had done it well. And the universal verdict of mankind is the counterpart of the Divine award, 'Well done, good and faithful servant, enter thou into the joy of thy Lord.'

Besides, the manner of his death is another element in the speciality of his calling. If his death had occurred from natural causes, his character would have been no less genuine, his work no less complete, our regrets no less sincere, but it would have lacked that finish which was needed to give uniqueness to his mission and effect to his life. Slavery wanted a victim. Liberty needed a martyr. Despairing of destroying the life of the nation, in its dying frenzy slavery took the life of the nation's preserver. But it little thought that in this it was answering the purpose of God. Slaveholding malignity gave to liberty a Martyr." [XXIX]

x   x   x

We might not have control over when we die, but there is so much more we can do. We can embrace the idea of death as inevitable to the process of life and make peace with it. In the first part of this chapter, we witnessed this process unfold in the lives of the Being Leaders.

You can also master the fear of dying that drives many around you. For many, the need for survival is the motive behind all their decisions. This fear has its own mind. Its motives are different from your logic. Looking at your own lives you can see how fear persuades you to narrowly focus

2. PASSAGE

on only yourself, stealing from you the magic of a living a heart-opened, fulfilling life lived in aliveness. This we saw in the section, OVERCOMING THE DEMON OF FEAR OF DEATH.

Finally, most of you cannot time your death, but you can choose for how you live your time alive. You can focus your thoughts, words and deeds on your self-realization and service to all. As Abraham Lincoln famously noted: "In the end, it's not the years in your life that count. It's the life in your years."

These steps are integral to the passage you undertake on your path towards personal mastery.

III. ARRIVAL:

Being in Mastery

In the previous section of 'PASSAGE: The Practice and Preparation', we came face to face with the apprenticeship of life that the Being Leaders went through in their passage of life.

As you notice, the Being Leaders' passage was never an overnight revelation, rather it was a long toil of years, if not decades, of learning and apprenticing in the art of mastery. Piece by piece, they went through the various lessons and learning of the self and the nature of humans. The whole process of confronting their identity, seeing themselves as a minute part of a larger whole and recognizing their own mortality of life is depicted in chapters 5 to 10.

This section, 'ARRIVAL: Being in Mastery', is fully a display of the Being Leaders' mastery. After departure and passage, in the 'arrival' phase, the Being Leaders had arrived at a place of inner mastery where they had fully accomplished all their faculties. This was the phase of their lives where they unleashed all their potential and, consequently, soared in greatness.

Though the Being Leaders were not warriors in the traditional sense of the word, they are heroes to us. They are larger than life. Historic. And they embody the highest within all of us.

So how does 'being in mastery' look like?

At a certain moment, when you have given up control of the course of your life and resign to 'fate', an inner shift will occur. You might feel like you have just surrendered in your powerlessness, instead you are amazed at the power of your quiet awareness. You feel like you are in your full strength in your restfulness. You become aware that you have mastered your demons and walked out of that chasm. That is the experience of 'being' in mastery.

Once you have accessed that 'being'ness, you will notice things different about you. The things that you had held important before—

3. ARRIVAL

like the pursuit of wealth and power—no more tickle your imagination. The people who used to trigger you in the past do not do so anymore.

You will also notice a shift in your values and ideals. Achievement gives space to giving. You start to believe that your victory does not mean another's defeat. When you win, another does not lose. All the illusions of fear that you carry in the mundane life suddenly presents itself in a different light.

You do not feel the need to justify yourself. You do not take it personally when others disagree with you or think in ways different than yours. You see yourself as a part of the ecosystem, but you are no more entangled with it. Your relationship with that ecosystem is based on mutual service.

Rather than cover comprehensively all the qualities of mastery seen among the Being Leaders, in this section I have carefully picked the qualities that were consistently seen in their lives. Secondly, the qualities I have picked for study in this section are the ones that have made the Being Leaders stand out in their 'being'ness, and as a result, made the Being Leaders stand out from the rest of the pack. The qualities studied in this section were the qualities that came to my attention through my own contemplation and experimentation that I speak of in the introduction chapter (see pg. 3).

In the upcoming chapters of this work, you will go through a study of Life Purpose and how it has been the beacon guiding the Being Leaders. The chapter 'YOU ARE THE SUM OF EVERYTHING YOU HAVE DONE' gives you the awareness to choose to become immortal, not simply for its own sake, rather to live with the same generosity and might as the Being Leaders.

The Highest Ideals were the uncompromising goals that drove the Being Leaders each day, even when they had to wake up to oppression and indignity. In chapter 14, 'BE LED BY YOUR HIGHEST IDEAL', you will find ways to script your own Highest Ideals.

It is imperative that each aspiring leader identifies her operating principle and thereafter consistently conduct herself in line with it. We will study this 'creed' in details in chapter 15, 'LIVE BY YOUR NOBLE CREED', and draw inspiration from the un-exhausting practice of the Being Leaders.

Chapters 16 until 20 studies pieces of the 'nature' of the Being Leaders while at their greatest. There are some consistent qualities of this 'nature' that is common to all, but prominent to some. These qualities are examined in details in these chapters.

11. RESURRECTING INTO MASTERY

"An individual has not started living until he can rise above the narrow confines of his individualistic concerns to the broader concerns of all humanity."

Dr. Martin Luther King, Jr.

'The University of Robben Island' became the only real source of stimulation that the black South African prisoners in the Robben Island prison enjoyed. Many attributed their ability to endure Robben Island to their study privileges. Studying brought Mandela mental stimulation, kept him preoccupied during the torturous life in prison, and offered him the much needed social contact. One of the early evidences of Mandela stepping into mastery was winning study privileges from the prison authorities.  Study privileges helped Mandela and his fellow prisoners battle their inner demons, for their isolation was the cancer gnawing within and killing them. This was the real problem. Studying was a way out of the ordeal. "At night, our cell block seemed more like a study hall than a prison," recorded Mandela referring back to that leadership moment in the collective lives of the prisoners.

"It is the one single thing that really keeps you together," said Dikgang Moseneke, a fellow political prisoner at Robben Island who graduated with a school-leaving certificate and then went on to obtain a degree in Political Science and English.

3. ARRIVAL

As Govan Mbeki recalled with pride, "we took people from the lowest level, who came to the island illiterate. I remember one group I had. I started with them when they were illiterate, started them up. And by the time they left Robben Island they were able to write letters home—they didn't require anybody to write letters for them and to address their envelopes. And they spoke English. Upon completing each stage of their courses, students were issued with certificates headed 'The University of Robben Island'."

In 1966, when the kitchens on Robben Island served food unfit for human consumption, the prisoners collectively revolted. They struck against the authorities and boycotted their meals for several days. Initially, the prison authorities punished the prisoners for their insolence. Then the authorities viciously pushed the prisoners to work in the quarries until they collapsed. And when the ill and the old reported at the prison hospital, the authorities turned them around.

As a last resort to break the will of the prisoners, the kitchen staff was ordered to prepare appetizing food, steaming hot, laced with vegetables and meat. To break the will of the prisoners would be another victory, and yet another assertion of the superiority of the Afrikaner race. Any last remains of self-respect that Mandela and the others had would be cleansed out of their spirit, and the prisoners would remain in eternal damnation.

But the resolve of Mandela and others held firm. Even those prisoners on the hospital beds refused their meals. The authorities drove them out of their hospital beds and told them to work in the quarry. Struggling, they stumbled along the road, some in bandages, some crawling, accompanied by the warders shouting, "No food, no medicine!"

But the prisoners did not give up their battle. Soon the prisons authorities relented and promised to improve conditions of the prisoners and to treat them with dignity. The food improved, the warders were more restrained and there were fewer beatings.

It was not long before the prison authorities took revenge. The prisoners who were considered the main instigators of the defiance against the authorities were sentenced to longer prison sentences. The authorities returned to their old ways. But they could not ever subdue the resurrected spirit of the prisoners. They had defied the administration and survived.

From prison Mandela boldly wrote several letters to the Minister of Prisons, Kobie Coetsee, asking to meet for discussions to end Apartheid. Though he never received a response to his various letters, he persisted. He expressed his mastery by taking the lead, and when Coetsee responded, he used that opening to instantly engage with the South African president P.W. Botha. It did not weigh him down that he had never worn a suit for decades, nor was he bothered that he had not knotted a tie or tied a shoe lace for decades.

As the number of prisoners on Robben Island grew, a new social organism started to form. In order to channel the collective power of the prisoners and to bring in harmony and teamwork, an elaborate network of committees was established. Committees were formed for disciplinary, political, educational literary and recreational areas to deal with every aspect of prisoners' lives and to keep open channels of communication between different sections.

At the apex was a committee known as the High Organ, consisting of four members of the old national executive of the African National Congress: Mandela, Sisulu, Mbeki and Mhlaba. Mandela served as its head. As a sign of the growing self-mastery of Mandela and his fellow activists, communication between the inmates started to take a new turn. Messages were hidden in drums of food, in toilets or in matchboxes discarded by warders. The prison hospital was a regular contact point to exchange information.

The penalties for being caught in possession of messages was severe: prisoners who were caught risked long solitary confinement and loss of privileges. Despite the risks, the prisoners grew in courage to reach out to each other and stand up against a system even when they could not enjoy the taste of freedom.

In order to assert his way with the prison staff, Mandela developed cordial relationships with a number of individual warders.

"With junior officers who knew their position, Nelson was charming and friendly," Michael Dingake, a fellow political activist of Mandela recalled. "Many young warders were friendly to him, occasionally soliciting advice from him in connection with their jobs or social problems." Mandela, from his ever-developing place of strength and clarity that came from his scars and sacrifice, was a mentor to many young warders. He encouraged warders, often poorly educated, to study so that they will develop a more enlightened approach towards other races. He could inspire more and more warders to turn to educated prisoners of African descent to help them with their courses.

In 1972, when three judges made a tour of Robben Island, Mandela was asked to act as a spokesman for the prisoners. When the judges asked him if he would like to speak with them without the presence of the prison authorities, Mandela—in all his presence and power—relied that he would rather speak in front of the prison officials so that they could have an opportunity to respond to his criticisms. He fearlessly related the incidents of beatings and torture going on in the prison, and the ongoing cover-ups.

When he was threatened by the Commanding Officer Piet Badenhorst (see chapter 4, THE FIERY ORDEAL THROUGH WHICH THE

BEING LEADERS PASS, pg. 59), "Be careful, Mandela. If you talk about things you haven't seen, you will get yourself into trouble," Mandela calmly turned to the judges and said, "Gentlemen, you can see for yourself the type of man we are dealing with as commanding officer. If he can threaten me here, in your presence, you can imagine what he does when you are not here."

Soon after, the Commanding Officer was removed. A more respectful regime was put in place. Living conditions were improved, study privileges were restored, hot water was provided, and the prisoners received extra blankets.

As Mandela resurrected from his old self and unfolded in his mastery, the prison routine did not feel anymore like shackles to him. His life became more purposeful, and he found himself serving and inspiring others all day.

He woke early, running on the spot for forty-five minutes, doing a hundred push-ups, two hundred sit-ups and fifty knee-bends. After dispensing with the tasks of tidying his cell and cleaning his toilet bucket, he jogged, skipped and shadow-boxed. He took his turn scrubbing and polishing the floors and cleaning the toilets of Section B along with everyone else. When a flu epidemic hit the isolation section in 1974, Mandela, who was spared the outbreak, made the rounds each morning collecting the toilet buckets of his sick colleagues, emptying them, cleaning them and then returning them to the cells. He gave lectures, participated in debates and listened to the grievances and discussions of fellow inmates.

When he was not working, he followed his own will, sometimes to the chagrin of the prison authorities. He studied and wrote letters. He also surreptitiously undertook legal work for prisoners in the general section who wanted help preparing judicial appeals. He used his privileges of receiving and sending more letters to help others who were in need. He used his guest visit privileges in a similar way.

In 1977, as a supreme sign of his growing self-mastery, Mandela had his way with the authorities on Robben Island. Mandela started gardening in a narrow patch of land alongside a perimeter wall of Robben Island. He assiduously nurtured plants in the dry, stony soil, studying horticultural techniques from library books.

It was in 1975 that he felt that he had a clear message to share with the world. So he boldly set upon writing his first autobiography. As such an endeavour was prohibited by the prison regulations, it was done secretly. He feigned illness and stayed back from the quarry writing in his cell during the day. Though he was later caught, Mandela's spirit could not be contained. A man prone to violence in the outside world, a world filled with hatred and inequality, had been turned into a man who was clear of what he stood for in prison. Ironically, the same system that the Afrikaners tried to preserve moulded the man who would fifteen years later be instrumental in dismantling that system.[XXX]

The adversities that Mandela faced were the greatest life-lessons that elevated him to inner mastery. This powerful connection between his life lessons and inner mastery may seem so unreal that when you look at the life voyage of the Being Leaders and connect the dots, it will seem as if there was some cosmic conspiracy that undressed the Being Leaders off their previous illusions and elevated them to inner mastery. How else could you explain the extraordinary set of events that would come together to strip off any comfort and certainty their old lives conferred upon them? (We will study this synchronous effect more in chapter 12, "BEING' ON PURPOSE', section 12.2)

Resurrecting into Mastery

There is a lot to be said about inner mastery. True inner mastery permeates thought, word and deed. Ultimate inner mastery would be when you can be in choiceful thought, word and deed. Doing Leaders spend a lifetime trying to gain mastery over their deeds. In organizational settings, they jostle for authority. They spend time on defining roles and responsibilities, and they fervently discuss control and authority. They want to know who falls under their control and the type of control they have over others. Defining territories is important to such leaders. Mastering their habitat gives them more autonomy and a sense of power to choose their actions. In conclusion, the locus of their practice of leadership is external to them.

The locus of the Being Leaders' practice of mastery was internal to them.

"In its positive form, non-violence means the largest love, the greatest charity. If I am a follower of non-violence, I must love my enemy. I must apply the same rules to the wrong-doer who is my enemy or a stranger to me, as I would to my wrong-doing father or son. This active non-violence necessarily includes truth and fearlessness. The practice of non-violence calls forth the greatest courage," Gandhi stated looking back at his practice of inner mastery.

His action of *Satyagraha*[26] was based on a detached stubbornness that gained strength from the quality of his daily practice. Unlike normal conflict, in which we get inflamed by emotion, Gandhi's practice of mastery made him measured and dispassionate in his approach towards civil disobedience and non-cooperation campaigns against the British.

All the Being Leaders had a strong attention on their inner life as a means of growing in power. Introspection led Gandhi to self-discipline.

---

[26] Gandhi coined the term Satyagraha, a Sanskrit word meant as 'Desire for truth'. We will study this form of non-violent resistance in chapter 15, 'LIVE BY YOUR NOBLE CREED'

3. ARRIVAL

It opened spaces for him where he found ways to sharpen his mind and will power. Lincoln's inner life gave rise to creative acumen and understanding of motives. Often sitting alone in his private world, he would make notes of future actions. Through notes made while seated in the telegraph office, he gave shape to the Emancipation Proclamation. His moments with himself was also his opening towards empathizing with his opponents.

Simple living and high thinking sprout out of the inner work of all the Being Leaders. Gandhi understood that to practice non-violence, he must first embody non-violence. For Gandhi, this was the beginning of his freedom struggle. Which meant for him to complement his ongoing movement against oppression and inequality with inner work. For Gandhi that inner work was his daily spiritual practice. Truth and non-violence were the main ideals that underpinned his daily spiritual practice. Spirituality—for Gandhi—meant a number of things; operating from the soul, non-violence, truth, non-stealing, chastity, non-possession, physical labour, control of palate, fearlessness, equality of all religions, and discarding untouchability. Gandhi took on hardships to practice all these principles in his *ashram*[27] irrespective of religion, creed and language, because many could not accept the fact that he admitted Muslims, Christians, Buddhists and people of lower caste, though he never attempted to convert them.

For the Being Leaders, the first step of stepping into mastery was taking charge of the world within. They strove to be choiceful in their thoughts and as a result their feelings as well. They recognized the power of their thought and the creative potential of their intentions (we will examine this in details in chapter 17, 'SHIFT THE MIND, SHAPE THE NEW ORDER'). They took responsibility for their realities and had enormous clarity of their ideals and values. They had a powerful realization of what they were here for, and that knowingness became their guiding light in

---

[27] Monastery

all their future choices. This we will explore deeper in chapter 12, "BEING' ON PURPOSE'. They had an exceptional clarity of what their service to humanity and beyond was. We will examine this more elaborately in chapter 13, 'YOU ARE THE SUM OF EVERYTHING YOU HAVE DONE'.

All the above assisted the Being Leaders to come into their own power, and their words and actions reflected that power. Their inner disputes around their purpose and sacred legacy resolved, they experienced a great sense of destiny and choice.

x   x   x

As the Being Leaders advanced on their inner path, they took natural command of the world around them.

On August 16, 1908, three thousand Muslims, Hindus and Christians led by Gandhi gathered outside the Hamidia Mosque in South Africa and burned their 'passes'. These were documents all people classified "non-White" by the Apartheid government were forced to carry or face imprisonment. The huge bonfire, lit in a cauldron, was the symbolic initiation fire for a young Gandhi stepping into his mastery. It was one of his first acts of non-violent resistance.

Against the order of Justice F. M. Johnson, Dr. King called on all men from across the U.S. Nation to join him on a march on March 9th, 1965, across the Edmund Pettus Bridge in Selma, Alabama. Only two days before, Alabama State Troopers had brutally assaulted peaceful marchers along the very same route in front of a horrified nation watching the brutality on live television. That day came to be infamously called "Bloody Sunday" (see chapter 17, 'SHIFT THE MIND, SHAPE THE NEW ORDER', pg. 283 for the full anecdote). "I say to you this afternoon that I would rather die on the highways of Alabama than make a butchery of my conscience. I say to you, when we march, don't

3. ARRIVAL

panic and remember that we must remain true to non-violence," Dr. King implored to the marchers that Tuesday, March 9th.

Paying no heed to fervent appeals from Governor Collins of the Community Relations Service and several others, Dr. King and another 1500 civil rights activists marched up to the spot where fellow activists were brutally assaulted by the State Troopers only two days ago. Upon arriving at the spot, Dr. King and the other marchers knelt down in prayer.

The "Bloody Sunday" on the Edmund Pettus Bridge in Selma, Alabama, made Dr. King resurrect in great determination to make the most irreversible move of the civil rights movement ever. His new direction would take him from the then familiar hotter pastures of the south to the harder, colder parts of the north as well. He more forcefully made his message heard and his vision felt amongst the more violent civil rights defenders in the north. These were great steps in his resurrection into his mightiest power over the reality around him.

Recognize that your power over your world is an automatic consequence of your elevation in consciousness. At the elevated consciousness, meaning and purpose drives your action. You are no more a victim of situations. Warders or oppressive regimes or white supremacists or any other force external to you does not dictate how your life should look. You choose, in spite of adversities, what your heart tells you is true. The world around you might retaliate, but it will not dislodge you from your choice. Whatever place or time, you present yourself in your choiceful presence.

For the Being Leaders, choiceful presence meant more than just honouring their core presence. It also meant remaining true to their values and ideals. It involved rising in clarity from all inner conflicts. In that state, you become certain of what you stand for and what you are willing to die for. This is the subtle essence of resurrection.

Resurrecting into Mastery

A resurrected individual can boldly face the turmoil around him. He is so firmly anchored in his values and ideals, and he has so painfully learned the key lessons gifted by life, that he feels with certainty the path he must take, the demons he must slay and the future he must help create. Every step he takes in the mastery of his thoughts, emotions, words and deeds, and all his alignments of his actions with his purpose and ideals will yield a corresponding positive shift in the world around him. In the midst of the storm, the resurrected individual remains the mountain. This we learn from the lives of the Being Leaders.

12. 'BEING' ON PURPOSE

"There is no passion to be found playing small—in settling for a life that is less than the one you are capable of living."

Nelson Mandela

∞ ☼ ∞ ☼ ∞

To understand Lincoln's purpose for existence, we must first understand the idea of the United States of America as envisioned by its founders and defended by the subsequent leaders.

The ninety years preceding Lincoln's presidency was a formative time for the United States of America. The Declaration of Independence was just a document expressing the concept of an ideal. The initial motive of the Declaration of Independence was to establish self-governance for the states, free and far from a foreign colonial power. The various states were simply together to secure the right to govern themselves.

Once that goal was achieved, the next natural question that arose was how the states would associate together as a Union. Recognizing that the welfare of all states would be best served by some form of association than by isolated independence, a contract was agreed upon called the United States of America. However, a few years of existence convinced all that the Articles of the Confederation were too loose, too indefinite and too inefficient to constitute the basis of a permanent and progressive nation. They left each state at liberty to withdraw from the Union and gave to no form of central authority. This led to the subsequent adoption of the constitution of the United States of America. It declared, "We, the People of the United States, in order to form a more perfect Union, do ordain and establish this Constitution for the United States of America."

Since then, the ongoing process of creating 'a perfect union' has been underway. The individual character of each state was placed in a balance against the harmonious whole of the Union.

Wary of the 'old world' centralization of power, the states were desirous of retaining their sovereignty that they achieved through their independence from the colonial powers. The founders of the Union were only willing to give as much power to the federal government as was needed for the preservation of the Union. Any concessions offered to the federal government were reluctantly given only after careful deliberation. Successive administrations and popular sentiment has continued to reaffirm that each state is indisputably and sacredly sovereign.

Yet, the whole idea of state rights could easily drive states off their orbits, throw the government into chaos or encroach on the rights and powers of other states. States' rights could deprive the federal government of its power to preserve the unity of the United States. The constitution was not designed to allow states to leave the Union at its own pleasure.

The secession and the subsequent Civil War over the four years of Lincoln's presidency settled it beyond dispute that no state can leave the Union. The war established that the United States is not a collection of independent state nations, but one American nation. Drawn by one central source of unity, the United States was defined as a unified collection of stars, each having its own orbit.

During Lincoln's presidency, any doubts or questions that any state had about its relationship to the Union was settled, though unfortunately through war. The result was the triumph of the national sovereignty over state rebellion. The Civil War clarified for the Americans —once and for all—the limits of each State's sovereignty. A State is sovereign in all accounts, but not to choose secession. All matters of affairs pertaining to the state can be determined by itself, yet that determination can only be done within the Union.

Henceforth it was declared that any grievances arising within the Union must be settled within the Union. Lincoln's war was essential to assert the supremacy of the national over the supremacy of the states' individual rights. Lincoln's mission asserted that the glory of an American will be that though he was a resident of a particular state, he is a citizen of the United States.

Until Lincoln's presidency, for years a restless and ambitious portion of Americans have demanded undue privileges, while others, driven by their desire for peace and harmony, and fearing the threat of secession, have submitted to the unjust demands of the more ambitious Americans. This only emboldened the rebellious few to imagine themselves as the autocrats of the nation.

Lincoln understood that this way of preserving the Union was a confession of its weakness and that it only encouraged conspiracies to destroy the Union's unity. The pride of American citizenship was sacrificed through dishonourable compromises. This Lincoln could not agree with.

It is possible to have one's own way by intimidation up to a certain extent. Most people are disposed to be peaceful and willing to make considerable compromises for the sake of the common interest. So was Lincoln. But when the demand meant surrender of the deeply held ideals of noble individuals, then self-respect became a stronger force

3. ARRIVAL

that the love of peace. The rebellion of the Confederates tested the sincerity of Lincoln to his ideals and tested the strength of his regard for the sanctity of the law.

Many obstacles could have appeared on Lincoln's purpose. It was possible for the American people to have refused its support for a war that meant loss of life, depletion of national wealth and possible defeat of ideals. In extension, that could result in a loss of faith in the government.

It was also possible for the citizenry to have refused to volunteer for the war or to be conscripted. It was possible for them to discourage the war and recognize the independence of the Confederates. Instead, in some divine manner, the people, the Congress and the Executive held together to empower Lincoln in his efforts to uphold the sanctity of the American Constitution and preserve the dignity and integrity of the nation. The citizenry and its representatives felt that no sacrifice was considered too costly for the preservation of the Republic, and no compromise was deemed inadmissible that would protect the Union.

As a result, not only was the war won and the Union saved, but also any delicate question or doubt around the legitimacy and viability of the United States Union was resolved by Lincoln's war once and for all.

Yet another natural outcome of Lincoln's presidency was the emancipation of labour. Lincoln carried the deep-held belief that servile labour would eventually disappear because it would not stand the competition of free labour, yet he felt that slaveholders wielded an unfair advantage on free market labour who relied on their own ingenuity and capacity to build a life of dignity.

Regrettably, there have been those who, out of self-interest, argued for the righteousness of the institution of slavery. This institution sold Blacks as cattle to plough the fields, denied them the right to the sanctity of marriage, robbed black women of their chastity, and deprived mothers of their offspring.

Many deplored slavery as evil, but could not find ways to eliminate it. Lincoln felt that while the rebellion needs to be put down, it was necessary to destroy its cause. Thus it became his sacred assignment to free four million slaves and vindicate the declaration of the United States that all men are created equal. While bringing justice to the slave, Lincoln's assignment also brought justice to the slaveholders. While the freedom of the slaves found its legitimacy through the war, the slaveholders were freed from the weight of barbarism that burdened them. Once that was achieved, men could travel anywhere they wanted, free to think and speak and act as free men without fear of banishment or death, free to pursue any honourable vocation, without being disadvantaged by the institution of slavery that gave an undue business advantage to an unscrupulous few.

If the grand design had been to dissolve the Union, let slavery flourish, and grow an unfair and unjust market system, then when Fort Sumter was attacked by the Confederates in 1861, someone other than Abraham Lincoln would have been president of the United States. But no, events had called upon the Union to soul-search, find its highest calling and resurrect as a Union, not just in geography, but also in spirit. We are able to say that Lincoln was brought to the presidency for precisely such a time of national calamity.

The circumstances of his nomination and election were unnatural. Lincoln was defeated as a candidate for the office of the United States Senator, so that he might be elected president. The American people stumbled upon him. By any conventional notion, it is not probable that his nomination or election would have happened. He did not belong to the group of presidential aspirants. His nomination came as political convenience to the Republican party, necessary as the rival factions could not unite around any of the acknowledged candidates. And when

3. ARRIVAL

the Civil War befell the United States, many doubted the untried president was the man for the hour. Some of Lincoln's own supporters considered replacing him with an appointed dictator. Yet, three years later the citizenry came together in near unanimity to re-elect Lincoln to continue on his purpose, and lead the US nation to its sacred destiny.[XXXI]

Your life-path follows a greater set of laws that is often hidden to you. Hence, most of you follow what is visible or known to you. You notice those around you follow a proven path, be it a rewarding professional track or life choice, so you follow. For many, that sense of familiarity is quite an attractive option. They recognize that others before them have taken that route before them and created pleasing outcomes. Others have set the course and have laid the paths. The rules have been established for them, and all they have to do is to take advantage of the predecessors' efforts. They are content with fitting as a small part of a larger order.

For the Being Leaders, that level of contentment was insufficient. Hence, they chose to step outside the comfort of familiar choices and make the steep climb of living a purpose-driven life. The sacrifices and effort involved in such a path was acceptable to them. Their ordeals, awakening and initiation were all part of that path. In some inexplicable way, the Universe conspired to bring them the ordeals they went through. The eighteen years Mandela spent on Robben Island, the discrimination that Gandhi and Dr. King experienced in their early adulthood, the late childhood experiences that Lincoln went through in his father's farm were all part of that Universal conspiracy.

'Being' on Purpose

Eventually the Being Leaders flourished on their path not despite their ordeals, but due to them. Those ordeals awakened them, trained them, hardened them and initiated them to follow their cause. In that path, they grew in awareness of their strengths and gained clarity of their Highest Ideals. Their ordeals infused them with a fire that shone through their hearts and roused their spirits. It mobilized them to follow a choiceful path that took them to the summit that they reached in life.

So what is Life Purpose? It is not some distant goal for you to strive towards in life. Instead, Life Purpose is a beacon that guides all your thoughts, words and actions each day.

Do not look at your Life Purpose as something that will actualize somewhere in the future, neither is it something that becomes glaringly clear to others after you have passed away. You recognize that you are living on purpose through the deep meaning you experience in every given moment you live.

All the Being Leaders are known today, after their passing, as legends who shaped our collective destiny. There were many who, during the lives of these Being Leaders, were limited in seeing their virtues. That would happen to you as well. So, do not go by others' view of your life. The only accurate scale to measure whether your life is being spent on purpose is to examine the moment. At this moment, as you read these lines, what state are you in? Are you in a state of elation and experiencing a sense of fulfillment? If so, you are expressing your Life Purpose at this moment.

The purpose of a seed could be to sprout into a plant, or it could also be to become food for another living being. In either of these acts, it finds the fulfillment of its reason for existence. The Being Leaders did not see their purpose as an inanimate statement scribbled on the wall or stuck on a poster, rather they experienced their purpose as a living

3. ARRIVAL

organism having its own spirit similar to that of the seed. Each interaction with their purpose gave them a boost of vitality. Each moment spent on purpose resulted in a flow of energy from the spirit of their purpose towards them and those they aimed to serve. It gave real meaning to their existence and filled them with anticipation for the moments to come.

x   x   x

Your Life Purpose is already assigned to you. Call it a preordainment; something that has been destined for you even as you were born. The only choice you have is how and when to express it. Whether you want to embrace it or resist it remains your individual will. You may choose to resist it, in which case you are simply postponing its manifestation in your life.

Many forces take you away from a life lived on purpose. Many of us are compelled by those around us, or by circumstances, to engage or disengage in an activity. Like when a parent compels a child to study against his or her will. Or when an employee is instructed to engage in tasks not to his preference. At that moment, he or she is not being in choiceful action, and hence is not living on purpose in that moment.

Then there are the internal compulsions that prevent you from living on purpose. When you are consumed by your pursuit of pleasure, or when you are propelled by your fears, then you can disqualify that pursuit as not being choiceful. That is being a victim to the ego.

Fear is the inhibitor of your life's passion. When you are propelled by fear in your life, you fail to live your passion. When your bodily survival is your priority, or your life is consumed by an urge to belong to others, or you are motivated by the need to receive respect and recognition, those are fears that discourage you from a life lived on purpose.

These fears have a legitimate role in your worldly existence. It is these fears that truly ensure your self-preservation. They act as indicators for where you are in your life and the needs that express themselves in your existence. These very same fears that ensure your self-preservation keep you away from self-realization. This is the irony of fear.

Mastering these fears is not an external action. Accumulation of wealth or packing your life with friends and family or putting yourself in situations where you will receive respect and recognition will not alleviate those fears. You must tackle them within, irrespective of your external situation.

In the early 2000s, when I started a programme within an organization to create alignment between employees' purpose and the organization's purpose, I received a massive push back from several organizational leaders. The loss of power was inconceivable among a minority of the leaders. But for the majority of leaders, the fear of their organization spiralling out of control was the leading reason to resist the programme. These were fears holding these leaders back from stepping into mastery.

In 1960, when Dr. King urged students to join the demonstrations in North Carolina[28], he was seeking of them to transcend their fears. "We will change these jails from dungeons of shame to havens of victory," Dr. King called out to the students. Students responded to his call by flocking to the jails.

∞ ☼ ∞ ☼ ∞

[28] Lunch counter sit-ins in downtown Greensboro, North Carolina (see 9.4 'LEARNING TO HUMANIZE ONESELF'; pg. 164)

3. ARRIVAL

12.1. FINDING LIFE PURPOSE

"Every event is a SETUP or a cause for UPSET," a great teacher once told me.

"It starts as a child," the teacher elaborated. "You are blessed with your childhood experiences to shape your awareness of Life Purpose."

The teacher was a great champion of finding purpose—and consequently meaning—in everything people did, whether in the workplace, or at home, or in the community.

"As a child, you were naturally attracted to what gave you deep meaning. Love gave you meaning, play gave you meaning, laughter gave you meaning." He paused for emphasis. "Experimenting and discovering gave you meaning. Exploring your limits gave you meaning."

"Yet many adults today live in disconnect from the calling of that child within them."

The teacher's comments reminded me of my conversation with Todd (see 4.2 "I AM NOT GOOD ENOUGH", pg. 70). With less than sixty days remaining for Todd in the political organization where he had served for twelve years, he was resigned to the fact that he had blown all opportunities within his political organization to create a new opening.

As I continued to coach him through his rut and dilemma, he disclosed that as a youngster he used to carry a dream of mentoring youngsters to become inspirational transformation agents in their field of play. "Even as a young adult, I started to feel very deeply about having the youth of society become voice leaders." I noticed a sparkle in his eyes and passion in his voice when he shared his dream. And then his voice lowered and his spirit sank, "I don't know where I lost that zest." He sighed.

Youth leadership had always been a passion for Todd since his college days, and he always made time to coach boys excel in hockey. He noted that it was a hobby that deeply fulfilled him and filled his life with meaning. As we started to analyze his hobby, powerful revelations started to present themselves. Todd recognized what inspired him most about his past hobby of coaching youngsters were the social element of being with others, assisting others grow, inspiring people to believe in themselves, teaching others to take responsibility for their lives, and helping children become human-oriented. He also had the exceptional ability to help the players identify what they did well in the past games and bring that learning into their future games. He was renowned for helping youngsters look inwards and become aware of their strengths, and apply that strength to excel in whatever they did. He had a way of challenging and confronting others to stretch themselves beyond their current limits.

Seeing youth excel and live magical lives inspired him. When he joined this political organization full time and took on the additional responsibilities of family life, he gave up his hobby.

With my support, Todd negotiated an extension with his organization and voluntarily chose to move to a less mainstream group within the party. He became responsible for grooming youth leaders for community organizing. All the gifts that he possessed in grooming youngsters in hockey came to play in this role and he felt a renewed sense of passion for his job. Within no time, Todd launched a youth wing which became the incubator for grooming future political leaders.

To the consternation of many veterans in the party, the youth wing started to become a powerful counterforce to the old school within the party. The youth wing started to be heard as a powerful new voice

3. ARRIVAL

demanding that the organization become more service-minded, futuristic and inclusive. Led by a powerful rush of fresh blood, he went on to launch the concept of conscious policymaking. During the next two years, new policies were drafted around the environment, people-development and economic development. The youth leaders—under the mentorship of Todd—went on to create a most vibrant and visionary grassroots organization with some superb leaders. As a tribute to Todd's mastery, the young adults' leadership team gratefully calls him the 'aged warrior'.

x   x   x

"Your life is enriched by the signs given to you by the Universe. These are not random signs. They are all pre-destined and calculated to open doors for you to flourish on purpose," the teacher spoke of how the world collaborated with us when we chose to live on purpose.

I could see some of his guests nod. Most were Westerners, some had professional backgrounds.

"While this purpose is being announced to you through your inner voice, the universe is also stacking signs around you," the teacher slowly and softly stated.

I could relate to that. I had observed many such signs in my own life that made it easier for me to choose the path I was on. Many such signs were visible also along the life arc of the Being Leaders.

Soon after Mandela and his fellow freedom fighters were transferred to Pollsmoor Maximum Security Prison on the South African mainland in 1982, Mandela was admitted to the Volks Hospital for surgery. After surgery, he was brought back to Pollsmoor, but the jailers moved him to a separate cell from his colleagues. Mandela was initially disconcerted by the change. Why had he been separated from his colleagues, he wondered. While Mandela was in the separate cell, he had a strong feeling of wanting to open discussions with the government. Given the right initiative and temperature, Mandela felt, there could be some form of negotiated agreement that could benefit the ruling Afrikaners and the majority Black South Africans out of the status quo. His feelings were inner signs speaking to him.

The Universe was also stacking signs around Mandela. Around the same time when Mandela was feeling like opening discussions with the government, South Africa was turning increasingly ungovernable. Also the Apartheid government was itself looking for a way out without losing face. President Botha had already declared to his countrymen that they had to accept the changing reality or die. Yet the government expressed hesitation to initiate such a discussion.

Mandela's move to the new cell was the setup awaiting history. Soon Mandela initiated communication with the government. First Mandela had the audience of the Prison Commissioner. That meeting led to an escalation. Mandela next met with the then South African Minister of Justice. Soon after, that meeting led to an appointment with President Botha himself. The chain of events led to the release of Mandela and his colleagues and to the first free democratic elections in South Africa's history.

x   x   x

"The Universe creates a studio setting around you to help you express purpose," the teacher spoke on how purpose reflects on our physical life.

3. ARRIVAL

"All you need to do is to give It a chance to do Its work," he stated, referring to the Universe. "For which you much stop resisting and surrender."

"Then, like a raft taken down river, the Universe shall take you along the path of purpose," he moved his hand in a flowing motion to mime the river.

"Life Purpose will be found along the path of least resistance. Resistance comes out of listening to external voices and the voice of fear. As adults you become more resistant to that natural flow, and life becomes effortful. When you stop resisting Nature and let go, a series of seeming supportive events will continue to support your life's path. Seemingly, random events will present you the lessons you need in order to flourish on your purpose. Like rows of little shops in a bazaar filled with delights, the Universe will organize a series of resources along your life path for you to use to express your purpose," again the teacher used both his hands to mime a row of shops.

"The money you need, the contacts you need, the love, the family, the knowledge, the tools, the materials, the essential resources, all will be brought to you once you choose to live on purpose." To make his point, he explained. "When you claim a life of purpose, the Creator conspires to make things happen for you. Things fall into place effortlessly. Money is given to you to do your life's work."

"As you continue on the inner path of living your Life Purpose, the Creator will assist you with a set of favourable events that will help you fulfill your purpose," he asserted. (We will study this phenomenon of the Universe in the section 12.2, 'SYNCHRONOUS EVENTS' of this chapter).

I understood what he meant. I have seen this phenomenon happen in my life and in the lives of numerous individuals who chose for a purpose-filled life. Everything that is needed in order to progress on purpose seems to appear long the way. The teacher's comments reminded me again what the Being Leaders had mastered in their eminent lives; the ability to attract towards them all the support they needed in order to achieve their noble cause. They received what they needed not by a special effort, but simply by embodying purpose.

It is from this mastery that Dr. King had urged his followers to "take the first step in faith."[29]

x   x   x

"Find your play in life." The teacher resumed after we were all served refreshments. We were seven of us seated against him. I could see most of the guests frantically making notes. I simply recorded his conversation. I knew that I would need to go back into what he was sharing, and find my own ways of bringing his wisdom alive in my life.

"Don't buy into the argument that play is only for children. If you kill play in your life, you have killed the dance of life." There was no drama in his voice as he spoke those words.

Then the teacher revealed something that brought the search for purpose into a new light.

"Hobbies...," he paused. "The constant criticism of hobbies is that it is purposeless. Hobbies are what you do to pass time, it is what you do for fun. It is play."

Yet here the teacher is, saying exactly the opposite. It is precisely because hobby is play that it has something to do with purpose, he claimed.

---

[29] Dr. King had a famous quote: "Take the first step in faith. You don't have to see the whole staircase, just take the first step."

3. ARRIVAL

"You engage in true hobbies for the pure experience of spirit. Financial gains or similar pursuits do not drive you to hobbies. While involved in your hobbies, time disappears, space disappears," he paused to look at his guests as if for consensus.

"Like when you read a great fantasy book. You are so absorbed in it that you don't notice time fly by. In that experience, you are living purpose.

You are so involved in the book that you become one of the characters. You depart your physical world and enter into another space, the world of fantasies. That is a sign that you are being on purpose."

I found his wisdom thrilling. I fell into thought. According to him, it is not in work that we are living purpose. Rather it is in play that we are being on purpose.

Late in Gandhi's life a Western journalist once asked him, "Mr. Gandhi, you've been working fifteen hours a day for fifty years. Don't you ever feel like taking a few weeks off and going for a vacation?" Gandhi laughed and replied, "Why? I am always on vacation."[XXXII]

As if reading my thoughts, the teacher remarked: "The need of the hour is to help leaders find play in work. When you can find your own play, or turn your hobby into your profession, you'd have found purpose in the workplace."

As I listened to the teacher, the seemingly disjointed, and often excluded, role of hobbies settled into clarity and ease.

X   X   X

"We are all given certain life experiences by the Creator to prepare us to serve our purpose. These life experiences are often life-altering." The teacher spoke on perhaps the most crucial piece of the Life Purpose puzzle. "For example, some serious illness or death in the family leaves you with lessons that prime you up to fulfill your purpose. These experiences are God's gift to you to help you fulfill your purpose.

We studied *life-defining experiences* in chapter 3, 'ORDEAL OF THE WARRIOR CHILD' (pg. 51). The teacher was referring to these experiences.

12.2. SYNCRONOUS EVENTS

"What we do not see in ourselves fate brings to us."

C. G. Jung

x   x   x

The Whigs party, to which Abraham Lincoln belonged, supported a system that promoted rapid economic and industrial growth in the United States. Whigs demanded government support for a more modern, market-oriented economy, in which skill, expertise and bank credit would count for more than physical strength or land ownership. Ironically, a party of such high ideals was ultimately destroyed by the question of whether to allow the expansion of slavery to new territories. Many in the Whig felt that slavery went against the idea of economic and industrial growth in the United States. Slavery, they claimed, went against the idea of equal rights where any individual by virtue of his efforts can built a life of success. Slavery offered some—the slave-holders—an advantage over those who relied

217

3. ARRIVAL

on their ingenuity and efforts. Lincoln was one of those against the idea of slavery.

As the party split, and later went defunct, Lincoln felt that it "was an act of fate" that a party of high ideals and many stalwarts would one day disappear. Hence he joined the new Republican Party in 1856. This new national party was comprised of many former Whigs who opposed slavery—referred to as "Conscience Whigs"—Free-Soilers, and antislavery Democrats. The Republicans took a firm stand against slavery. They were dedicated to the repeal of the Kansas-Nebraska Act and the prevention of the further extension of slavery westward.

Looking at the long arc of history it might seem as if the sole purpose of Lincoln moving to the new Republican party was to be later nominated as the republican candidate for the presidency.

As Lincoln sat in his office in Illinois while the Republican convention was underway in 1860, a telegram arrived announcing that his name had been placed in nomination as the Republican candidate for the Presidency of the U.S. Lincoln was told that his nomination was received with great enthusiasm. The entire Illinois delegation were in support of Lincoln, and many delegates from other states were inclined towards Lincoln as well. He was not the choice candidate, but was introduced as a replacement choice after the party could not come together behind their first choice candidate, William H. Seward.

Seward, the biggest prospect to be elected the Republican candidate for President, could not close the deal in the first ballot. A determined opponent of the spread of slavery in the years leading up to the American Civil War, he was a dominant figure in the Republican Party in its formative years, and was widely regarded as the leading contender for the party's presidential nomination in 1860. But delegates from several American states were not very inspired to fall in behind him, instead choosing to lend their votes to Lincoln and get him nominated as the Republican presidential candidate in 1860.

As fate would have it, a similar issue befell the opposing Democratic party. After the historic debates with Lincoln, Stephen Douglas found himself vilified by southern Democrats. He tried unsuccessfully to argue that his middle way would enable the nation to pass over the momentary issue of slavery in the territories and thus preserve the Union. But southern radicals would have none of it. They nominated John C. Breckinridge as the candidate of the Southern Democratic Party for the presidency.

During the election, the opposition votes were split by the two rebelling candidates. As a result, the un-fancied Lincoln became president. It was a providential purpose that brought Lincoln to the Presidency at such a time as that which marked the epoch of his administration.[XXXIII]

x   x   x

During the Civil War, a series of *synchronous events* came together to facilitate the declaration of the Emancipation Proclamation (see chap 17, SHIFT THE MIND, SHAPE THE NEW ORDER). There was not only majority support for the Emancipation Proclamation, there were several champions of such action within the Congress. The war was inflicting huge losses upon the union army and enough Congressmen were feeling that there was no way out except through a proclamation. Through the whole process of scripting and later declaring the Emancipation Proclamation, Lincoln felt that he had been called by the "Providence of God" to achieve an important mission because he faithfully discharged the trust committed to him.

In chapter 3, 'ORDEAL OF THE WARRIOR CHILD', we examined a set of painful experiences that moulded the Being Leaders to step into their true being. I called these experiences the *life-defining experiences*. A

3. ARRIVAL

second type of events, situations and circumstances almost magically came together to enable the Being Leaders to reach the pinnacle of their lives. I call these experiences *synchronous events*. Like an invisible greater power orchestrating events around them, circumstances came together—as if by coincidence—to place the Being Leaders in the right place at the right time to take up the right role that seemed perfectly designed for them to take on.

If all the *synchronous events* seemed like a universal conspiracy to get Lincoln to become president, and later the author of the Emancipation Proclamation, then that is precisely how it was. This universal conspiracy is one attribute of a life lived on purpose. It accompanies you all through your path. As a result, the improbable becomes probable and the impossible becomes possible. Your responsibility is to forge ahead with your plans however farfetched they may seem and remain open to accept these synchronous blessings of the universe.

We can look back and connect the dots and say, "Ah! Lincoln's past experiences make sense. We can see why that particular experience or event was so essential to his achieving his purpose in life." You can notice a similar phenomenon of synchronicity in the lives of the Being Leaders.

Dr. King's dad was himself a minister, and that served as an inspiration for him to become a minister. His father won the grudging respect of the Whites, a fact that explains why Dr. King took an attraction to the life of a pastor.

Church helped Dr. King develop his ability to connect with people and build relationships. Dr. King's life as a pastor brought his several lessons to lead and inspire. It reinforced his belief of love and non-violence as an instrument of conquering the hearts and minds of the segregationists. The church also offered an easy pulpit for him to air his views. In church he found a receptive audience who battled the scourge of racism everyday.

The church also offered him a meeting space for the many meetings that were to take place over the later decade to shape the civil rights movement. It was a valuable resource given to him "by God to do God's work."

You can admire the perfection with which *synchronous events* have unfolded in the lives of the Being Leaders in order to facilitate their grand mission. Soon after his return from England, Gandhi attempted to launch his law career in India. By his own admission, his practice was not developing in spite of several attempts and the help of many.

Soon he picked up the assignment for one Dada Abdulla to help his activities in South Africa. It was during that trip to South Africa that the scourge of discrimination affected Gandhi's life.

Over two decades of his experiments to counter discrimination, he developed his creed of *Satyagraha*[30]. He perfected the methodology of *Satyagraha* in the Phoenix settlement in South Africa. Much later in India, he effectively applied *Satyagraha* against the British to force them to leave India. As a result, he became the legend that he is now due to it.

To the Being Leaders, mastery involved finding their Life Purpose and living on it. There was no nobler cause, no greater road for them to take

---

[30] Gandhi coined the term Satyagraha, a Sanskrit word meant as 'Desire for truth'. We will study this form of non-violent resistance in chapter 15, 'LIVE BY YOUR NOBLE CREED'

3. ARRIVAL

than to execute what was called of them in that moment in history. The Universe conspired to place them in those eras where their voice and actions were needed most.

You could say that the Being Leaders were accidental soldiers caught in the revolutions they were involved in. Yet, so were many others of the same era. Walter Sizulu, Mandela's mentor, and Henry Clay, Lincoln's role model are two examples.

'Being' in mastery results from a life lived in alignment with Life Purpose. The life examples of the Being Leaders demonstrate precisely that. They made sacrifices rather than deviate from purpose. That is not to say that a 'being' leader does not err. There can be mistakes made. We know this from the numerous self-acknowledged shortcomings of the Being Leaders. The Being Leaders were legendary, but there were not perfect.

This chapter examined why finding and living Life Purpose was fundamental to the Being Leaders becoming who they were. The section 'FINDING LIFE PURPOSE' looked at a number of pointers that will guide you to find your own Life Purpose[31]. That is only the beginning of walking the road that the Being Leaders walked before you. Each day consciously choosing thoughts, words and actions that align with your Life Purpose is the next step. This is a lifelong practice. Yet, it is also a fulfilling practice in each moment.

---

[31] In the Being Leader Workbook, I will dive into a few specific questions that will help you find your Life Purpose

13. YOU ARE THE SUM OF EVERYTHING YOU HAVE DONE

"The quality, not the longevity, of one's life is what is important."

Dr. Martin Luther King Jr.

On Thursday, April 4, 1968, Martin Luther King Jr. had retreated to room 306 of the Lorraine Motel, worrying about a sanitation strike in Memphis and working on his sermon for Sunday.

For Dr. King, whose focus had shifted from civil rights to antiwar agitation and populist economics, the 'Dream' was turning dark. He had been depressed, sleeping little and suffering from migraines. In Memphis, Dr. King's first march with striking garbage men had degenerated into riot when young black radicals—not, as before, angry state troopers—broke Dr. King's non-violent ranks.

Always fastidious, Dr. King shaved, splashed on cologne and stepped onto the balcony. He paused; a .30-06 rifle shot slammed Dr. King back against the wall, his arms stretched out to his sides as if he were being crucified.

So what is the real legacy of Dr. Martin Luther King Jr.?

Dr. King was an unlikely leader of the cause to begin with. On December 1st, 1955, Rosa Parks declined to give up her seat to a white

3. ARRIVAL

passenger on a Montgomery bus. Dr. King was not quite 27 then; his wife Coretta had just given birth to their first child. Yolanda E. D. Nixon, another Montgomery pastor, wanted to host a boycott meeting at Dr. King's Dexter Avenue Baptist Church, not because of Dr. King but because his church was closest to downtown. It is amusingly noted that when the session ran long, a frustrated minister got up to leave, whispering to Dr. King, "This is going to fizzle out. I'm going." Dr. King replied, "I would like to go too, but it's in my church."

Dr. King took up the burden that was inexplicably brought upon him, however, and his greatness emerged. Over the next many years, he led waves of courageous ordinary people on the streets of the American South, from the bus boycott to Birmingham to Selma to the Freedom Rides.

What makes Dr. King's story accessible is that he was a common man. Behind his public dignity, Dr. King was roiled by inner conflicts and self-doubts. He worried for the safety of his family and friends, he questioned if he was the perfect torchbearer of such a moral cause as social justice, and he sometimes wondered if non-violence was the right path for an already wounded race. He made powerful enemies: J. Edgar Hoover, the FBI Director, obsessed over Dr. King, wiretapping and harassing him from 1962 until his death. On one occasion, he told his congregation that "life is a continual story of shattered dreams." Yet he lifted himself up like any of us would do. "We must turn a minus into a plus," Dr. King said, "a stumbling block into a steppingstone—we must go on anyhow."

His legacy is the triumph of good over evil. Dr. Martin Luther King Jr., created the promise of the greatest moral crusade on the American nation's racial battlefield. For most of humanity the story seems quite straightforward. He was a prophet, the American Gandhi, who led the nation out of the darkness of racial segregation. His 'Promised Land' was the one he conjured on the steps of the Lincoln Memorial in 1963, a place where his "four little children [...] will not be judged by the color of their skin but by the content of their character."

His Christian socialist vision may have proved too radical to affect white mainstream Americans and his non-violent tactics may have remained too peaceful to satisfy the rising tide of black militancy, but more than any other leader, Dr. King had been responsible for the many concrete achievements of the Civil Rights Movement. Dr. King had dreamed and he had acted. Perhaps Dr. King's concrete legacy was the pieces of federal legislation passed in 1964 and 1965. As a result, American minorities enjoyed a flurry of political empowerment in the late 1960s and early 1970s, when the Voting Rights Act of 1965 began to affect local elections.

Dr. King's legacy does not end there. He tried to build an interracial coalition to end the war in Vietnam and force major economic reforms—starting with guaranteed annual incomes for all. That was different from his past battles. He understood that the victories of Birmingham and Selma were gone forever, and sensed the tricky racial and political terrain ahead. He knew the country was embarking on a long twilight struggle against poverty and violence, necessarily more arduous than the fight against racial segregation. Once the target shifted to poverty, he knew that it would be tough to replicate the drama that had led to the Civil Rights and Voting Rights Acts in 1964 and 1965.

Yet, he took on those battles, because he felt that the world needed him to. "We've got some difficult days ahead," he preached the night before he died. According to David J. Garrow's Pulitzer Prize-winning Dr. King's biography, "Bearing the Cross," while reading Ramparts magazine at lunch one day in 1967, Dr. King came across photos of napalmed Vietnamese kids. Dr. King pushed away his plate of food noting, "nothing will ever taste any good for me until I do everything I can to end that war."

3. ARRIVAL

Look at Dr. King's legacy through the eyes of a world inspired by his life and death. Dr. King is a hero because he opened the doors for humanity to look at each other as equals. When most Americans were caught up in a collective hysteria around the Vietnam war, he advocated against the morality of the war. And he vociferously spoke of the sacrilege of poverty to a prosperous nation. Dr. King has been one of the very few men with the standing to frame the issue of the ghettos in moral terms. Today, Dr. King's legacy resonates worldwide.[XXXIV]

History judges men on the entirety of their lives. And that means two things.

Firstly, what you do in each moment is important, but in the long arc of history, it will be only one speck. No one action defines a man. Many specks together define you in the eyes of history.

"No one is as noble as the best thing he has done or as venal as the worst," Mandela said.

The good you do and the goodness you be far outweighs the bad. There is always room for redemption. However, you must demonstrate to those around you that you are conscious enough to embrace the lessons from these experiences. Prove you are a leader because you have the openness and capacity to internalize lessons offered by your experiences. Prove that you can give hope to those around that there is a path out of mistakes made. Prove that people are not doomed once and for all with one careless action. Then you are redeemed.

Secondly, you cannot seek and find your legacy, you can only identify the field where your spirit yearns to make a difference (we will examine the field of legacy under section 13.2, 'FIND YOUR PLAYGROUND', later in this chapter). Your legacy writes itself in history when you live to fruition your Life Purpose. If your Life Purpose represents the guiding beacon that takes you to the summit of life, your Noble Legacy is what you have shaped in the hearts of others as you walk towards the summit of life. So work out what your Life Purpose is and live your life congruent with that purpose. When you are following your Life Purpose, you are being led by your spirit. And that spirit ignites those of others. Those others end up feeling the same intensity, and they will want to join you. They will want to be part of your mission. You inspire them to want to help you shape your Noble Legacy.

This phenomenon you see profoundly in the lives of the Being Leaders. Beneath all their differences, Mandela's fellow prisoners were deeply wedded to the cause and means propounded by Mandela.

13.1. SPEAK YOUR EULOGY AND READ YOUR EPITAPH

In this temple
As in the hearts of the people
For whom he saved the union
The memory of Abraham Lincoln
Is enshrined forever

Epitaph of Abraham Lincoln

x   x   x

There are eulogies and then there are curriculum vitae (CV). What the eulogy speaks of you is different from what your CV says of you.

3. ARRIVAL

Your CV speaks of what you have achieved, your eulogy speaks of what you have given. While your CV will highlight your consistent achievement of your deadlines and your addition to profitability, your eulogy will glorify you making the difference in a refugee's life. While your CV will gloat the positions you have made, your eulogy will announce the recognition you have given to others. Your CV will state how you made department head, while your eulogy will speak of how caring and giving a human you have been. While your CV will speak of the very many gainful years you spent, your eulogy will speak of how considerate and humble a human you were.

Though the Being Leaders were not living towards an epitaph in their glorious lives, they were living a life which was boldly and fondly spoken of in their funerals. They have immortalized themselves, not because they wanted to. They simply made a choice to live their greatest meaning and dedicate themselves to joyful service. They walked the trails that others before had chosen not to, they undertook sacrifices that others were not willing to undertake, and they chose with their spirit. As a result, their spiritual presence forever dominates our lives.

So, live life mindful of what your eulogy will speak and what your epitaph will read. You will never hear your eulogy, but even as you are reading this, you are scripting yours. You are the author of your epitaph. One day you will be dead in your flesh. But there will be others around you who will outlive you. And within them, a small part of you will remain alive. That memory is your legacy. The realization that after your death a part of you will remain alive in the thoughts of those around you—your family, friends and beyond—adds a responsibility upon you to live a life of meaning and magic. The countless moral choices you make will forever remain in the collective memory of humanity. That involves saving your legacy before choosing to save your life.

You are the Sum of Everything you have Done

Jawaharlal Nehru, the first prime minister of independent India and Gandhi's protégé spoke at Gandhi's funeral: "Great men and eminent men have monuments in bronze and marble set up for them, but this man of divine fire managed in his lifetime to become enshrined in millions and millions of hearts so that all of us became somewhat of the stuff that he was made of, though to an infinitely lesser degree."

I once visited a great sage seeking his wisdom. After a few minutes of conversation with him, he confidently stated, "You are destined to become a legend." Before I could get inflated by his remark, he added, "because that is each human's destiny". After a careful moment, he added, "You can only postpone your destiny, you cannot avoid it."

Those words have always remained with me.

So use your power of choice to shape a life that will be spoken off proudly by those who have known you. What you have achieved for your personal gains will not be spoken in your eulogy, the difference you have made in others' lives will be. When your daily practice is to be the moral conscience of your ecosystem, be it your home, your family, business or an entire nation, that is when you are on your path of shaping your Noble Legacy. It is easy to achieve power and rule over a group, but that does not make you a Being Leader. That explains why certain founders' legacies have outlived the company itself.

13.2. FIND YOUR PLAYGROUND

In 1915, when Gandhi returned to India from South Africa to join the freedom movement, he noticed a particular dynamic among the various players in the Indian independence movement. He noticed a good number of local British administrators who had good intentions for the Indians they ruled. The rulers and the Indians would come to compromises on how much autonomy the Indians were given to live a life of limited choice. Many local British administrators had a fair amount of empathy  for the Indians they ruled and stood for giving freedom to the Indians to follow their religious practices and rituals. In return, the Indians did not collectively and actively revolt against the local administrators. In return for limited rights, the Indians limited their push for equality. On occasions, the local administrators employed by the British government were overruled by the powers in Britain and the local decisions were replaced with draconian and insensitive laws. That would lead to a brief outcry from the Indian subjects, but to no avail.

The only token form of resistance to British rule that existed in colonial India was the Indian National Congress (INC). In 1915, the INC was a club of affluent Indians who held animosity against the ruling colonialists. These elite Indians were those who traditionally owned large swaths of land across the country and were used to have numerous lower caste people in servitude to them.

Like in all other walks of pre-independence India, there was a clear hierarchy in the INC. You could join the party as long as you joined the appropriate rank. If you were from the labour class or lower castes your role was to clean, cook and serve. If you were from the elite class, you automatically assumed a senior position within the political fabric of the party. All talk of independence were entertained by these elites only as long as the talks were held under the auspices of the INC. All grand talks of resistance were conducted in posh parties held in mansions belonging to the rich Indians. There were annual meetings held in any one of the major cities where all these elites came together to pledge their allegiance to the cause of freedom.

Outside the INC were the Indian royalty. Before the colonial invasion, India was an assortment of dozens of little kingdoms, each with its own royal families. The royalty were forbidden by the British rulers from organizing against the rulers. Royals paid "tax" to the British and were expected to pledge their allegiance to the British monarchy in return for the "protection" that was extended to them. Most of the rulers pretended allegiance to the British but in their hearts wanted to see the rulers gone. Their hearts lied with the INC. A small number of valiant royals rebelled against the mighty British army, and were swiftly eliminated.

The majority of Indians were poor and were resigned to their fate and led a subservient life. They expected nothing from either the administrators or the INC. Lack of access to resources and the natural wealth of the land kept the majority of Indians in existential mode each day. This majority have never experienced solidarity or have ever engaged in patriotic expression. They never organized themselves and never participated in community or civics.

This was the world into which Gandhi arrived. As he slowly started to find his place in the movement, he sensed the possibilities lying ahead for a nation to stand up for its highest ideals. So Gandhi made the conscious decision to change the rules of the game. It was important—he felt—that a new consciousness be created within the Indian independence movement, and that could be done only when the walls of hierarchy and discrimination were torn down. There was a need for change in "heart", that if the independence movement were to go ahead, a shift needed to occur from the existing practice of exclusivity towards

3. ARRIVAL

inclusivity. That meant bringing together the aristocracy together with the poor souls in the villages, creating convergence in vision between Hindus and Muslims, and a merger between movements that were more centered around the north and those centered around the south of India.

Gandhi saw that there was an urgent and important need to reverse the roles, that the masters need to become the servants and the servants the masters. All the ideals from his younger years, from having spent hours listening to the stories of the pious Indian king Harishchandra and studying the principled life-lessons of the *Bhagavad-Gita*[32], and all his *life-defining experiences* and knowledge that he gained from his years in South Africa he applied for reinventing the field that he had entered.

x   x   x

Mrs Annie Besant, a distinguished Englishwoman, was a theosophist, socialist and a women's rights advocate. Over the years she had become an accepted and respected leader of India. She became a passionate advocate of self-rule for India, and in 1917 she was elected president of the Indian National Congress. When the British were entangled in World War I, she famously raised the cry: 'The moment of England's difficulty is the moment of India's opportunity.'

The prominent INC members had bought into that call. However Gandhi felt differently. He felt that the British were in a righteous war, and as such, India had an obligation to support Britain in its moment of need. Besides, such support would only present India in a positive light among the British monarchy when the moment of choice arrived. He also felt that as a result of the agitation for freedom, when the inevitable self-rule came it would be on friendly terms.

---

[32] A treatise on life from ancient India

Gandhi's views went against the existing paradigm of the INC, but the place of strength from which he came and the unwavering power with which he stood in his ideals, placed the INC in a deep dilemma.

The INC had over the years become the figurehead of the Indian independence movement. But here was a man, Gandhi, who was drawing the attention of the everyday man of India and the prominent newspapers in the East and the West.

The INC was used to convening in mansions where the only presence of any foot soldier were the orderlies who catered to the needs and comforts of the rich. And here was Gandhi who insisted on travelling 3rd class among the poor in train, and slept, ate and drank with commoners. As a result, when he made a call to disobey the colonial rulers, people joined him irrespective of caste or religion. When others argued in favour of the numbers on their side—the Indian population was 300 million—Gandhi spoke about non-violence and civil disobedience.

Until Gandhi's return to India and many years thereafter, English was the medium of instruction used by most in the independence movement. Gandhi insisted on addressing the gathering of patriots in Hindi, much to the dismay of many veterans of the erstwhile resistance club. Gandhi knew that for India to earn self-rule, it must express its own identity and character. And making Hindi the medium of communication expressed that character.

Gandhi also shocked British and Indians alike by eschewing western clothing and wearing simple sarongs of homespun cotton. This act was one of defiance to a British stranglehold on the Indian economy, but also to express a distinct Indian character to the independence movement.

3. ARRIVAL

It is noted that in the meetings in which Gandhi participated, he would unhesitatingly take the tea set and serve the participants (see chapter 9, section 9.1, 'MAKE YOURSELF SMALL'), a task usually reserved to the servants and orderlies hailing from the lower castes.

In another anecdote of how Gandhi changed the rules of the game in his playground, Gandhi was visiting a city to give a lecture to an organization he supported (see chapter 9, section 9.1, 'MAKE YOURSELF SMALL'). He noticed that a certain area of the floor needed sweeping. So he found a broom and began sweeping. He wanted to break the notion that menial jobs are only for the poor.

On April 13th, 1919, a crowd of non-violent protesters had gathered in the Jallianwala Bagh garden in Amritsar, Punjab, to protest the arrest of two leaders despite a curfew which had been recently declared. On the orders of Brigadier-General Reginald Dyer, the fifty riflemen fired on the crowd for ten minutes, directing their bullets largely towards the few open gates through which people were trying to run out. Dyer continued the firing for about ten minutes, until the ammunition supply was almost exhausted. The dead were estimated around thousand, possibly more.

In the aftermath of the massacre the Lieutenant Governor of Punjab, India, Michael O'Dwyer convened a meeting between his staff and the leaders of the Indian freedom movement. In the opening statement, the viceroy reiterated the unspoken agreement that each party should arrive at a compromise that will permit both parties co-exist with each other. Gandhi immediately interrupted him with a firm no. In a calm but firm voice Gandhi stated that it is time that the colonial power leave India. The viceroy was left shocked and speechless. That was the moment that the British knew that the rules governing the occupation have changed forever.

Gandhi created his own movement, his own following, and changed the rules of the game. In the process, he planted the seeds of his own sacred legacy. And soon enough, his principles started to become the principles that governed the Indian independence movement.

Once your have identified and defined your field of legacy, you must endeavour to master it thoroughly. You must understand its lifeblood. You must learn its condition, how your predecessors have shaped it, what are the laws that govern this field...and then go ahead and redefine those. The Being Leaders superseded the physical laws with the non-physical ones. They brought more meaning, more ownership, more collective pride and a higher purpose to it.

The field of legacy must be known to you. And this knowing must not be limited to an intellectual understanding rather it must be a knowingness that originates from your very core. You must know it in your heart, it must fire you up when you think about it in the morning. It must infuriate you when you notice justice not being done to it. It must frustrate you when you cannot advance in that field. All this, not because you want to become famous or you want to become wealthy harnessing it but simply because it speaks to your highest truth.

Look at the lives of some of the renowned personalities you might know. Sigmund Freud has shaped his legacy in the field of psychology. Picasso in arts. Einstein in the science of matter. Florence nightingale in the field of serving. Wright brothers in the field of transportation. Henry ford in automotive. Mozart in music compositions. The Being Leaders in the field of social justice. Could you see all these eminent personalities excel in any other field as they did in their chosen fields? Did they possess the Unique Gifts to excel in any other field than their field of legacy? The answer to both questions is no.

So once you identify your field of legacy, selflessly apply yourself in that field. Gandhi once quoted from the *Bhagavad-Gita*[33] to the American author and traveler Vincent Sheean: "Renunciation of the fruits of action does not mean that there can be no fruits. Fruits are not forbidden. But no action must be undertaken for the sake of its fruits." He further explained to Sheean that by detachment he meant that one must not worry whether the desired result follows from one's action or not, so long as one's motive is pure and one's means correct.[XXXV]

That is the mindset you must possess while in pursuit of your Noble Legacy. Once you choose, your Noble Legacy becomes inevitable and unstoppable.

---

[33] A treatise on life from ancient India

14. BE LED BY YOUR HIGHEST IDEAL

"I desire so to conduct the affairs of this administration that if at the end [...] I have lost every other friend on earth; I shall at least have one friend left, and that friend shall be down inside of me."

Abraham Lincoln

In August 1965, during the annual convention of the Southern Christian Leadership Conference, Dr. Martin Luther King surprised his audience by publicly expressing his regret at the United States' participation in the Vietnam war. The U.S. was deeply involved in a war in distant Vietnam against a perceived threat of communism across the Far East. Dr. King appealed to his colleagues to take a stand for peace, join in a call to end the war and an immediate halt to U.S. bombing operations in Vietnam.

"I'm not going to sit by and see the war escalate without saying anything about it," Dr. King spoke. "It is worthless to talk about integrating if there is no world to integrate in. The war in Vietnam must be stopped."

Dr. King's Highest Ideal was a nation where every man had the same rights as the other, where there is no violence perpetuated against the other and where there is enough economically to let all individuals live a life of choice. The public pronouncement of his ideal of a non-violent world did not play well with his audience, and his aides and advisers were deeply divided over his stand for his ideals. Friends and foes alike condemned that his ideals could only be selectively applied, and that they were contextual.

His stand certainly did not play well in the U.S. White House. Dr. King and the U.S. President Lyndon B. Johnson were on the best of terms, and taking a stand for ideals over relationship was ill-advised, many felt.

"They told me I wasn't an expert in foreign affairs," Dr. King recalled of the warnings he received from the administration. "And they were all experts. I knew only civil rights and should stick to that."

Plus, a nation consumed by the collective hysteria of war turned against Dr. King, both the right and the left. The country was extremely hawkish over the war so many reviled him. But Dr. King would not be restrained. Racial injustice, poverty and war were all "inextricably bound together," he asserted.

In December 1966, President Johnson announced plans to divert antipoverty funds to Vietnam and Dr. King again asserted his opposition to what he considered an immoral and ill-advised war effort. It was cruel and outrageous, Dr. King said, for the U.S. government to use the most vulnerable and poor in American society to fight and die for a nation that has refused to seat them in the same schools together. Dr. King, led by his ideal of equality—racial and economic, refused to stand aside as those in the American ghettos, to whom he had preached that guns and Molotov cocktails were not the answer, were dragged halfway around the world to spread violence. For the sake of those young men and of the soul of the United States, Dr. King refused to remain silent.

"Somehow this madness must cease," he declared. "We must stop now. I speak as a child of God and brother to the suffering poor of Vietnam. I speak for those whose land is being laid waste, whose homes are being destroyed, whose culture is being subverted. I speak for the poor of America who are paying the double price of smashed hopes at home, and death and corruption in Vietnam. I speak as a citizen of the world, for the world as it stands aghast at the path we have taken. I speak as one who loves America, to the leaders of our own nation: The great initiative in this war is ours; the initiative to stop it must be ours."

Most of Dr. King's contemporary men and women did not have the elevation to see what he saw. He was a man who had entered the chasm, had overcome his demons and had come out in an ever stronger clarity of his ideals. He just did not settle for equality among the races, he urged a whole nation to live up its ideals.

By the Spring of 1967, Dr. King's bold but controversial stance seriously fractured his national support and standing.

"I don't determine what is right or wrong by taking a Gallup poll of a majority. Ultimately a genuine leader is not a searcher of consensus but a moulder of consensus," was Dr. King's response when it was pointed out to him that two out of three Americans disapproved of his stance on the war.

Among his fellow civil rights leaders, there was consternation and anger that he had wedged the antiwar movement into the civil rights struggle. Roy Wilkins of the National Association for the Advancement of Colored People (NAACP) and Whitney Young of the Urban League chastised Dr. King. On April 1967, the NAACP's sixty-member board unanimously opposed any effort to fuse the civil rights and anti-war movements.

Black Congressman Adam Clayton Powell derided Dr. King, calling him Martin Loser King. Jackie Robinson, the Hall of Fame baseball player and long time civil rights activist, pleaded with Dr. King not to

3. ARRIVAL

weaken the call for racial justice with a political position that was certain to alienate a large percentage of the American people.

"I am convinced he is making a very serious tactical error which will do much harm to the civil rights movement," asserted Ralph Bunche of the United Nations. "King should realize that his anti-U.S. Vietnam crusade is bound to alienate many friends and supporters."

By late 1967, the war in Vietnam was not going well, but it hurt Dr. King that most Americans were not ready for a change of course. Many urged him to join the majority as they felt that such a compromise would salvage his reputation and that in turn should help the civil rights movement. Even Dr. King's own father did not approve of his stand for his ideals.

All this clamour against him by those who he wanted to transcend the tactical view of events crushed Dr. King. The *New York Times* scathing editorial against him wounded him deeply. The *New York Times* was the most prestigious paper in America and Dr. King had great respect for it. Only recently, he had given it an interview about Vietnam, and he was totally unprepared for its hostile editorial. He was so distraught and hurt, his advisers said, that he sat down and cried.

But it never occurred to him that he should alter his Highest Ideal or stop living by them.[XXXVI]

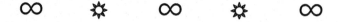

One sign of 'being' in mastery is how resolute you are about living by your highest ideals. To many, this is easy when things are going well. However, it is in the face of adversities that your resolve to hold true to your ideals is severely tested.

Be Led by your Highest Ideal

The Being Leaders always carried higher ideals. They recognized that their primary job was not merely worldly fulfillment. It was something greater. It was beyond oneself. It was not merely taking for oneself what is available to take. It is about being in service to a greater good.

See your Highest Ideal as a standard of perfection, a principle to be aimed at. Your Highest Ideal cannot be confined to just you or your near ones. You might not outlive its unfolding, but when you have departed, you would have made a difference to your Highest Ideal. For the noble self within you, an ideal is an ultimate object of endeavour, an honourable or worthy aim. In fact, an ideal is one of such high or noble character that many consider it exists only in the mind and lacks practicality or the possibility of realization.

The Being Leaders have shown us otherwise. Gandhi's Highest Ideal was *Purnaswaraj*[34]. To him, *Purnaswaraj* involved not just the independence of the nation in abstract terms. It involved the emancipation of all Indians from the colonial rulers of India, even more so for those toiling in the Indian soil. That included—but was not limited to—improvement of health, education of the worldly ways and public hygiene. *Purnaswaraj* to him meant material and spiritual renewal for one and all. It meant not only the purging of the Colonial powers but also a cleansing of caste and discrimination.[XXXVII]

Following are a few pointers to get you towards your Highest Ideal and embed your life in it. In embedding your life in your Highest Ideals, you are transcending the tugs and distractions of daily living and being in mastery, as the Being Leaders did.

---

[34] *Purnaswaraj* is a Sanskrit compound of *Purna*, or "complete", and *Swaraj*, meaning "self-rule"

14.1. EXCAVATE YOUR HIGHEST IDEAL

Lincoln saw the free market system as the system that helped each individual to preserve her personal dignity and live a profession of choice. A free market economy was crucial to each adult individual's pursuit of happiness as was enshrined in the United States constitution. It "gives hope to all, and energy, and progress, and improvement of condition to all," he claimed. Beyond the constitution, a free market economy was at the core of Lincoln's life story.  It served as a ticket to any man's dignified existence. At an early age, Lincoln left a life of physical labour in the farms in order to be his own man free from the disgrace piled upon him by his father. Lincoln dreamt of a life lived in choice and personal fulfillment.

There was yet another reason for him to leave his home farm at an early age. The farm did not quench his undying passion for intellectual growth, fuelling his desire to live a life in service. He credited the free market economy for offering such a choice to uplift himself.

As a young adult, not only did Lincoln see slavery as a moral failing, he also saw it a threat to the free market principles that lifted him in his later years from being a measly farm boy into a successful lawyer and later into the president of the United States. He viewed the free market system as a generous, just and dignified system where every man's pursuit of happiness was in his own hands.

When you look at Lincoln's life through the lens of his childhood experiences and the ideals that inspired him through his early life hardships, you can instantly see why he was dead against slavery. Lincoln saw the rise and spread of slavery an end to the free market system—an ideal—that he so cherished. Slavery, he felt, could spread from the west of US to even back into the north and consume and destroy his ideals. On the one hand, it robbed the honour of the slaves, on the other hand the advantage to a life of personal dignity would become more unfairly skewed towards the slave owners which in turn would further enslave other free men, leaving them at the mercy of the powerful slave owners. This was a blot to Lincoln's ideal of a dignified world.

The undivided heart and the unrelenting defence of his Highest Ideal turned Lincoln into the legend that he today is. As you see from the above chronology, it is a sequence of several *life-defining experiences* that wedded Lincoln to his Highest Ideal. We can look back and connect the dots to see with clarity his Highest Ideal.

His Highest Ideal was a 'Perfect Union' that was preserved by a collective principle, where all men were made equal. This Union "gives hope to all, and energy, and progress, and improvement of condition to all" in the pursuit of his happiness. Lincoln's Highest Ideal was a principle so sacred to him that he was willing to leave his party to which he remained loyal all his political career. To defend the U.S. constitution and to uphold the founding fathers' vision, he was willing to turn friends into enemies and proponents into opponents.

x   x   x

Seek your Highest Ideal with such an undivided heart that you will unfailingly uncover it. And once you have uncovered it, reconfirm it. Practice consciously aligning your thoughts, words and deeds with your ideals. Set your intentions towards fulfilling your Highest Ideal even when the odds seem slim. Fill yourself with optimism and resolve.

If you do not feel a wholesome connection with your Highest Ideal, question yourself. Examine if your life reflects the voice of your spirit. Ask yourself if that ideal is something worth dying for. Find out if it infuriates you to see the world not reflecting your Highest Ideal. As you continue to align your thoughts, words and action with your Highest Ideal, you would have acquired such a profound level of personal mastery that even in the midst of the most trying adversity you act in alignment with your Highest Ideal.

Such belief protects you from losing faith even in dire circumstances like Mandela faced on Robben Island. It was very easy for him to lose hope and sink into darkness, devoid of hope. Instead in small deliberate steps, Mandela populated his imagination with his Highest Ideal of a nation where all citizens were treated equally, and each person was entitled to one vote each. He wove that ideal into every action and every routine that he followed in prison. He noted to himself—without any resentment towards the prison warders—that he was a political prisoner put in prison for standing up for his Highest Ideal.

Here are two questions straight from the sages that will help you gain clarity of your Highest Ideal. Ask yourself what noble principles when violated by others infuriate you the most. Secondly, when you are most disappointed with yourself for what you have done (or failed to do), what value did you fail to live by? In the emotions you experience when you see your Highest Ideal being dishonoured you will receive a clue.

14.2. LET YOUR IDEALS EVOLVE

Worldwide demands for the release of Nelson Mandela from imprisonment began to shape following the infamous Rivonia Treason Trial of 1963. As time went on and an international anti-Apartheid movement grew, demands for Mandela's release, and the scores of freedom fighters imprisoned by the South African Apartheid regime became hallmarks of the global anti-Apartheid movement from the nineteen sixties through his actual release in 1990.

Initially Mandela, along with both rank and file and leadership cadres from the African National Congress and other South African parties were held in Robben Island. In 1982, Mandela and other key leaders were transferred to Pollsmoor Prison. On January 31st, 1985, the State President of South Africa, P. W. Botha, speaking in parliament, offered Mandela his freedom on condition that he 'unconditionally rejected violence as a political weapon'. This was the sixth such offer, earlier ones stipulating that he accept exile in the Transkei. His daughter Zinzi read Mandela's reply spurning Botha's latest offer to a mass meeting in Jabulani Stadium, Soweto, on February 10th, 1985. This was the text of his response as read publicly by Zinzi:

"I am a member of the African National Congress. I have always been a member of the African National Congress and I will remain a member of the African National Congress until the day I die. Oliver Tambo is much more than a brother to me. He is my greatest friend and comrade for nearly fifty years. If there is any one amongst you who cherishes my freedom, Oliver Tambo cherishes it more, and I know that he would give his life to see me free. There is no difference between his views and mine.

3. ARRIVAL

I am surprised at the conditions that the government wants to impose on me. I am not a violent man. My colleagues and I wrote in 1952 to Malan (D.F. Malan, was the Prime Minister of South Africa from 1948 to 1954) asking for a round table conference to find a solution to the problems of our country, but that was ignored. When Strijdom (Hans Strijdom was Prime Minister of South Africa from 1954 to 1958) was in power, we made the same offer. Again it was ignored. When Verwoerd (H. F. Verwoerd was Prime Minister of South Africa from 1958 to 1966) was in power we asked for a national convention for all the people in South Africa to decide on their future. This, too, was in vain.

It was only then, when all other forms of resistance were no longer open to us, that we turned to armed struggle. Let Botha show that he is different to Malan, Strijdom and Verwoerd. Let him renounce violence. Let him say that he will dismantle Apartheid. Let him unban the people's organisation, the African National Congress. Let him free all who have been imprisoned, banished or exiled for their opposition to Apartheid. Let him guarantee free political activity so that people may decide who will govern them.

I cherish my own freedom dearly, but I care even more for your freedom. Too many have died since I went to prison. Too many have suffered for the love of freedom. I owe it to their widows, to their orphans, to their mothers and to their fathers who have grieved and wept for them. Not only I have suffered during these long, lonely, wasted years. I am not less life-loving than you are. But I cannot sell my birthright, nor am I prepared to sell the birthright of the people to be free. I am in prison as the representative of the people and of your organisation, the African National Congress, which was banned.

What freedom am I being offered while the organisation of the people remains banned? What freedom am I being offered when I may be arrested on a pass offence? What freedom am I being offered to live my life as a family with my dear wife who remains in banishment in

Brandfort? What freedom am I being offered when I must ask for permission to live in an urban area? What freedom am I being offered when I need a stamp in my pass to seek work? What freedom am I being offered when my very South African citizenship is not respected?

Only free men can negotiate. Prisoners cannot enter into contracts. Herman Toivo ja Toivo (he is considered the father of the Namibian independence struggle), when freed, never gave any undertaking, nor was he called upon to do so. I cannot and will not give any undertaking at a time when I and you, the people, are not free. Your freedom and mine cannot be separated."[XXXVIII]

x   x   x

With the years, however, Mandela's ideals evolved. As he grew and became more inclusive and more nobler, his ideals evolved and subsequently reflected his shift in consciousness.

The increasing social unrest in South Africa that swept through the country in the 1980s, and the changing geopolitical circumstances on the international political scene forced the Apartheid government of South Africa to enter into negotiations with the African National Congress (ANC). Sensing the opportunity, Mandela used the greater access to the government and the secrecy offered by Pollsmoor prison to deviate from his long-held principle of non-negotiation to open up negotiations with the Apartheid government.

In July 1986, Mandela wrote to the Commissioner of Prisons, requesting a meeting with Kobie Coetsee, the Minister of Prisons. During the meeting with Coetsee, the idea of negotiations between the National Party led government and Mandela was raised. Immediately there after, a request to meet President P.W. Botha was tabled. That same year Mandela was visited by the Eminent Persons Group from the

3. ARRIVAL

Commonwealth Groups of Nations. Coetsee continued to visit Mandela to negotiate on behalf of P.W. Botha.

In August 1988, Mandela contracted tuberculosis and was admitted to the Tygerberg Hospital, where he was hospitalized for a month and half. On December 9th, 1988, Mandela was transferred from Pollsmoor Prison to Victor Verster Prison, much closer to the seat of the Apartheid government, where he was held in a house formerly occupied by a prison warder. After almost three years of meetings between Coetsee and Mandela, in 1989 Mandela wrote to P.W. Botha acknowledging the need to negotiate. As a result, on July 5th, 1989, South African president P.W. Botha secretly met Mandela. Soon after, Botha was replaced by F.W. de Klerk. F.W. de Klerk moved to implement reforms that would enable a negotiated settlement to take place. In December 1989, he met with Mandela in prison to discuss his release.

On his opening speech to parliament on February 2nd, 1990, De Klerk announced the unbanning of political organizations and the release of imprisoned political leaders. This was followed by another announcement at a press conference on February 10th, 1990, that Mandela would be released the next day. On February 11th, Mandela was finally released from Victor Verster Prison after spending a total of 27 years in prison. These events set the stage for a long process that led to the first democratic election in South Africa.[XXXIX]

x   x   x

At the summit of their lives, all thoughts, words, actions, all commitments and all positions that the Being Leaders took remained always aligned with their ideals. However, they have let their ideals evolve with time and experience. By the end of their lives, the Being Leaders' ideals had grown to the 'highest'; their ideals truly reflected their spirits.

Gandhi always told his followers that if two of his sentences contradicted each other, and if they thought he was sane at that time, they should ignore the first one and accept the second one. This remark reflects his ongoing evolution.

It is a man with self-awareness who can grow and evolve his ideals. For the Being Leaders, this evolution was never driven by any expediency. Before going to prison in 1964, Mandela carried an ideal in his heart, that of a South Africa that is led and ruled by its indigenous black population. He resolved to himself that he would never negotiate with the government except as equals as individuals having the same freedoms at both sides.

As Mandela himself has acknowledged, he went into prison an angry man convinced that the only way of achieving his people's freedom was by force of arms. This was neither an original nor a morally opprobrious approach back then, in 1962, given every attempt to negotiate with successive white governments over the previous half century had been contemptuously rebutted; and given, too, the enormity of the injustice to which the eighty-five percent of the population who were not white had been subjected since the arrival of the first European mariners in 1652.

It was behind bars that he learnt his most valuable lessons in leadership. Prison shaped him. What the experience of prison did was elevate Mandela to a higher political plain, setting him apart from the great mass of ordinarily brave, ordinarily principled freedom fighters within his country and beyond. He learnt that succumbing to the vengeful passions brought fleeting joys at the cost of lasting benefits; he learnt, through studying his jailers closely, that black and white people had far more in common, at the core, than they had points of difference; he learnt that forgiveness and generosity and, above all, respect were weapons of political persuasion as powerful as any gun.

3. ARRIVAL

In prison, Mandela let his Highest Ideal take form. *He saw a society where the Blacks, Whites, Indians and other Asians co-existed harmoniously and synergistically. He started to speak of a rainbow colour nation that upheld the dignity of all, gave equal rights to education and land to all and where each man's vote counted as equally as the others. This ideal spoke of a citizenry who would not have to carry discriminatory passes or else be arrested. In that country, different races were not geographically segregated from each other, and where no one would have to ask permission to live in an urban area. Where no citizen would have to ask for permission to seek work and feed his family.*

His Highest Ideal was visible in his subsequent actions. He opened negotiations secretly with the government because he could accept that he had a responsibility in shaping a new reality, this new ideal where many races coexisted as one. He knew that he was living in a time where the change was inevitable. The outcome of these meetings was that he was released from prison and the process of negotiations began that led to his people's freedom and his rise to the highest political office in the land.[XLI]

14.3. HOLD FOREVER TRUE TO YOUR HIGHEST IDEAL

The Being Leaders recognized and accepted that truth is relative. But whatever truth they believe in, they claimed it with an undivided heart. They remain steadfast in their truth in the face of extreme adversity. The adversity that the Being Leaders have faced are different in nature from those faced by today's leaders in business and politics. It is not the erosion of market share, or product recalls, or re-election prospects that kept them awake. It is the shaming of human dignity—and that of nature itself—that offended them. Yet, in the face of such adversities, they never flinched. They remained steadfast in their truth, never wavering when the odds were against them and even when their lives were threatened. In the defence of their Highest Ideal, pain felt trifle to them.

Dr. Martin Luther King's stand against the American involvement in the Vietnam war created a fierce attack on him by the war hawks and several so called 'patriots' of the day. Yet, in the face of abandonment, he never retreated from living for his Highest Ideal. He—like the other Being Leaders—was not beyond pain, he simply chose not to waver in the face of pain. The Being Leaders understood that every word that is uttered is controversial, that there is someone who will take offence with words that have been spoken, actions that have been taken, intentions that have been set and ideas that have been championed.

Many times Dr. King doubted if his ideals of a nation, where every man had the same rights as the other, where there is no violence inflicted upon each other, and where there is enough economically to let all individuals live a life of choice, were a pipe dream. When many friends admonished him and well-wishers turned against him, he doubted if his ideal was an unrealistic illusion. Yet he remained bonded unwaveringly to his Highest Ideal. When you have righteousness on your side, why do you need majority opinion on your side? This was his thinking.

As Lincoln reminded us of his position, "I desire so to conduct the affairs of this administration that if at the end [...] I have lost every other friend on earth; I shall at least have one friend left, and that friend shall be down inside of me."

x   x   x

When Gerald (name changed) first asked to meet me, I was instantly struck by the defeated demeanour about him. For many years, he had

3. ARRIVAL

been active in politics in one of the developed European countries and he held the ideal of a new, noble and conscientious political world. In his ideal world, politicians unified around the noble aim of serving the greater good, where consensus was built around people, planet and prosperity.

Years of being active in national politics, he had arrived at the conclusion that the existing political system and the current political class were not equipped to shape a new reality for a society that was demanding a more conscious outlook from politicians. He felt that irrespective of his current position, it was his prerogative to act on his ideals. He pressed ahead with turning his ideals into his manifesto and started to attract a sizeable following and valuable press attention.

In late 2000s, with great determination, Gerald stepped out on his own to launch a new party. His previous attempts at new launches had failed, and that had already affected his reputation. Similar political experiments by others in the past decade had also met with negative outcomes. Yet, in his core he felt that he must follow his passion. When he started to go about setting up his own party, the true nature of the political fraternity became visible to him.

From the rank and file of the existing establishment many fully identified with his ideals, yet few joined his party. More significantly, he was ostracized en masse by the power brokers within the establishment. There seemed an unspoken collective pact among the establishment to give him no presence. They were determined to give him no air time and his views were not to be publicly discussed. Their position was that his views were already part of the establishment's manifesto, and that he was essentially imitating what there already is. They also started painting him as an unrealist.

He felt mentally blocked by all the pressure that he was putting upon himself by virtue of the games played by the establishment. At some unconscious level, he felt trapped in the judgments of those around him. How others saw him was important to him. He was conditioned to believe that it was important for him to belong to that fraternity, and the establishment's acceptance of his initiative was crucial for its success and his wellbeing.

"In the face of such adversity, I am not inclined to pursue my dreams," Gerald lamented. "Its time has not come yet," he sighed.

There is a lesson to learn here.

Note: You do not create pain in others. They create it themselves. You might be a trigger to their pain, but ultimately their pain is their own. It is never who you are being, or your words or actions that create that pain, it is their interpretation or judgment of who you are, or what your words and actions meant that create their pain.

For the Being Leaders, the intention behind being unbending in principle and unwavering in spirit was not to inflict pain and see their foes suffer, it was to live their own Highest Ideals. In that process they were heavily tested, mostly by their near and dear ones. After all, it is the suffering of the near and dear ones that most unsettles you. Would you continue to live for your ideals in the presence of suffering within those nearest to you, and in the face of objections? That will be the test of your mastery.

If you can muster the courage to stand long enough by your principles, and weather the strong winds, and have the patience and faith in the voice of your spirit, I know that you will prevail, not only because you are stronger, but also because you stand for the ultimate good of yourself and all.

3. ARRIVAL

It is attributed to Lincoln; "I am not bound to win, but I am bound to be true." As Gandhi's life taught us, if I am bound to be true, I am bound to be victorious.

Identifying your Highest Ideal is a first practical step towards living a life of personal mastery, organizing your life in conformity with those ideals is the next. This step of articulating and living by the Noble Creed of your life we will examine in-depth in the next chapter.

15. LIVE BY YOUR NOBLE CREED

"There is no royal road except through living the creed in your life, which must be a living sermon."

Gandhi wrote in the late 1930s on this creed

"Satyagraha[35] *is a force that may be used by individuals as well as by communities. It may be used as well in political as in domestic affairs. Its universal applicability is a demonstration of its permanence and invincibility. It can be used alike by men, women, and children."*

M. K. Gandhi

For Gandhi, *Satyagraha* was not simply a technique or theory, but the Noble Creed of his life. *Satyagraha* was not just a tool suited to certain situations. It applied equally in all his interactions, whether it involved removing the British colonialists from India, or removing the scourge of discrimination from the hearts of the upper class Indians, or his daily lifestyle. *Satyagraha* was for Gandhi a way to approach conflict and resolve it non-violently, on any level of human interaction.

In Gandhi's life, at the personal level (internal level) *Satyagraha* assumed the role of the pursuit of truth and a firm adherence to non-violence. Gandhi knew human nature and felt that, by itself, the pursuit

---

[35] Gandhi coined the term *Satyagraha*, a Sanskrit compound of *Satya*, or "truth", and *Agraha*, meaning "desire"

of truth can become self-centered. So his personal practice of *Satyagraha* involved the systematic reduction of self-centeredness. This he called, "reducing yourself to zero."

In his own words, Gandhi was a domineering, sometimes petulant husband early in his marital years. He believed, as he recounts, that it was his right to impose his will upon his wife. But Kasturba—his wife—had an intuitive grasp of the properties of non-violent love, and during those tumultuous years of domestic strife, she proved to be an even greater practitioner of the principles of *Satyagraha* than was Gandhi.

"I learnt the lessons of non-violence from my wife, when I tried to bend her to my will. Her determined resistance to my will, on the one hand, and her quiet submission to the suffering my stupidity involved, on the other, ultimately made me ashamed of myself and cured me of my stupidity...in the end, she became my teacher in non-violence."

For Gandhi, family *Satyagraha* is founded, like all *Satyagraha*, on this delicate balance of patience and determination, which, when correctly practiced, can become a cornerstone for deep personal relationship between man, woman and child. His Noble Creed simply said; forgive, forbear, support the other always, and when it becomes necessary to resist, do so lovingly and without rancour. The apex of the practice of this creed is reached when the spouse's welfare becomes more important to the other than one's own happiness.

The "irreducible minimum" with children is that the welfare of the children comes first; their growth and development take precedence over everything else. Practice of *Satyagraha* involves setting the example that is true to their ideals.

When Gandhi moved to the Phoenix settlement, he took all the children in the farm under his fatherly wings.

"I saw," he writes, "that I must be good and live straight, if only for their sakes."

As in his personal life, in his activism to achieve Indian independence, Gandhi's actions are a testimony of his Noble Creed, from its conception in South Africa at the turn of the century to the final clashes with the British colonialists during the World War II times. During those times *Satyagraha* assumed many forms; marches, strikes, boycotts, but most importantly, civil disobedience.

Gandhi shocked British and Indians alike by eschewing western clothing and wearing simple sarongs of homespun cotton. This act of humble defiance was his response to a British stranglehold on the Indian economy, the demand that only British-made textiles be produced and sold.

To motivate Indians to become self-sufficient, but also as part of his eating habits, Gandhi cultivated his own food. He believed that each Indian deserves a dignified life, a life where they do not have to depend on the government or the largesse of the barons in the villages. And if each Indian could cultivate his own food, it would leave him free from subjugation. Besides, the British can only tax food traded in the market, they could not tax food harvested from one's own backyard.

In early 1930, Gandhi mounted a civil disobedience movement against the British law preventing the colonized Indians from making their own salt[36]. Gandhi continued his Satyagraha against the salt tax for the next two months, exhorting other Indians to break the salt laws by committing acts of civil disobedience. Thousands were arrested and imprisoned, including Gandhi himself in early May. News of Gandhi's detention spurred tens of thousands more to join the movement. The Dandi March drew worldwide attention to the Indian independence movement through extensive newspaper and newsreel coverage.

---

[36] See chapter 9, 'HAVE A TRUE MEASURE OF THE SELF', pg. 143)

3. ARRIVAL

Satyagraha, soon after, became chosen by all Indians as their main tactic for winning Indian independence from British rule. Perhaps for the first time in human history, this event demonstrated the effective use of civil disobedience as a technique for fighting social and political injustice.[XLI]

x   x   x

"I believe implicitly that all men are born equal. I've fought this doctrine of superiority in South Africa inch by inch. And it is because of that inherent belief that I delight in calling myself a scavenger, a spinner, a weaver, a farmer and a labourer," in 1927 when campaigning in India against untouchability, Gandhi referred to his doctrine in life.[XLII]

For Gandhi, removing the British from India was the easier part, like all external cleansing in life is. Removing the scourge of discrimination from the hearts of the Indians who called themselves higher caste was a much greater task, because this was discrimination of their own.

He called the so called lower caste *harijans*[37]. Whenever he travelled, he travelled by 3rd class compartment in train, the class usually taken by the *harijans*. He stayed and ate with them, and mostly shunned richer homes and mansions, many belonging to friends and benefactors of his movement. In his *ashram*[38], he found place for many *harijans*, in spite of the protest of closest relatives and other well-wishes.

Gandhi felt that the power of his Noble Creed was that it could resolve conflicts without annihilating the opponent. As he stated succinctly, the practice of his Noble Creed "seeks to liquidate antagonism but not the antagonists themselves." Bringing about the conversion of the opponent

---

[37] Meaning 'Children of God'
[38] Monastery

is always a primary aim of *Satyagraha*. His Noble Creed did not involve excluding the adversary from the solution. On the contrary, it tried to transform the opponent, drawing him in as a participant and beneficiary of the new reality. Before he turned his attention to full independence for India, for years Gandhi aimed for autonomy for India while remaining a part of the British Empire.

Gandhi felt that the *Satyagrahi*[39] who has risen above self-interest, who can see beyond his own opinions, is in a position to view conflict with some objectivity and therefore able to look for common ground. So the task of *Satyagraha* here is to work silently and steadily to minimize self-interest in the work environment through the appeal to a broader, unifying purpose.

"Only one individual is necessary to spread the leavening influence of *Ahimsa*[40] in an office, a business, a school, or even a large institution," Gandhi pointed out. "One dedicated *Satyagrahi* can alter the climate so that work can proceed in an atmosphere of mutual trust and cooperation."

"This," Gandhi echoed the Buddha, "is the highest kind of work."[XLIII]

Your creed is your operating principle. See it as an authoritative, formulated statement of your personal beliefs. Creeds are not intended to be comprehensive, but to be a summary of your core beliefs. You acquire it through your life's experiences, first and foremost, your *life-defining experiences*. Consider your creed a system that underpins all your actions and is foundational to you.

---

[39] Aspirant of Satyagraha
[40] Non-violence

3. ARRIVAL

A creed—also called credo sometimes—is not self-preserving. If self-preserving, it will be rooted in fear and will arise from a place of low self-worth. Adolf Hitler held the doctrine of Aryan supremacy. And if he had not carried low self-worth, he would not have felt the need to assert that the Aryans were a mighty race. The same can be observed with religious extremists; they feel lowly of themselves and compensate for that low self-worth through aggression.

On my path, I meet many leaders from politics, business and NGO who have set high ideals. Yet, they find it challenging to practice noble means. For example, I have met many modern day managers profusely make commitments fully well knowing that they are not going to honour those. This trait of using less than noble means is not confined to leaders in high places or belonging to particular cultures. Across many countries that I have lived, I have met people who act that way.

Using noble means to achieve noble ends is more difficult than setting high ideals. Taking a stand for noble means entails unfailing practice every time, each day. Leaders who claim that the end justifies the means are only deluding themselves. Often unnoticeable to themselves, they testify to their own low consciousness while excusing themselves for their lack of competence to operate by a noble creed. Inevitably, history will forget such leaders and often punish him.

Choosing to live your Noble Creed each day is to live by noble means. Make your life an incessant spiritual practice. Align your actions with your Noble Creed. Living by your Noble Creed is more difficult because each day you must hold yourself steady against many winds of adversity. Temptations, shortcuts and opportunities for instant gratifications will come your path. And each failure to stand by your Highest Ideal can seem like a defeat.

Here is a prescription that has served me well. Enjoy the process and never lose sight of the big picture. Draw inspiration from the lives of the Being Leaders. You do not have to be perfect each moment, you simply need to recognize that every moment is a test. All the choices in front of you fall into either of two categories; good or bad. When you choose the bad, ask yourself what the lesson is from that capitulation. Learn the lesson and move on.

I take great inspiration from the Noble Creeds of the Being Leaders. Earlier in this chapter, we studied the Noble Creed of Gandhi. Below are the Noble Creeds of the remaining three Being Leaders.

x   x   x

Lincoln's Noble Creed was honesty combined with forbearance.

"Resolve to be honest at all events," Lincoln once said in a law lecture in 1850. "And if in your own judgment you cannot be an honest lawyer, resolve to be honest without being a lawyer. Choose some other occupation."

In that speech he acknowledged that there is a popular belief that lawyers are dishonest. He spoke, "let no young man choosing the law for a calling for a moment yield to this popular belief." As a lawyer, he felt very passionate about honesty.

Jesse Fell, an Illinois lawyer and real estate developer insisted that "if there was any traits of character that stood out in bold relief in the person of Mr. Lincoln it was that of truth and candour. He was utterly incapable of insincerity, or of professing views of this, or any other subject that he did not entertain."

In the aftermath of the US Civil War, Lincoln—a true man of forbearance—spoke thus in his second inaugural address as the US

3. ARRIVAL

President; "Neither party expected for the war, the magnitude, or the duration, which it has already attained. Neither anticipated that the cause of the conflict might cease with, or even before, the conflict itself should cease. Each looked for an easier triumph, and a result less fundamental and astounding. Both read the same Bible, and pray to the same God; and each invokes His aid against the other. It may seem strange that any men should dare to ask a just God's assistance in wringing their bread from the sweat of other men's faces; but let us judge not that we be not judged. The prayers of both could not be answered; that of neither has been answered fully. The Almighty has his own purposes."

Lincoln closed his inaugural address with an impassioned plea to all, "We are not enemies, but friends. We must not be enemies. Though passion may have strained, it must not break our bonds of affection."

Mandela's Noble Creed could be well summarized with 'Ubuntu' (see section 8.1, 'BRANCHES OF THE SAME TREE', pg. 138). Within that context, you can easily understand the motives behind his activism. Dignity and the rights for all regardless of race, class or gender was non-negotiable to Mandela. To achieve that end, no amount of sacrifice was considered sufficient. No amount of compromise, concession or change was considered sufficient for the cause of *Ubuntu*. In later chapters, we will see more of Mandela's Noble Creed.

Dr. King's Noble Creed was to be God's instrument of love.

To truly understand Dr. King, you must understand that he was—first and foremost—a preacher. Yet, he was more than a preacher. He saw himself foremost as a foot soldier. Examples of Jesus as a foot soldier touched him more than Jesus the moral teacher.

Unlike other ministers and churches, he preached an active social gospel. "[...] the church must incessantly raise its voice in prophetic warning against the social evils in all the institutions of the day. The church must not try to be a state or an economic order, but remaining in its own role as conserver and voice of the state and the economic order. In all its judgements it must avoid even the appearance of being one organisation competing for power and prestige among other organisations. Its peculiar power lies not in self-seeking but in searching for truth and justice and peace for all, in the spirit of Jesus Christ. For this, too, is part of being 'first' by being 'slave of all'."

Born to a father who was a minister, he grew up listening to the hymns of Jesus. He said that he would gladly suffer like Jesus to uphold the dignity of humanity. He grew up fully indoctrinated by God's intend for all of humanity, and that was that all humans were created equal as children of God. Racial discrimination, the Vietnam war and persistent poverty across America were social evils, and as an instrument of love, he found it a normal thing for him to fight against.

In the previous chapter, we studied the Highest Ideals as a high choice and revered quality of the Being Leaders. In this chapter, we examined Noble Creed and the unwavering practice of those who have attained personal mastery. There is no metric for success in your practice of your Noble Creed. Each day you must continue in the spirit of your Noble Creed, and after a lifetime of practice history will reward you for it. That is an un-gratifying imperative of 'being' in mastery.

16. THREE SIDES OF A COIN

*"Rarely do we find men who willingly engage in hard, solid thinking.
There is an almost universal quest for easy answers and half-baked
solutions. Nothing pains some people more than having to think."*

Dr. Martin Luther King, Jr.

In 1906, The white government of the Transvaal, a South African province, had just introduced new legislation to deprive South African Indians of what civil rights they still retained under the law (see chapter 9, section 9.3, 'HISTORY MAKES MEN', pg. 160). If the 'Black Act' was passed it would mean the end of the Indian communities in South Africa.

The South African Indians were faced with two evident options; one was to accept that they had no choice than to accept the draconian and humiliating laws brought out by the Afrikaner government of South Africa. The second option was to resort to violent retaliation. Some folks felt that they had the numbers, means and the passion to counter the administration.

Gandhi saw a third way that others could not. The plan was to refuse to obey such degrading legislation and accept the consequences without violent retaliation but without yielding an inch in their demand for fair and equal treatment under the law.

3. ARRIVAL

The movement spread swiftly through South Africa. What Gandhi proposed was an entirely new method of fighting. Instead of fanning hatred with hatred and violence with violence, he argued that exploitation could be overcome simply by returning love for hatred and respect for contempt, in a strong, determined refusal to yield to injustice. It was a style of resistance which demanded the highest courage and such depth of commitment that every temporary setback only strengthened the resisters' determination more. Thousands of men, women and children courted jail sentences in open but disciplined defiance of South African exploitation.

In 1914 the laws most offensive to the Indians in South Africa were repealed and basic civil rights voted into law.[XLIV]

Note: There is always a third way out of any dilemma. This we learn from the lives of the Being Leaders. Gandhi—like the other Being Leaders—exhibited a certain subtle finesse when it came to how he addressed the challenges he faced.

Gandhi carried many wounds from the discrimination he faced in his early years in India and his young adult years in South Africa. These wounds were so deep that retreat or subservience was not an option. His wounds called out to him to act. They reminded him of a world that was distant from his Highest Ideal of *Purnaswaraj*[41].

At the same time, aggression was not part of Gandhi's native structure. Many people close to him had screamed retaliation and vengeance, first against the South African white regime and later against the colonialists

---

[41] See chapter 14: 'BE LED BY YOUR HIGHEST IDEAL', pg. 241

in India. But the values he imbibed from the childhood stories of pious souls like the Indian King Harishchandra and Lord Krishna, an Indian deity, left no space within him for aggression.

When confronted, most humans tend to either retreat or attack. That is the primate nature within us. In a split second we will assess the threat we are faced with, and based on that assessment we will either retreat or attack. These two options form the most visible two paths we take when confronted. However, when you can transcend that primate self, multiple other responses appear to you. The most elevated among you can access multiple solutions beyond the primitive two. Yet, the ability to access even a third solution to your dilemmas is a huge leap in awareness.

Satyagraha, for Gandhi, was his Noble Creed[42]. In a reactive world where your responses are predicted to be either retreat or attack, *Satyagraha* was also Gandhi's Third Way. In February, 1922, a large group of peaceful protesters participating in the Non-cooperation movement turned violent, leading to police opening fire and in retaliation the burning of a police station. The incident led to several deaths of both civilians and police. Many expected Gandhi to take advantage of the tension and ratchet up the conflict. Others all but expected him to give up the struggle. When the news of the violence reached Gandhi, his response was to suspend all protests and go on a five-day fast as penance for what he perceived as his culpability in the bloodshed. Loss of any life was inconceivable to him, honouring and accepting life was.[XLV]

The Third Way is the capacity to transcend the primitive consciousness and access a realm where love and compassion becomes the operating principle for the self and humanity. In love and compassion, the Being Leaders found the solution to all inner, transpersonal and social evils. That consciousness was innate to the Being Leaders.

---

[42] See chapter 15: 'LIVE BY YOUR NOBLE CREED', pg. 255

3. ARRIVAL

x   x   x

The reason why the Confederates from the south of the United States were so vengeful against the anti-slavery North is simply because they felt threatened. Their way of life included the slaves, and slavery offered them a life of comfort, and that way of life was being challenged by the Union. Hence they waged war.

Lincoln had an elevated view of the confederates and their fear that slavery would soon be banned by a Lincoln administration. Even as many around him were expecting a ringing call to arms, in his inaugural address, he earnestly stated, "so far as possible, the people everywhere shall have that sense of perfect security which is most favourable to calm thought and reflection."

Rather than rattling his presidential authority, Lincoln closed his inaugural address with an impassioned plea to the southern states to rethink there rash actions. "We are not enemies, but friends," he declared. "We must not be enemies. Though passion may have strained, it must not break our bonds of affection."

Though Lincoln abhorred the idea of slavery and carried raw wounds from the terrible indignity he suffered as a child growing up in a farm, he still could transcend his wounds to see things as they really were. He was not entangled in his pain and he did not lash out against the perpetrators of slavery. Instead, away from his wounds and its war cry, he stepped back and dispassionately explored the possibilities.

Wounds are part of the *conditioned self*[43], and it is the imperative of every true leader to uncover the wisdom of these wounds. What is the wound trying to teach you? What is the wrong that must be righted?

---

[43] See chapter 4, 'THE FIERY ORDEAL THROUGH WHICH THE BEING LEADERS PASS', section 4.3, 'BATTLE OF THE SELVES' pg. 76 for more on the *conditioned self*

It is when you have embraced that wisdom and discharged the emotions that you have accumulated through your past wounds that you are truly free from those wounds. Then you can start harnessing the immense power of the wisdom of your wounds.

With all the emotions and energy attached to that wound cleared, you become present and choiceful. The wound does not dictate your choices, instead your awareness does. From that space, you are able to access more solutions than just the default two responses that humans are conditioned to; attack or retreat. You start seeing the landscape around you and the people operating in that landscape for who they truly are. You stop seeing them as perpetrators, instead you see them as normal individuals motivated by their own self-interest. In that moment, you are mirroring the Being Leaders and expressing their awareness.

Once you become free from your wounds, you become unlimited. This unlimited nature in children leads to an explosion of possibilities when confronted with problems. In the DNA of the Being Leader they held two genes of this unlimited nature that helped them repeatedly evolve Third Ways;

> ➢ The ability to operate in the third person
> ➢ The ability to see all sides

3. ARRIVAL

16.1   OPERATING IN THE THIRD PERSON

The kitchens on Robben Island were notorious for turning out food that was barely edible, but was also experienced as being corrupt and discriminatory. They were manned by common-law convicts who ensured that the tastiest foods were kept back for themselves, their friends and the warders who supervised them. The official rations allowed to prisoners were meagre enough, but what emerged from the kitchens was even less adequate.

"Lunch and supper, especially the supper of African prisoners, were sometimes so full of sand and miscellaneous kinds of dirt and insects that even the strong stomachs of the most hard-bitten would somersault," said Neville Alexander, a fellow political prisoner of Mandela. "Hungry people would sometimes leave food uneaten."

Complaints about food were commonplace, but nothing was ever done to improve the system. A particular grievance of political prisoners was the discrimination the authorities applied between food for Africans and food for Coloureds and Indians. African prisoners received what was termed an 'F diet'; Coloureds and Indians were placed higher on the scale with 'D diet'. Both diets were based largely on maize, but D-diet prisoners were given bread and extra helping of meat, vegetables and coffee. The regulations were quite specific. D-diet prisoners, for example, were allowed two ounces of sugar a day; F-diet prisoners, one and a half ounces. Sharing food with prisoners with different diets was forbidden and resulted in punishment.

At the stone quarry where about 600 prisoners worked, food for lunch arrived in half drums transported on two wheeled trolleys. When the bell for lunch rang, the prisoners would form queues, with Coloured and Indian prisoners in front and Africans behind, waiting patiently while a common-law convict doled out food on plates set out in long rows, starting with Coloured and Indian plates and moving on to the African ones. No one was allowed to take a plate until all the food had been laid out.

Often the food ran out and many plates would stand empty. The usual routine when this happened would be for warders to send prisoners back to the kitchens for more food, but on some occasions the warder in charge of the quarry simply gave the order to reduce the F-diet rations already doled out.[XLVI]

Many young prisoners often complained that Mandela was not moving fast or challenging the authorities forcefully enough. Mandela himself was offered the F-diet and it was justified for him to stand up against the system. The unpalatable food that the black prisoners were given was not just about cost management or a power game by the authorities. It was an expression of the centuries old racial discrimination that Blacks in South Africa have faced. He got the F-diet food not because his crime was different from those committed by others, but because the colour of his skin was different from the colour of others.

Yet Mandela was able to transcend his wounds and look at the landscape and its stakeholders in its entirety. He approached the issue as if it was foreign to him. In the characteristically dispassionate way in which he would meticulously make the bed or methodically tie his shoe lace, he would look at the challenge presented in front him.

Such an approach made some young prisoners doubt his commitment to their cause. Why else would someone remain so distant to the problem? Why else would someone not feel the same indignation that they felt against the discrimination? Why else would someone not express the same rage that many young freedom fighters showed in the face of such indignity? They wondered. Yet, history shows that no other man has made a greater sacrifice for the cause of anti-Apartheid or given his utmost to serve the cause, including his family, friends and freedom.

After careful deliberation, the prisoners collectively struck against the authorities and boycotted their meals for several days. Initially, the prison authorities punished the prisoners for their insolence. Then the authorities viciously pushed the prisoners to work in the quarries until they collapsed. And when the ill and the old reported at the prison hospital, the authorities turned them around. As a last resort to break the will of the prisoners, the kitchen staff was ordered to prepare appetizing food, steaming hot, laced with vegetables and meat.

But the resolve of Mandela and others held firm. The prisoners did not give up their battle. Soon the prison authorities relented and promised to improve conditions of the prisoners and to treat them with dignity. The food improved, not only for the black prisoners, it improved for the Coloured and Indian prisoners as well.

x   x   x

The Being Leaders impart some lessons on what it takes to operate in the third person. In every situation, you must refuse to see yourself as stakeholders. You must not have any vested interests. You can be involved, but not entangled. Whatever the cause, you must be passionate, but not passion-ridden. And you should have the inner mastery to accept any outcome, whatever it may be. From such a place, you notice various doors open. Once you can step above the fray, where you could see only problems, you start seeing solutions.

Note. You cannot fix a problem at the same level of consciousness at which the problem was created. If a rift has been created in a fit of anger, that rift is not going to be mended in the same emotional state at which it was created. You will need to lift yourself out of that state of anger before the problem can be fixed. This you see recur in the lives of the Being Leaders.

∞　　☀　　∞　　☀　　∞

16.2　SEEING ALL SIDES

Many in the Republican Party from Lincoln's days vehemently fought against the evil of slavery. But most could not envision a day when the Whites and free Blacks could live side by side as equals in the same streets and the same community. Yet, they constantly sought ways to limit the spread of slavery from the south to the west and perhaps even back to the north of the United States. The reasons for eliminating slavery were many.

Many in the Republican Party of that time saw slavery as a threat against the free market economy that offered anyone who had the resolve a dignified life. A free market system allocated resources efficiently, and any man who was willing to serve others and apply his strengths, however lowly he may be at the beginning, could grow in life in a free market system. That was the promise of the free market system. In such a system, slave owners, riding on the back of their slaves, could accrue undue advantage and leave other hardworking white Americans at a disadvantage. Such accumulation of strength and power in the hands of slave owners would takeaway the freedom of other Whites, practically turning them into slaves.

To many others within the Republican Party, abolishing slavery was a constitutional necessity. The U.S. Declaration of Independence

3. ARRIVAL

stipulated that "All men are born free and equal", and to treat one race as slave-masters while another as slaves went against the spirit of the Declaration of Independence. To overlook such a grave inequality was a certain threat to the constitution. "Who is to say that if such an unconstitutional practice was tolerated and promoted other constitutional breaches would not come up in later times?" Many within the Republican Party wondered.

To a large minority in the Republican Party, abolishing slavery was a moral imperative. Many felt that slavery was not a Christian thing to do, others felt that it was not within the will of man to treat another as different. Lincoln himself was fiercely against the idea of slavery.

In the North, many suspected that there was this secretive, tyrannical slave power out to grab power in the federal government. Many Republicans claimed that the Southerners wanted to take control of the Executive and Legislative. The worries got more severe when they felt that the slave powers of the South now wanted to take over the Judiciary as well. The slave powers had already hijacked the Democratic Party of the time, the reason why many northern Democrats had fled the party to join the Republicans. The slave powers twisted the arms of the Democratic presidents for the past 60 years to support and protect their way of life. The slave owners of the Confederate states was ferocious in their earnestness to protect their way of life. They were using their muscle to pack the courts with judges who would overturn any restrictions on slavery and maybe even change the laws that prevented slavery in the North, something unthinkable to the Republicans in the North.

On March 26, 1864, former Senator Archibald Dixon, Governor Thomas E. Bramlette, and Albert G. Hodges, editor of the journal Commonwealth in Frankfort, Kentucky, travelled from Kentucky to meet with Lincoln to discuss the recruitment of slaves as soldiers in Kentucky. There was considerable dissatisfaction in Kentucky on the issue because, although the Emancipation Proclamation did not apply in the border states—of which Kentucky was one—runaway slaves could gain their freedom through military service. The idea of Whites and Blacks living side by side as equals in the same streets and the same community was unthinkable to many in Kentucky.

Slavery existed in the border states between the Union states and the Confederate states, yet they saw themselves as an essential part of the Union. They expressed their allegiance to the Union and sided with the Union army during the Civil War. To preserve their way of life, though, they wrenched out a commitment from the federal government that slavery would not be abolished from the border states even as such law would be passed in due course in the Confederate states.

Lincoln heard their complaints and went on to state that "I am naturally anti-slavery. If slavery is not wrong, nothing is wrong. I can not remember when I did not so think, and feel." He went on to outline the benefits for Kentucky of allowing Blacks to serve in the Federal Army.

As presented earlier in this chapter, the Southerners felt threatened by the new Republican administration in the federal government. Their comforts were built upon the sweat of slaves, and given the strong anti-slavery sentiments in the Republican party, they felt that the slaved will be banned by the party. This they could not swallow. For these Southerners, their personal comforts came ahead of the ideal of a perfect Union of which they were a part of.

x   x   x

Lincoln could distance himself from the harsh rhetoric among many within the Republican party and the Southerners. He could also empathize with the concerns of the border states. Yes, his allegiance lay with the Republican party, but he took an oath to be the president of the entire Union. He was first and foremost a president and then a Republican.

Lincoln had the ability to see a mixture of motives.

"Slavery," Lincoln, who was himself anti-slavery, insisted, "had its own economic logic. Southerners are just what we would be in their situation. If slavery did not now exist amongst them, they would not introduce it."

He went on to say, "When southern people tells us they are no more responsible for the origin of slavery, I acknowledge that fact."
His remarks show his ability to see the reality of all sides, their self-interests and their motives. Seeing the grays is to truly understand human nature. As we examined in chapter 7, 'LOOK IN THE MIRROR: SEE THE TWO SELVES', the moment you can understand the motives that drive each side, you can transcend the trap set by the obvious choices of all sides. This transcendence does not mean latching on to a compromise that keeps all sides less than satisfied. It means looking for a third way that forges partners and shapes noble legacies. This is what Lincoln achieved amongst the various stakeholders.

Lincoln's Third Way was a system of gradually abolishing slavery in the United States. Succumbing to the pressure of the Republicans and abolishing slavery outright would have lead to a potential threat to the existence of the Union and even further violence, which also was against the spirit of the U.S. Constitution. This was not any less hurtful to the letter of the constitution as the proponents of slave expansion were trying to do to the constitution.

The Being Leaders understood that it is human nature to defend one's own truth and preserve one's way of life. They had the ability to not only understand the motives of all sides, but also to look at all motives through a non-ideological lens. Looking through that lens, they could transcend partisanship and divisive politics. They became the forgers of relationship and promoters of collective thinking. They stop identifying with an external locus around which ideologies are built, instead their thoughts, words and actions were anchored around an inner locus around which deep bonds are built.

"The old system is outdated, it has failed to serve the needs of the current times," Gerald (see chapter 14, 'BE LED BY YOUR HIGHEST IDEAL', pg. 237) claimed to me vehemently. "It needs to be replaced. Like a phoenix rising, a new system must arise out of the ashes of the old system. That is why I have chosen to start a new establishment. The values of the new establishment are vastly different from that of the old system."

Over the previous eight months, Gerald had gone through a process of mastering his rejection pains triggered by him being ostracised by the establishment. He had succeeded in convincing himself that his life was not entangled with the views of others, and that had hugely lifted his self-confidence and made him more choiceful.

"The old and new are like oil and water, they don't mix. So we must keep them separate. The new system must grow to reach a critical mass so that it can take on—and eventually replace—the establishment." Gerald was adamant that the only way ahead to manifest his Highest Ideal was a create a new movement.

He had for many years attempted to convert the thinking of his previous party. He noticed that many of the noble ideals that were part of the vision and mission of the previous party were just plaques on the wall. These ideals were just buzzwords used in their annual conferences

3. ARRIVAL

but were hardly part of their daily activities. For three years before his departure from the party he had taken on the additional title of 'Chief Values Officer', with the added responsibility of bringing alive that party's noble ideals. When he failed to make an impact in that role, he had stepped out convinced that the existing establishment cannot be reformed.

"The old system is not redeemable," Gerald sighed visibly in disappointment.

In the course of our conversations, I invited Gerald to explore other ways besides the two obvious ways he had seen. The first option seen to him was to organically grow a new party, the second was to transform the current establishment. I opened up his attention to a third way. I urged him to look more deeply into the inner work that lay ahead of him.

As he progressed on his self-examination, he arrived at some profound conclusions. Firstly, his Highest Ideal was still a script for him. He had yet to organize his life along his Highest Ideal. Secondly, he had never put any serious thinking into how he was perceived by others. So, he decided to ask for anonymous feedback from many who have known him for years.

"Gerald is someone who tries hard to look different. He wants to come across as non-conformist." This was one of the anonymous feedbacks he received.

"Gerald wants to create his own personal brand. His words are different from the rest, but his actions aren't." Said another.

"Gerald is all for reducing our environmental footprint, but he still drives a gasoline driven car," said yet another.

He was seen as someone who speaks of a new reality, but who does not live it. This incongruence between his intentions and his own lifestyle was glaring to others. In spite of his good intentions, others found it difficult to take him seriously.

Gerald did his assessment three years before the release of this manuscript. Since then, Gerald's life has transformed in numerous ways. His inner work became his primary focus, and his political activities secondary. He had given himself ample time to develop his Noble Creed. 'Be the change you want to see' underpins his Noble Creed today. He tries to live each day by that Noble Creed. He has since replaced his gasoline driven car with a smaller hybrid car. He also takes public transport on occasions.

His political activities have followed the beat of his inner work. The inner path of leadership that he has taken has become his Third Way. This path has acquired a form of its own, and he has been attracting a steady stream of individuals who share his vision and values. His own party has since grown significantly, attracting many new participants into the political process. His party has since forged alliances with a few small regional parties, and the depth of the partnerships has steadily grown. The party has been slowly growing towards a critical mass. His party was on the ballot in the past election. More significantly perhaps, he is a part-time consultant and interim manager within one of the leading parties with the responsibility for launching and growing conscious policymaking initiatives. This has helped him make his Highest Ideal a part of the mainstream political conversation.

Numerous are the examples of the Third Way seen in the lives of the Being Leaders.

3. ARRIVAL

On the matter of voters rights, the Third Way that Dr. King championed was ingenious. He was faced with the two options visible to most. One option was to leave it to the mercy of the court, respect its will however coloured its view of the world was. The other option was to let the violence erupt until it leaves such a deep scars in the collective hearts of the nation that sooner or later out of resignation the powers shall relent.

The Third Way was to press forward peacefully demanding civil rights. This way did not leave room for any alternative proposal to be considered, but still offered a way to save the pride of the law enforcers and honoured the constitutional right to peaceful demonstration. All parties felt validated. U.S. President Johnson felt that he was heard, the court felt that the constitution was not violated, the law enforcers felt that their demands were met and the law not broken. The surging masses of young Whites and Blacks whose blood was raging felt their voices heard.

During his short law career, Gandhi was always inclined to resolve differences outside of court. He did not believe that the answers to life's questions were all black or white. He did not believe that one was wrong and the other right. Both were right on their own accord. He noticed that it was their firm convictions that prompted each party to take the heavy step of going to court.

Neither did he believe that he was the right arbiter or he possessed a greater wisdom not available to the judges or either party that made him more suitable to solve cases to all party's satisfaction. Instead he believed in the power of collective thoughts. When he could bring all together in speaking terms and collective thought, a third way would emerge. This third way would be one that acknowledges the truth of each party...and find a win-win.

Three Sides of a Coin

During a time when the color of the skin with which you were born determined your destiny, Mandela took a seemingly naïve position that the Whites who perpetrated a culture of discrimination are as much a part of this renewal of the system as were the Blacks. He felt that his movement was a movement to resurrect the Whites as much as it was to resurrect the Blacks.

It was an easy choice to leverage the popular black anger against the white settlers to accelerate the movement. But he chose for a Third Way, and that way involved forgiveness and healing. The healing way not only righted the wrong, but also created heroes on both sides, heroes who have helped write a noble history for South Africa and helped usher in the dignified future that South Africa deserved.

The Being Leaders are not let down by the adversities that life threw at them. In the face of setbacks, the Being Leaders could transcend normal human reactions and access solutions at a higher level. This ability is a sign of mastery. It involves being in your full presence in the face of a problem and recognizing that problems can be viewed through the eyes of all stakeholders. When done so, solutions that serve the concerns of all appear. That is you being in mastery.

17. SHIFT THE MIND, SHAPE THE NEW ORDER

"Free at last, free at last,
Thank God almighty, we are free at last."
 Dr. Martin Luther King's final words of his 'I have a dream' speech

Early in 1965, U.S. President Lyndon Johnson believed Southern states needed time to absorb the Civil Rights Act of 1964—with its comprehensive ban on segregation—before any further action could be taken. Dr. King, however, believed a second bill was necessary to secure voting rights for African Americans. Toward this end he decided to launch a major Southern Christian Leadership Conference (SCLC) voter-registration drive. Student  Nonwiolent Coordinating Committee member Jim Bevel suggested the drive take place in Selma, Alabama, where an unsuccessful voter-registration drive had been going on for months.

Selma was at the heart of Alabama's 'black belt'. It provided everything that made a media event: a segregationist mayor, a Klan-affiliated police chief, and a very low percentage of Blacks registered to vote. Of 30,000 people, slightly more than half were black, but only 350 Blacks were registered. And Blacks who had tried recently to register had been deflected by slow service, odd courthouse hours, excessively difficult literacy tests, and, of course, the threat of violence.

3. ARRIVAL

Dr. King first visited Selma with other SCLC members in January 1965, shortly after he returned from Oslo, Norway, after accepting the Nobel Peace Prize. Early protests were small in number, and resulted in arrests, both in Selma and in nearby towns. On February 1st, Dr. King and Ralph Abernathy led a march of about 250 people to the Selma Courthouse to protest slow voter-registration. Both Dr. King and Abernathy were arrested and spent five days in jail.

During the march, the Selma campaign became bloody on the evening of February 18th when a protest march headed for the jail of the town of Marion was attacked by a mob of Whites. The streetlights shut off and violence commenced in the dark. A young black man, Jimmy Lee Jackson, was shot, and died eight days later.

On March 5th, Dr. King flew to Washington to encourage Johnson to introduce a Voting Rights Bill. Johnson declined, and Dr. King immediately announced plans for a massive march from Selma to Montgomery, Alabama's capital, which was 54 miles away. Governor George Wallace issued an order prohibiting the march, but the SCLC proceeded, though Dr. King did not lead the march himself.

On March 7th, over 500 people began walking up the four-lane highway toward Montgomery. When they reached the Edmund Pettus Bridge, which crossed the Alabama River, they encountered 60 State troopers, some cavalry, and the sheriff of the town. White civilians also stood by. The authorities ordered the crowd to disperse, but it refused. Moments later, the troopers began attacking the protestors with teargas, clubs, whips, and electric cattle prods, while the white spectators yelled encouragement. By the time the scuffle had ended, sixteen people had to be hospitalized, and at least fifty others were injured. This day eventually came to be called 'Bloody Sunday'. Reporters captured images that were subsequently broadcast nationally. These images inspired protests in Detroit, Chicago, Toronto, New Jersey, and other cities, and caught the attention of the White House.

Dr. King announced plans for a second march, which he would lead himself. This time Governor Wallace obtained a federal injunction against it and President Johnson himself had requested Dr. King not to undertake the march because the voters right was under consideration in the court and if they attempted to march they would be stopped, even if that meant using force. Despite these requests, and despite the admonition of the Attorney General, Dr. King was firm and knew already he was going to march. The collective spirit of the masses— which included in good measure both Blacks and Whites—was calling for its voice to be heard. In Dr. King's heart that march had already taken place and no human force could alter the inevitable passage of history.

"We have no alternative but to keep moving with determination. We've gone too far now to turn back. In a real sense, we are moving and we cannot afford to stop, because Alabama, because our nation has a date with destiny," Dr. King declared.

"I say to you this afternoon that I would rather die on the highways of Alabama than make a butchery of my conscience. I say to you, when we march, don't panic and remember that we must remain true to non-violence. I'm asking everybody in the line, if you can't be non-violent, don't get in here. If you can't accept blows without retaliating, don't get in the line. If you can accept it out of your commitment to non-violence, you will somehow do something for this nation that may well save it. If you can accept it, you will leave those state troopers bloodied with their own barbarities. If you can accept it, you will do something that will transform conditions here in Alabama." Dr. King made a ringing call to all the marchers.

He reminded the marchers that this march was not a response to the brutal actions of the Alabama State Troopers. He called on the marchers to choose to act from love instead of act from the wounds inflicted by decades of indignity inflicted upon the Blacks. Instead, this march was

3. ARRIVAL

a movement for voting rights for the Black, not simply a response to the troopers' barbarities.

About 1500 people participated in the second march, more than half of them white. Clergypersons from around the country had rallied in support, and clergypersons constituted almost a third of the crowd. When the march reached the Edmund Pettus Bridge, it again confronted State police. They were standing there, battle-ready with batons, tear gas, whips and other weapons, ready to receive orders and pummel the peaceful marchers. On the bridge the marchers prayed and as they locked hands to start to walk, and the troopers stepped back. Soon after, Dr. King ordered the protestors to disperse and leave the march. By doing so he freed the segregationist mayor and the Klan-affiliated police chief of Selma from eternal damnation in the eyes of history. He relieved the troopers and history from the burden of violence.

On May 15th, in a televised address to a joint session of Congress, Johnson compared events in Selma to events in Lexington and Concord during the Revolutionary War, and at Appomattox during the Civil War. He then proceeded to unveil his Voting Rights Bill to legislators and the nation.

As Birmingham had led to the Civil Rights Act of 1964, Selma led to the Voting Rights Act of 1965, which Johnson signed into law in August. The legislation prohibited the kind of tactics that had been used in Selma to hinder black voter registration (deliberately slow service, odd courthouse hours, excessively difficult literacy tests, etc.) and gave the federal government more power to police local instances of abuse. Insofar as federal legislation was concerned, Selma marked the final stage of the Civil Rights Movement.[XLVII]

Shift the Mind, Shape the New Order

Through thought, unblemished with doubt and unwavering in the face of adversities, the Being Leaders created the conditions for miracles to occur. Through unwavering thought, they have made their chosen reality to unfold.

Lincoln attracted an opportunity to take a huge step towards achieving his ideal that all men would be free and equal. He conceived the Emancipation Proclamation while waiting in the cipher room of the War Department telegraph office. But to get it passed into law, he needed the right conditions.

The Confederate Army was advancing northwards and there was a real threat of European support to the Confederates. Lincoln needed a decisive Union victory to lend credence to the proclamation and got one at the Battle of Antietam on September 17th, 1862, which had ended Confederate general Robert E. Lee's first Northern invasion. On September 22nd, 1862, Lincoln signed the preliminary Emancipation Proclamation, which informed both the Confederacy and the Union of his intention to free all persons held as slaves in the rebellious states.

In their mental world, the Being Leaders had envisioned a new order for the world they lived in even before anything actually happened. They had already created a vision of the ideal outcome they sought and lived their lives in accordance to that reality.

Before his historic meeting with President P.W. Botha, Mandela lived that meeting in his mind. In his mind's eyes, Mandela saw every detail of the conversation. As if seeing on a silver screen, he saw the meeting play fully in front of his eyes. He saw the suit he was wearing, the way he introduced himself, the way he greeted and conversed with P.W. Botha, the then premier of South Africa, he saw himself being his own mighty self, humorous and self-assured. He heard Botha's responses and remarks, and he felt the outcome of the meeting.

3. ARRIVAL

Before the meeting between Mandela and Botha had occurred, Mandela had been through the experience fully, without yet physically participating in it. This is important. When we can create a powerful vision of an experience yet to happen, later when it happens in real life, the real life event tends to imitate the imagined version. This power of visualization was innate to the Being Leaders.

Long before the civil rights legislation was passed in the U.S, Dr. King declared with passion, "Free at last, free at last, thank God almighty, we are free at last." In thought and feeling, he was already a free man long before the world around him had accepted his truth. So it was inevitable that his inner reality would soon express as the reality around him.

"Full effort is full victory," said Gandhi. "You need not be troubled if you have made mistakes, or if your ideal has slipped away. Just continue to give your best, he reminded. If you fall, pick yourself up and march on. If you cannot run, walk. If you cannot walk, crawl. Nothing in life is more joyful or more thrilling. The effort alone brings a continuing wave of joy in which every personal problem, every suffering and humiliation, is forgotten."[XLVIII]

Gandhi used to cite from the *Bhagavad-Gita*[44], "Do your allotted work, but renounce its fruit. Be detached and work—have no desire for reward and work." By detachment he meant that you must consider the fruits delivered. So do your allotted work with pure motive and using the correct means. There is an element of faith involved in such a practice; faith that the outcomes will be taken care of by the greater presence in return for your efforts.

---

[44] A treatise on life from ancient India

Shift the Mind, Shape the New Order

When faith is reflected in your thoughts, your thoughts turn into intentions. In intention all your faculties fuse together until your mental picture of the future event fuses into an intuitive knowing. At the level of normal thought your reality is uni-dimensional. But when your thoughts get reinforced with emotions, your reality becomes multidimensional. The difference between a simple thought and an intention is like a color painting and a grey scale picture of the painting. The color painting has depth and it fills the imagination with a knowing that cannot be put into words.

True intention is when your thoughts, words and deeds reflect that intention. Inversely, if your thoughts, words and actions do not reflect your intention, it is not truly an intention. It is simply a fleeting mental activity devoid of any energy.

When you practice true intentions you are no more a victim of your external reality. Your inner state is not tied to outer events (it is the reverse actually). Everything that you experience and all events that appear in your life become a matter of conscious choice. You do not give away your power to those around you, nor do you attribute blame upon others; government, markets, competitors, consumers, environment, nature, action groups, your family, your neighbours, etc. You claim authority. You experience yourself standing in your full power.

You see this happening in kids always. Sometimes they get wedded to an idea so much that it is difficult to convince them otherwise. You lose your patience trying to convince them otherwise. You even wonder if they are delusional and living outside reality. Many adults even go as far as to label some kids mentally unsound because their 'illusion' is so profound that they have difficulty accepting a different truth. A kid who is fully engrossed in the fantasy of a sunny day refuses to be let down by a rainy day. Her reality continues to be sunny. Her faith remains strong and in that faith she finds her contentment. Not only do kids reside in that inner contentment, when they operate from such deep conviction, they attract to them external events and experiences that reflect their inner state. Unfailingly, in time their intention becomes an external reality. That is the power of intention.

The Being Leaders knew this. Even before the Civil Rights Bill came into reality, Dr. King passionate declared, "Free at last, free at last, thank God, we are free at last." In the full depth of his inner world, he was already a free man.

I often meet leaders who are thick on goals and thin on intentions. Due to that mix up, they experience enormous exertion in their lives. Life is effortful, and getting things done takes energy. They prefer the controllability that goals offer over the uncontrollability of intentions. Achieving goals involve taking control, manifesting intentions involve letting go and surrendering in faith.

In this, most leaders of today differ from the Being Leaders. Goals, the Being Leaders see, as being embedded in the future. The practice of intentions happen in the present. The future and the past is irrelevant to the practice of intentions. Let me elaborate this further.

The focus of goals is on a future outcome and working towards achieving it. You organize your people, time and money based on your goals. When consumed with goals, we ask: What needs to be done next? Where do we go from here? Who and what needs to be leveraged in order for us as individuals or as an organization to get to the goal? Thus the future becomes the point of reference for all individuals and organizations.

Intention is very focused on the present. It is not tied up with a future result. All thoughts, feeling and emotions that each individual experience in the present lends into what they create for themselves in the future. In the practice of intentions, there is no recognition of the future. Instead, you recognize there are only present moments, one after the other. So it asks of you to remain focused on the present in the constant evolution of life. And once you have expired the current 'now' you will continue to remain in the next present moment. That means that you do not set an intention one day and then forget it; like the Being Leaders, your intentions become a matter of daily practice.

The practice of intentions has serious implications for an organization. When each individual's thought has an impact on the future of the individual and his concerned world, imagine what impact the collective thought of all individuals within an organization can have on what the organization creates. It is significant.

Your efforts are tightly interwoven with your goals. Your efforts take you towards your goal while your goal gives direction and meaning to your efforts. Together with effort, goals make you efficient in harnessing the various resources within an organization, while your intention makes you effective in the game of life. Intentions unify your energy and create a foundation you can fall back on in moments of chaos and confusion. While goals synchronize the actions undertaken by each individual within an organization, intentions synchronize the thoughts of all participants within an organization. The goal unifies the outward view of an individual or an organization. Intention on the other hand, unifies the inward view of each individual within the organization.

Goal relates to your doing, intention relates to your being. Your intention involves your daily practice focusing on your being. Goal relates to your want, intention relates to who you are. What you do with yourself in order to live a life aligned with your deepest values and ideals is at the core of your practice of intentions. Intention is not simply confined to a thought that is devoid of feeling, it is rich in experience and vivid in imagination. We all carry desires. So did the Being Leaders. Learn from them, they have conducted themselves as if their desires are fulfilled even before they have actually manifested.

Why is the understanding of the distinction between goals and intentions important? While goals are in the realm of 'Doing' leaders, intentions are in the realm of the Being Leaders. Even when the Being Leaders were shackled and imprisoned, their intentions could not be subjugated by their antagonists. As a result, even when the Being Leaders were physically restrained, their power could not be subdued.

Personal mastery involves taking charge of the infinite resources the human mind offers. At the peak of their lives, the Being Leaders had attained mastery over the resources of their minds. Thoughts became choiceful. Consequently, so were their emotions. This is the essence of mastery that the Being Leaders lived from.

17.1 WHEN YOU PERCEIVE THE GOOD, YOU AWAKEN THE GOOD

Richard Stengel, the co-author of Mandela's autobiography narrates in his book, Mandela's Way:

"Some call it a blind spot, others naiveté.

But Mandela sees almost everyone as virtuous, until proven otherwise. He starts with an assumption that you are dealing with him in good

faith. He believes that, just as pretending to be brave can lead to acts of real bravery, seeing the good in other people improves the chances that they will reveal their better selves. It is extraordinary that a man who was ill-treated for most of his life can see so much good in others.

In fact, it was sometimes frustrating to talk with him because he almost never had a bad word to say about anyone. He would not even say a disapproving word about the man who tried to have him hanged. I once asked him about John Vorster, the Nazi sympathizing president of South Africa who tightened Apartheid, and rued the fact that Mandela and his comrades have not been executed.

"He was a very decent chap," Mandela said with complete sincerity. "In the first place, he was very polite. In referring to us he would use courteous terminology."

This might seem like praising Saddam Hussein because he was kind to animals. But it is not that Mandela does not see the dark side of someone like Vorster. It is that he is unwilling to see only that. He knows that no one is purely good or purely evil. We were talking one day about a prisoner who had been a rival of Mandela in Robben Island, and who had put together a list of grievances about Mandela.

When I asked him about the fellow, Mandela did not address the man's hostility, but said, "what I took from him was his ability to work hard."

"What I took from him." Mandela seeks out the positive, the constructive. He chooses to look past the negative. He does this for two reasons. Because he instinctively sees the good in people, and because he intellectually believes that seeing good in others might actually make them better. If you expect more of people, whether they are co-workers or family members, they often contribute more. Or at least feel guilty, if they do not.

3. ARRIVAL

The worst he might say about someone is that they are operating in their own self-interest. I remember once listening to him talk on the phone with the editor of South Africa's largest black newspaper. The editor was planning to run a piece on the negotiations[45] and Mandela asked him to hold off because the matter was sensitive. Afterward, Mandela assured me that the editor would pull the story. The following day, though, the story was as big as life on the front page. I pointed it out to him, and he smiled and said, "These people do these things, you see, without an ulterior motive. They do it from the point of view of their own interest. So I didn't get cross about it."

The editor had not misled him. He had simply acted in his own interest. There was no point in taking it personally, and Mandela didn't. "[XLIX]

x   x   x

In 1972, when the then prison commander Colonel Piet Badenhorst, was transferred from Robben Island (see chapter 4, THE FIERY ORDEAL THROUGH WHICH THE BEING LEADERS PASS, pg. 59), Badenhorst spoke to Mandela, "I just want to wish you people good luck."

"He said this like a human being. And I was a bit taken aback by his moderate—and even considerate—tone. I must say, that was a bit of a surprise," Mandela noted in his autobiography.

"No one is born prejudiced or racist. No man," Mandela suggests, "is evil at heart. Evil is something instilled in or taught to men by circumstances, their environment or their upbringing. It is not innate. Apartheid made men evil, evil did not create Apartheid."[L] [LI]

---

[45] Negotiations between Mandela and F.W. de Klerk were underway to shape the new constitution of the post-apartheid South Africa

Shift the Mind, Shape the New Order

The Mandela who came out of prison always maintained that circumstances made men behave in terrible ways. This view that he carried, in turn, awakened the goodness within those around him. Unconsciously, those around him wanted to reflect his perception of them.

When you expect only good from others, they will automatically display the good within them. Now, it is easy for you to see goodness in those you love, your near and dear ones and those who do good to you. Are you able to replicate the same practice with those who are not close to you? With strangers? What about those you bump into on the street? What about individuals unknown to you who you must interact with at work? Can you see the goodness in them?

How much goodness you can see in others is a good measure of how much goodness they will step into in your presence. For example, if you include trust as an operating principle in your life, people around you will place their trust in you. In summary, the quality of the relationships that you have in your life is a reflection of your own way of being. That gives you a measure of the personal mastery that you have achieved. When you resonate with the consciousness of the Being Leaders, your love is aflame for all, not just a meagre few who are closely related to you.

x   x   x

This understanding has brought great meaning and has paid rich dividends in my own life.

Bill (name changed) was the lead sales executive for an American medical devices company. This company had a portfolio of products and services valued by a specialized group of the medical clients of the company that I served. Our organization was the preferred name for

3. ARRIVAL

many in the healthcare industry. So we had the reach, the medical devices company had the products. An evident win-win.

Having a strategic partnership was a natural choice, something recognized by the boards of both organizations. So, at the turn of the century, I led a team to setup an agreement that would lay the foundation for this partnership. During our first appointment with the Global Sales team of the medical devices company, we sat across the table from a passionate team of sales professionals responsible for partnerships. Bill headed the team.

Within the first ten minutes it became clear to us that we are seated against someone who did not value a partnership with us as much as we valued a partnership with them. Bill made several derogatory remarks about our organization and its objectives. He more than once explicitly remarked that he was bound by a passion to see us at the losing end of any bargain. He acted condescendingly towards some of the women in the room. I recollect him making a comment about how manly one of my female team members was dressed. The comment left her feeling deflated. Some minutes later, in the midst of the negotiation he commented that I must take myself—including my "slick hair"—into the next room and rethink my offer. Though I maintained a smile, I felt offended. Within two hours, I concluded to myself that I did not see any prospects in this collaboration.

We were in absolute shock when the meeting was over. Our team found Bill to be condescending, rude and mocking. Some of Bill's own team members seemed apologetic as we bid our goodbyes with vague commitments to resume the discussions soon. "I hope that the circumstances were different. We may have achieved different results," one of Bill's team members privately remarked to me clearly referring back to the distasteful discussions of the morning.

Shift the Mind, Shape the New Order

The whole afternoon our cross-global team of six felt weighed down by the uncouthness of the sales executive. We, in our own immaturity, labelled him to be ill-suited for the corporate world. We consoled ourselves that he did not belong to the corporate world of protocols and etiquettes. He occupied our thoughts and our dinner table discussions that evening. Though physically absent, he was fully present in the midst of us.

We claimed that he was only suited for some remote bush away from civilization or to remain in the barbaric era. By the end of dinner, we were convinced that he represented everything that was wrong in business today. I still remember clearly that his 'rude' behaviour continued to remain in my thoughts when I went to bed.

The next day I made a resolution to myself. I told myself that I will accept Bill as a person filled with good intentions. "If I am capable of goodness, so is he," I told myself. I believed in my virtues when it came to conducting myself in my personal, professional and social lives, yet I had been blind towards his virtues. If I could not see them, I simply had to look harder. I was aware of the motives and self-interest that propelled me in my career, similarly I needed to gain visibility into the motives that led him to act the way he did. It was my prerogative to keep in my sight the goodness that was contained within him. I told myself that I will make an effort to understand his motivations to act a certain way with us.

Over the next several months, some of my team members retreated from all engagements with Bill and his immediate team. They concluded that they could not stand him, and it was best left to me to tolerate his insolence. Partly due to business reasons and partly due to personal growth reasons I continued to engage with him. During the early stages of our engagement, I forced myself to counter his unpleasant attitude with a pleasant countenance. When he made a condescending remark, I

3. ARRIVAL

responded with a smile. When he taunted me, I pointed out to him that he deserved the fun he was having at work.

Three months after our first unpleasant meeting, our companies foreclosed a far-reaching contract. During that time, I came to know Bill much closer and found him a caring individual towards his friends and family. His family strongly relied on him and his two children felt his presence brought strength and stability in their lives. He carried a strong sense of solidarity towards his company and fiercely stood by his team. These were his attributes that I chose to carry with me in every interaction I had with him.

During the signing ceremony of the agreement, my team members were amazed to see the genuine connectedness that Bill and I had with each other. They were awed by the gentleness and attention with which he engaged me during discussions. "I am amazed how deferentially he received your personal and professional concerns," remarked one of my team members to me after one dinner gathering to celebrate the milestone of finalizing the agreement.

How I developed my relationship with Bill always remains a fulfilling experience in my life. I must admit, it was not easy in the beginning. The safe solution was to disqualify that partnership and initiate negotiations with another partner. Yet, I decided to persist with the lessons I gained from the Being Leaders. I am glad I did.

x   x   x

Next time you are in the presence of someone who is not seeming pleasant towards you, use a different tack. Frame his behaviour as being pleasant. It will seem unauthentic for you to frame someone as being pleasant when that person is acting insensitive and rude. Never mind that behaviour. Frame his behaviour in relationship to his motives, both conscious and unconscious. And continue engaging him from that inner place. As time goes by, he will mirror that intention that you carry with you. This is a very profound demonstration of the power and practice of intentions.

Note: A person is only as unpleasant as you judge him to be. It is your judgment that colours your perception of someone as being unpleasant. Suspend that judgment. Replace it with a positive perception of that individual. Your perception belongs to you and has little to do with your external circumstances. So the choice of perception is yours[46].

Soon you will notice that the person who has seemed to behave in unpleasant ways will respond to your perception. This is either a conscious or an unconscious response. The goodness that you see in him is the goodness that he will start to see in himself. And when he sees it, he will become it. As the saying goes, perception is reality. Change that definition. Expand that saying to mean perception creates reality.

There are opportunities to step into greatness all around. Most of the world operates from a fear-based consciousness, and the world is yearning for leaders who can present a different consciousness to the whole world.

This specific practice of intentions is a very practical application of intentions in your daily life, whether at work, or at home, or in your community. The dividends are enormous. And, it is an effortless opportunity to represent the mastery of the Being Leaders.

---

[46] In the next chapter, we will examine in-depth the standard of choicemaking the Being Leaders applied in their lives

18. ENGAGING IN CHOICEFUL ACTION

"The chain reaction of evil—hate begetting hate, wars producing more wars—must be broken, or else we shall be plunged into the dark abyss of annihilation."

Dr. Martin Luther King Jr.

In early 1917, Gandhi arrived at a little known town in Northern India called Champaran. His choice to visit Champaran was a result of the persistence of one man, a simple farmer by the name of Rajkumar Shukla. Shukla had impressed upon Gandhi the plight of indigo farmers whose land was exploited by wealthy planters. Indigo was an extract used to raise the brightness of clothes while laundering, and it seemed Champaran was the only place in India where indigo was cultivated.

Gandhi was called upon to put a stop to the exploitation of the farmers by the planters. As he arrived in Champaran, he received a rousing welcome from the farmers who heard of his arrival. The local lawyers also offered their undivided support to the cause. Gandhi's immediate step was to inquire into the condition of the Champaran farmers and truly understand their grievances against the indigo planters. But first he wanted to know the planters' side of the story.

As he approached the planters' representatives to study the problem, he received a cold reception from them and the town administration who were controlled by the planters. The Secretary of the Planters' Association told Gandhi plainly that he was an outsider to Champaran and that he had no business to come between the planters and the farmers. The Commissioner of the Division on whom Gandhi called proceeded to bully him. The Commissioner instructed Gandhi to immediately leave Champaran. Gandhi became aware of the likelihood of the white government officials stopping him from proceeding further with his investigations, and that he would end up in jail if he continued.

The very next day, on his way to meet a farmer, he was stopped by a government courier and served a notice to leave Champaran. On being asked to acknowledge the receipt of the notice, Gandhi gave the local administration its first shock. He responded that he did not plan to comply with it and leave Champaran until his inquiry was completed. The local administration, used to its people obeying its laws, was thrown into confusion at Gandhi's position. On rare occasions, they were used to citizens who legally resisted the summons served upon them, prompting court action. But this was the first time someone would accept the summons and choose to submit to the penalty imposed by law.

Within 24 hours he was tried for disobeying the order to leave Champaran. The news of the notice and the summons spread like wildfire, and the town witnessed unprecedented scenes. The courthouse overflowed with people who wanted to pledge their support for the struggle that has come to their town. Uncharacteristically, the District Collector, the Police Superintendent and the Magistrate were very good-natured towards Gandhi for him having accepted the summons and acting in a non-offensive and courteous manner. Yet, their authority was shaken. Gandhi's civil resistance to their orders emboldened the simple folks of Champaran and momentarily took away any fear of punitive action they would have otherwise had.

As the trial began, the government prosecutor, the Magistrate and other officials were at a loss to know what to do. The prosecutor pressed the Magistrate to postpone the case, but Gandhi jumped in and declared that he pleads guilty to having disobeyed the order of the administration to leave Champaran.

"With the permission of the Court I would like to make a brief statement showing why I have taken the very serious step of seemingly disobeying the order passed under section 144 of Cr. P.C. In my humble opinion it is a question of difference of opinion between the Local Administration and myself. I have entered this country with motives of rendering humanitarian and national service. I have done so in response to a pressing invitation to come and help the ryots[47], who urge they are not being fairly treated by the indigo planters. I could not render any help without studying the problem. I have, therefore, come to study it with the assistance, if possible, of the Administration and the planters. I have no other motive, and cannot believe that my coming can in any way disturb public peace and cause loss of life. I claim to have considerable experience in such matters. The administration, however, have thought differently. I fully appreciate their difficulty, and I admit too that they can only proceed upon information they received. As a law-abiding citizen my first instinct would be, as it was, to obey the order served upon me. But I could not do so without doing violence to my sense of duty to those for whom I have come. I feel that I could just now serve them only by remaining in their midst. I could not, therefore, voluntarily retire. Amid this conflict of duties I could only throw the responsibility of removing me from them on the Administration. I am fully conscious of the fact that a person, holding, in the public life of India, a position such as I do, has to be most careful in setting an example. It is my firm belief that in the complex constitution under which we are living, the only safe and honourable course for a self-respecting man is, in the circumstances such as facing me, to do what I have decided to do, that is, to submit without protest to the penalty of disobedience.

---

[47] Those who hold land as cultivator of the soil

3. ARRIVAL

I venture to make this statement not in any way in extenuation of penalty to be awarded against me, but to show that I have disregarded the order served upon me, not for want of respect for lawful authority, but in obedience to the higher law of our being, the voice of conscience."

The Government Prosecutor and the Magistrate were taken by surprise. The next day the Magistrate ordered the case against Gandhi withdrawn, and the District Collector wrote to Gandhi saying that he was at the liberty to conduct his proposed inquiry, and that he might count of whatever help he needed from the officials.[LII]

Each of us possess the capacity for choiceful action. Yet, to live in choiceful action takes conscious choice. This choice is one of stepping into true leadership. The Being Leaders—out of necessity—stepped into it because they were called upon to. Even when Mandela was incarcerated for twenty-seven years in prison, he was practicing choiceful action. Prison physically restraint him, but not spiritually. Ironically, it was when he was physically restrained that his spirit broke free.

The University of Robben Island and the prison revolt against the inedible food in 1966 (see chapter 11, RESURRECTING INTO MASTERY, pg. 189) were supreme examples of a human's capacity to practice choiceful action even under extenuating circumstances.

The Being Leaders always operated on their own terms. They were not being reactive to events external to them, but engaging in creative action. When the British resorted to violence, Gandhi did not react with violence. He engaged in creative action, independent of their action.

Engaging in Choiceful Action

"An eye for an eye only makes the whole world blind," Gandhi reminded those inclined to violent agitation.

In the midst of the freedom movement, Gandhi was ordered by a local judge to leave the state where he was agitating. He refused to. So the judge let him out on bail. He plainly refused to pay bail. This created an embarrassing situation for the judge whose authority was questioned and gave rise to a dangerous situation for the local administration. If Gandhi were to be put in prison, that would only further energize the local uprising. The administration knew that in no time the jails would become full and overflowing and an uncontrollable situation would ensue. Forced to concede, the administration requested the magistrate to drop the charges and let Gandhi go.

The Being Leaders recognized that they reserved the choice of how to lead their lives. They did not relinquish their power of choice-making to others. At the same time, they did not attribute blame for their life circumstances upon others, be it their bosses, spouses, parents, government or any other external entity. They felt self-empowered to exercise choice, and they owned the consequence of their choices.

x   x   x

You have a choice. You live by choice. You are your choice-maker. You are a consequence of conscious choice. The life you live is a consequence of your past choices. That is the way of the Being Leaders.

On Easter day in 1963, Dr. King and his team were seated making plans to have mass in church. There were clergymen who believed in the cause that Dr. King espoused. Seated among them was also his father, another minister. They wanted this Easter to be the time for all Blacks to recognize themselves as children of God, to honour themselves as the Whites expected to be honoured, to love themselves as they loved their neighbours.

3. ARRIVAL

In the midst of the meeting, Dr. King suddenly stood up to change up. In a few minutes, he returned in a pair of jeans instead of his priest attire. Instead of going to church to pray and offer prayers, he got ready to go to jail. On this Easter, he said, he could be of greater service to God and His children by going to jail instead of going to church. His decision took the others by surprise. They were prepared for some protest on Easter day, but such an action was beyond their thinking.

That Easter he went to jail as he had chosen to.

X   X   X

The Being Leaders were unflappable in thoughts, words or deeds. Even against extreme odds, they never felt the desire to lean forward—retaliating to events around them—or lean backwards in retreat. Instead they continued remaining stable and forbearing, untouched in their clarity by the chaotic and conflicting forces around them. They remained true to their Highest Ideals, and their noble mission always continued to be their guiding power. They stood erect, on their own two feet as statues erected in the land of history.

The Being Leaders did not lean forward in response to the events unfolding around them. They were not reactive to the force exerted upon them or events unfolding around them. They were not acting in response to the pressures of circumstances. That—for them—was the equivalent of leaning forward, and even that leaning forward was a deviation from their centre. Instead, each action for them was creative action originating from the Noble Creed they were living by. They were guided by their deepest knowing and Highest Ideals.

When Mandela was on Robben Island, the younger prisoners often complained that he was not moving fast enough or challenging the authorities forcefully enough (see chapter 16, THREE SIDES OF A COIN, pg. 265)

When he advised them not to force an issue, or when he argued with them about a policy that was longer term, they would challenge him, "what about right now?"

"Look, you might be right for a few days, weeks or months," he would say. "But in the long run you will reap something more valuable if you take a longer view."

Neither were the Being Leaders the ones to lean backwards. This we know from history. They were not the retreating kind, except tactically when essential. Such tactical retreats was simply a temporary retreat from confrontation, not a retreat from their greatest aspirations. Nor did the Being Leaders lean backwards because they felt lesser than those who they were seeking to persuade. There were neither disengaged nor indifferent, even to those who differed with them.

In August 1861, Union major general John C. Fremont, commander of the Department of the West, issued an order declaring martial law in Missouri and freeing all slaves held by Missouri secessionists. Foreseeing that linking abolition of slavery with the war would cause the slave-holding border states to rebel, in September Lincoln ordered Fremont to change his order. When Fremont refused to revoke or amend the order, Lincoln removed him from command and revoked the order himself.

Lincoln's actions came as counterintuitive to many in the North who have known and elected Lincoln as an anti-slavery president. The border states of Delaware, Kentucky, Maryland, and Missouri were on the side of the Union, and were valuable allies in the logistics of the Civil war. Lincoln, though, had concluded that it was essential to revoke Fremont's order for a greater good.

3. ARRIVAL

A second unauthorized emancipation proclamation was issued on May 9th, 1862, by Maj. Gen. David Hunter. This proclamation not only declared freedom for all slaves in areas of South Carolina, Georgia, and Florida, it authorized the arming of able-bodied Blacks. Lincoln again issued a public statement revoking the order, but urged the slave-holding border states to "adopt a gradual abolishment of slavery."

Yet again, Lincoln's actions were a source of consternation for many in the North. Many had viewed the actions of local commanders as stepping stones towards the greater plan to abolish slavery. Lincoln, with forethought, knew that these local initiatives from the local commanders were well-intentioned, yet wrongly timed.

The same Lincoln, on July 22, 1862, surprised his Cabinet by reading his first draft of the Emancipation Proclamation. Until his announcement, many had considered Lincoln leaning back on the issue of slavery abolition. He was patiently waiting for its time.

X   X   X

The Being Leaders followed their own internal rhythm. They refused to be coerced by the artificial demands of situations.

When you look at one moment as pleasurable and another one as painful, you are not in equanimity. There is still attachment; attachment to pleasure or attachment to the ideology of escaping pain. And as long as there is attachment, it does not create space for you to express your Unique Gift[48]. Instead you are still trapped in your cravings. Your ego is leading the charge, and you are led by your sensations.

For your gifts to express, you need to habituate yourself with equanimity. And when you have achieved that, you will notice that

---

[48] See chapter 3, ORDEAL OF THE WARRIOR CHILD, pg. 51

every act—be it writing a simple note or something as grand as making risky decisions—will remain as precious to you as any other.

When you are in inner peace, your creative self is delivering big. That is because you are accessing all faculties of the brain, your resources, and of your complete self. There is very little inner conflict. This reflects a higher level of consciousness. This consciousness offers you a higher elevation to view the reality of the opponents or adversaries.

This quality of non-reaction was a big thing with the Being Leaders. They simply would not react to all the little fluctuations and turbulences happening around them. Instead, they simply remain aligned around their values and ideals. At the peak of their mastery, they never could be dislodged from that alignment.

Prison taught Nelson Mandela non-reaction; the thing he considered essential to leadership. One of the sharpest criticism he ever levels at anyone is that they are emotional, or too reactive. One word he would use to praise others was balanced.

The Being Leaders were able to successfully be in equanimity not because they suppressed their emotions, but because they were free from triggers. It was not that they were suppressing their anger or resentment. They simply did not get affected by the reality of those around them and how opponents were acting. They recognized that the reason why one sees another as evil was simply because of their own judgments. Such individuals were filled with resentment inside and would judge those around them against their past wounds.

Caution: My words that label you as imperfect are simply expressions of the resentment that I carry within me, or my fear that I carry within, or my hate, or the pain or the wounds that I carry within me.

3. ARRIVAL

This understanding of human nature gave the Being Leaders the capacity to feel compassion for their detractors or enemies[49]. At the peak of their personal mastery, they were never blinded by their rage, instead they were in full equipoise when in the presence of or in consideration of their enemies. This equipoise originated from their elevated self-awareness. They could take full responsibility for their emotions while assigning ownership of others' emotions upon others.

x   x   x

Every reaction contains within it the potential to be the start of a new interaction. The energy can be new and the emotions can be chosen.

Recognize this: Most individuals you come across in your everyday life are emotionally reacting to your last statement. Chances are, so is your reaction to others.

If that is the case, you are both reinforcing each other's emotional state through both your unconscious responses. That makes you a follower. In that state of victim hood, you have relinquished your power to disrupt the continuous cycle of negativism or violence that is projected upon you. With every response, you possess the power to begin the process of constructing a new relationship, no matter how toxic a relationship has been in the past.

That is the context of Dr. King's statement, "I don't know what the future holds, but I know who holds the future."

In April 1865, the Union army had captured the Confederate capital of Richmond. Lincoln visited Richmond soon after, and as he left he

---

[49] We will study this capacity of the Being Leaders in chapter 20, 'CAPACITY FOR COMPASSION AND FORBEARANCE'

ordered the band to play *Dixie*[50], saying that the tune was the best he had ever heard, and it was now federal property. "And its good to show the rebels," he added, "that with us in power they'll still be free to hear it." More than the humour, this action demonstrated that Lincoln wanted clemency for the Confederates.

After Mandela became president of post-Apartheid South Africa, there was a need to free the Blacks from bondage as there was a need to free the Afrikaners from fear. There is nothing more subtle and abstract than freeing someone from fear. Mandela used Rugby for it (see chapter 9, 'HAVE A TRUE MEASURE OF THE SELF', Pg. 143).

Rugby was racially charged in South Africa. It has been the favourite sport of the white Afrikaners and a symbol of oppression. After Mandela became the president, there were attempts by some of his deputies to change everything about this traumatic symbol of white oppression, including attempts to even ban it.

Away from the wounds of the past, Mandela undertook choiceful action. He donned the Springbok jersey and visited the South African team in their locker room to wish them luck. And when the South Africans won the world cup, Mandela presented the trophy to white captain Francois Pienaar, while wearing the player's spare No. 6 shirt and a Springbok cap. In one day, Mandela helped heal the bitter wounds of racial division in a wounded nation.

Being in mastery is your capacity to transcend your wounds and triggers. In that state of transcendence, you are non-reactive. All thoughts, words and actions become choiceful and creative.

At the summit of their lives, the Being Leaders possessed the quality of equanimity, unruffled by the dramas of their opponents and the world

---

[50] An American folk song. During the American Civil War, "Dixie" was adopted as a de facto anthem of the Confederates

3. ARRIVAL

around them. In the Being Leader Workbook, we will look at practices that help you elevate in equanimity and ground yourself in non-reaction.

19. THE BEST WAY TO EAT AN ELEPHANT

"We should not be in haste to determine that radical and extreme measures, which may reach the loyal as well as the disloyal, are indispensable."

Abraham Lincoln

"Our nation is on the brink of ruin," Joseph Medill, President Lincoln's close political friend, lamented to Lincoln. "Mr. Lincoln, for God's sake and your Country's sake rise to the realization [...] that this is a Slave-holders rebellion." Medill wanted Lincoln to act against slavery.

Many in the U.S. Congress also criticised Lincoln for not attacking slavery, the cause of the war between the North and the South. In Congress these criticisms were often subtle and indirect, as when Congressman Thaddeus Stevens complained that in this war there had been "no declaration of the great objects of Government, no glorious sound of universal liberty."

Lincoln's view on slavery was not different from those of his critics. Throughout his career, he made no attempt to disguise his anti-slavery feelings. During his presidency and before, he took small but significant steps in abolishing slavery. He signed a law prohibiting slavery in all the U.S. national territories, he foreclosed a new treaty with Great

3. ARRIVAL

Britain to suppress slave trade, he refused to commute the death penalty for the first American slave trader.

Focussed on the efforts of preserving the Union, he did not adopt more sweeping changes to slavery. He warned his party against hastily adopting "radical and extreme measures, which may reach the loyal as the disloyal."

"I have been anxious and careful that the inevitable conflict for this purpose shall not degenerate into a violent and remorseless revolutionary struggle," Lincoln told Congress in December 1861. Throughout the course of his career, Lincoln always maintained that in time slavery would die out. So, he did not feel it was wise to strike violently at slavery, especially since nothing he could do or say would have any practical effect on the South.

Even as it seemed that Lincoln was not inclined to take a big leap to emancipate slavery, Lincoln had quietly been looking into the possibility of rehabilitating slaves when freed. On consideration was an idea to return the freed slaves to Africa. He patiently listened to the ideas of abolitionists to set up a free colony for the slaves under the protection of the United States somewhere in Central America or the Caribbean. In 1860, Lincoln appointed someone to investigate the viability of Panama as a destination for the freed slaves.

So long as the border states between the North and the South—Delaware, Maryland, Kentucky and Missouri—maintained slavery, Lincoln knew that any act of abolishing slavery might drive the border states to join the Confederacy. He was also aware that the continued existence of slavery in the North complicated foreign policy; so long as the border states remained slave states, European nations could not view United States as a land of the free. Thus, Lincoln concluded that emancipation of slaves could strengthen the Union cause abroad, but disintegrate the Union itself.

314

In such a sensitive situation, Lincoln carefully recruited two conspicuous spokesmen of slavery abolition, Senator Charles Sumner and Secretary of the Treasury Salmon P. Chase. Patiently he allowed Sumner to lecture him, sometimes two or three times a week, on his duty to act against slavery. Lincoln cajoled and consoled them, keeping them on his side fully knowing that the time was not right for any big step in emancipating the slaves. In Winter 1861 Lincoln told Senator Sumner, "Well, Mr. Sumner, the only difference between you and me on this subject is a difference of a month or six weeks in time."

Over the course of 1862, Lincoln began to think of emancipation as a question to be decided on grounds of policy as much as of principle. During Spring 1862, he started to formulate his ideas for a proclamation of freedom. He started to share some of his ideas with members of his administration.

Late in June of that year, in the cipher room of the War Department telegraph office, which Lincoln frequented while anxiously awaiting dispatches from the army, he asked Major Thomas T. Eckert for some foolscap, because he said, "he wanted to write something special." Then and there, sitting at Eckert's desk in the quiet telegraph office, facing on Pennsylvania Avenue, Lincoln started to make his first notes of the now historic Emancipation Proclamation.

That first day, Lincoln filled less than a page, and as he left he left his notes with Eckert for safekeeping. Almost everyday during the following weeks, he developed further the proclamation. Only when he had finished writing the complete proclamation did Lincoln tell Eckert that he had been drafting a proclamation "giving freedom to the slaves in the South."[LIII]

3. ARRIVAL

19.1 ONE NOBLE STEP AT A TIME

There is an ancient saying that the best way to eat an elephant is...one bite at a time. Paradoxically, those leaders who fill our collective imagination for having lifted an entire race or nation out of darkness were those who approached their movement one issue at a time. They were masterful enough to know that when the cause was noble, it took a small step to awaken the collective heart.

Apartheid-era laws required black South Africans to carry a passbook. It identified their race and where they lived. Anyone required to have a passbook was forbidden to travel to another area of the country without it. The passbook controlled the movements of the Blacks and kept them out of white areas. Failure to carry the passbooks risked arrest and imprisonment. The black South African population vehemently hated the pass laws.

In 1952, long before the black South Africans moved against the passbook, Mandela rose against this deeply humiliating practice. He decided that he would not carry the passbook and would rather risk arrest. When authorities notified Mandela and other black South Africans of the consequences of not carrying their passbook, he publicly burned his passbook. Emboldened by his action, several others followed suit, until the burning or the surrendering of the passbook turned into a movement, the first civil disobedience action of the Mandela era in South Africa.

x   x   x

On March 9th, 1965, Dr. King led men and women across the U.S. nation on the Selma march for one thing; voters' rights (see chapter 11, 'RESURRECTING INTO MASTERY', pg. 189).

The Best Way to Eat an Elephant

In early 1930, Gandhi mounted the demonstration against the repressive salt tax imposed by the colonial British by marching from the western Indian state of Gujarat, India, to the town of Dandi on the Arabian Sea coast. There he produced salt in defiance of British rule. (see chapter 9, 'HAVE A TRUE MEASURE OF THE SELF', pg. 143).

On September 22nd, 1862, Lincoln patiently waited for one victory in battle for the Union Army before announcing the preliminary Emancipation Proclamation (see chapter 17, 'SHIFT THE MIND, SHAPE THE NEW ORDER', pg. 283), which informed both the Confederacy and the Union of his intention to free all persons held as slaves in the rebellious states.

There were those who urged Lincoln to rush through the announcement and create momentum. But Lincoln knew better. To rush the Emancipation Proclamation through would show weakness and desperation. He first ensured that all stakeholders were fully taken into consideration and all aspects were fully studied before a step was taken.

Such an approach often goes against the grain of modern leadership where time is often considered of the essence. In the "quarterly performance" culture of the business world, full effort is imparted into ensuring that time is saved. When you contrast modern leadership against the Being Leaders', one remarkable insight appears; ***When you consider your cause to be grand, your entire life becomes the timeline in which to make a difference.***

Remember, your Noble Legacy[51] is not crafted in one day. It is a lifetime of work.

x   x   x

---

[51] See chapter 13, 'YOU ARE THE SUM OF EVERYTHING YOU HAVE DONE'

3. ARRIVAL

Haste brings regret. Now, if the feeling of future remorse is the only side effect of haste, that would be easy. More severe is that hasty decisions erodes your equity in the heart of those you lead. You lose consistency. In the eyes of those you seek to lead, it minimizes the altitudes that you have scaled in your journey of sacrifice and suffering. You become seen as one who is a victim of time, not the shaper of timelessness. Your desperation shines through and you are not seen to be standing in your own power. You are seen as not giving space to your internal voice to speak for itself.

So take time and ask yourself what you stand for. When chosen to decide on important matters, study your choices against your values. Ask if your choice is aligned with your Highest Ideal. Is it still in line with your Noble Creed? Give it plenty of thought, and once convinced, remain aligned with what you stand for. Circumstances will test you. See those tests as what they truly are, tests. Consider them tests of the strength of your conviction. Test of your alignment with your Highest Ideals. Stay rooted. Do not get swayed by the emotions around you. Recognize simply that you did not create those emotions in others, and hence are not responsible or tied to it.

Many years ago, I was witness to a young MBA, Filip (name changed), brought in to lead a leading business in the medical appliances industry. He was recently promoted to this role and he was eager to prove himself.

After a series of management meetings, Filip declared his top three priorities to the entire organization—many hundreds strong; reducing cost of their products, improving the quality of the products and raising the speed at which the organization would introduce new products into the market.

The Best Way to Eat an Elephant

Some seniors advised him to take it one step at a time. Filip was urged to start a trial with a small section of the organization, understand the challenges they face and the effectiveness of the approach, learn from the trial, and once convinced that it is the right way ahead, roll it out across the whole organization.

Past experiments of the kind undertaken by Filip had proven successful in improving quality and speed and reducing costs in other organizations that Filip had studied in business school. Armed with the lessons from those case studies, he pressed forward with the new priorities for the organization, convinced that this experiment would be beneficial.

He had foreseen that this new alignment would create pressure in the organization to reinvent its current way of working and become more focussed. Instead the opposite happened. An organization that used to operate at a decent level of harmony was suddenly thrown into chaos. The three priorities demanded were too broad and were often in conflict with each other. Teams that used to deliver some output before the change of vision ground to a halt, waiting for the managers to announce which of the three priorities to focus on. Significant time was lost and quality compromised due to the lack of forethought on the part of Filip on how to best implement his priorities.

Department managers, who were primarily focussed on people management suddenly found themselves become issue managers and trouble-shooters. Top management—including Filip—were forced to leave behind their long-term priorities and instead become micromanagers. As a consequence, some younger managers who were used to autonomy and high productivity before the failed experiment started turned against Filip. Trust in his ability to lead the business eroded, and subordinates began to challenge his authority.

3. ARRIVAL

Filip had failed to sense the pulse of the organization. And much later, when he recognized his mistake, he made light of it claiming that shaking up the existing culture of the organization was his intention during the entire experiment. Unconvinced, the board soon replaced him with a more considered type of leader.

Contrast this example with the patient steps taken by Mandela in prison while in the midst of the protests against the dismal food (see chapter 16, 'THREE SIDES OF A COIN', pg. 265). You notice two critical differences between the approach of Filip—a typical stereotype of the modern leader, quick in action—and the Being Leaders. Firstly, the characteristic amount of forethought and careful consideration that has gone into the Being Leaders' actions versus the haste shown by Filip. Secondly, the outcome from Mandela's leadership of the rebellion against the kitchen on Robben Island is vastly different from the results achieved by Filip.

19.2   TO BE LOVED OR TO BE RESPECTED?

Abraham Lincoln was not a very popular man among the folks in Springfield, Illinois, where he practiced law, but he was highly respected. *Honest Abe* was not a mythology in the minds of those who knew him. Jesse Fell, an Illinois lawyer and real estate developer insisted that "if there was any traits of character that stood out in bold relief in the person of Mr. Lincoln it was that of truth and candour. He was utterly incapable of insincerity, or of professing views of this, or any other subject that he did not entertain." That trait of Lincoln however did not befriend him many who felt uncomfortable in his presence.

The Best Way to Eat an Elephant

His own life practice was part of his ideal of a society operating at its highest moral substance under every circumstance. In a law lecture in 1850 he acknowledged that there is a popular belief that lawyers are dishonest. He spoke, "let no young man choosing the law for a calling for a moment yield to this popular belief."

"Resolve to be honest at all events," Lincoln continued. "And if in your own judgment you cannot be an honest lawyer, resolve to be honest without being a lawyer. Choose some other occupation."

Often the choice of living your Highest Ideals involve mastering the temptation of instant gratification. This has been the way of the Being Leaders. Pleasing others and seeking their approval can be tempting. But if you can overlook temptation you can transcend any weakness in the moment. Free from having to commit to something as frivolous as others approval, you can practice forethought as part of your Noble Creed.

In our lives, we come across those whose truth we cannot seem to handle at that moment we face it. Yet it is implicit in our nature to feel a sense of awe or admiration for those who stand by their truth. That is human nature. At the moment of being confronted by their truth, we might experience resentment or defiance. Or—to cope with your sense of rejection—you attempt to minimize their truth or even ignore it. This I often notice within collective settings like organizations.

The above responses from your environment towards your truth drives many of you to seek instant gratification. In an attempt to not 'lose' those around you, you might slip into a 'nice' archetype thus compromising on your own ideals. This you do out of fear of loss or a perceived sense of opportunism.

3. ARRIVAL

Taking the long view, on the other hand, involves postponing gratification. Postponing gratification also takes mastering our fear of losing those who disagree with us.

Note: For each short-sighted individual you lose today because he cannot handle your integrity to your truth, there would be numerous looking at you with awe and admiration. This is an undisputable truth that shines out of the lives of the Being Leaders.

In the midst of the civil war, along with some fellow administrators, one evening Lincoln visited the home of George B. McClellan, the General-in-Chief of all U.S. Federal armies. McClellan was out. So Lincoln and the rest waited. After about an hour, McClellan returned home, and paying no attention to the distinguished visitors he went upstairs and to bed. Lincoln's fellow administrators fully expected McClellan to be censored and even removed from his post for such a snub. Instead Lincoln said, "It was better at this time not to be making points of etiquette and personal dignity."

Lincoln could transcend the snub, because to him the indignity of the snub was minor than the greater cause, a cause for which he was willing to swallow such an insult. Lincoln famously said that he was willing to hold McClellan's horse if McClellan would give the Federation a victory against the Confederates.

Had Lincoln become myopic due to the insult, the history of Emancipation Proclamation and anti-slavery might have been different. Myopia leads to opportunism. You grab what is visible in front of your eyes, because you are driven by a sense of scarcity in everything you do.

Note: When your are unconsciously motivated by scarcity, that says of your inability to take the long view. You become limited to imagining your life as mortal, and as a result your cycles of vision get narrowed to the minimum. Within organizations in the Western hemisphere often this scarcity manifests itself through quarterly performance cycles. While this is not damaging in itself, when the long view gets sidelined by the quarterly view it leads to blindness towards the greater purpose of an organization.

x   x   x

To be loved and to be respected are not mutually exclusive. Yet, what you receive from the life example of the Being Leaders is that if any aspirant of such iconic leadership has to choose between being loved and being respected, he would choose to be respected. In the long run, respect attracts genuine love.

The best way to eat an elephant is...one bite at a time. Your whole life is your timeline. When you look at your work through the whole arc of your life, you will start to see beyond the quarterly view if you are in business, or outside the Gallup polls if you are in politics. In that practice you will become the Being Leader.

20. CAPACITY FOR COMPASSION AND FORBEARANCE

"We must develop and maintain the capacity to forgive. He who is devoid of the power to forgive is devoid of the power to love. There is some good in the worst of us and some evil in the best of us."

Dr. Martin Luther King Jr.

Lincoln's quality of forbearance shines through one of Lincoln's most-admired doctrines, his "charity for all" and his "malice toward none," from the defeated Confederate leadership down to the sentry caught asleep on duty. Many commentators have ascribed his forbearance to a mysterious, godlike reservoir of virtue in Lincoln; yet Herndon, Lincoln's law partner, felt that it was closely linked to Lincoln's fatalism[52]. "Lincoln's patience sprang from his  philosophy," Herndon explained, "his charity for men and his want of malice for them everywhere, all grew out of his peculiar philosophy." Since Lincoln was a "thorough fatalist" and "believed that what was to be would be, and no prayers of ours could arrest or reverse the decree." Therefore, "men were but simple tools of fate," and no one "was responsible for what he was, thought, or did."

This might not seem like a very useful attitude for a case lawyer like Lincoln. He was against the idea of legal punishment for crimes as

---

[52] See chapter 8, 'PART OF A GREATER SEA', pg. 131 about Lincoln's belief in fatalism

retributive justice rather than as an opportunity for moral exhortation and rehabilitation. Punishment, Lincoln believed, should not be "an expression of hatred, but a means of exciting in the mind of the delinquent a motive to do right, and thereby [...] remedying his deficient moral state."[53] Laws should therefore be "remedial" rather than retributive. Lincoln was a proponent of the reconstruction of the English penal system, including the architecture of prisons, to promote penitence rather than to inflict pain. Not surprisingly, Lincoln often took the same line of argument in asking for the revision of sentences for wartime criminals. "Five years at hard labour in the penitentiary is not at all necessary to prevent the repetition of the crime by himself and others," wrote Lincoln in remitting the sentence of William Yocum in 1864. The valuable thing to note in that judgment was Lincoln's conviction that the purpose of punishment was not to even scores, instead to present a sufficient motive to deter repetition.

In 1854, he had remarked that southern slaveholders "were neither better, nor worse than we of the North" because "if we were situated as they are, we should act and feel as they do; and if they were situated as we are, they should act and feel as we do; and we never ought to lose sight of this fact in discussing the subject." Later, when reviewing the appeals of war deserters, Lincoln liked to look for reason rather than sentiments as the grounds for granting a pardon.

"Well, after all, Judge, I think I must put this case with my 'leg cases'," Lincoln remarked on one occasion amusingly to Judge Advocate General Joseph Holt: "They are the cases that you call by that long title, 'cowardice in the face of the enemy,' but I call them for short, my 'leg cases.' But I put it to you, and I leave it for you to decide for yourself: if Almighty God gives a man a cowardly pair of legs how can he help their running away with him?"

---

[53] Quote attributed to an American, Benthamite John Allyn

This capacity for compassion and forgiveness accounts for much of Lincoln's actions and underlying motives in his splendid life. Lincoln's philosophy comes through with great clarity in his most eloquent statement on the meaning of responsibility, in his second inaugural address. Our hearts are drawn to the final paragraph, with its benediction-like exhortation to end the Civil War "with malice toward none; with charity for all; with firmness in the right, as God gives us to see the right."

In that speech Lincoln also noted how little of freewill God had actually given people. Even though the Confederate cause had been dedicated to an injustice—that of "wringing their bread from the sweat of other men's faces"—even this injustice had been part of "the Almighty's purposes." Lincoln was loath to pass too severe a judgment of his own on Southerners even when slavery was the crime that started the war. Much as he liked "that this mighty scourge of war might pass away," Lincoln also felt the necessity of the four years of bloodshed, that the war was something that "God wills to continue." Hence Lincoln warned against judging each other. This again gives us a view into Lincoln's capacity for compassion.

There was one another relationship that brought Lincoln's capacity for compassion to the forefront. In November 1861, President Abraham Lincoln appointed George B. McClellan the General-in-Chief of all U.S. Federal armies. In giving this responsibility to McClellan, Lincoln expected to move swiftly against the rebelling Confederate army. But the general failed to launch an advance against the Confederate army, and his relations with Washington started to deteriorate.

After his first few weeks in Washington as a general, McClellan stated to his friends that the president was an idiot. He wrote to his wife that Lincoln was "nothing more than a well-meaning baboon." On one occasion Lincoln poured over the map of Virginia making strategic suggestions and McClellan pretended to listen deferentially. After the

3. ARRIVAL

President left, McClellan turned to his subordinate and laughed, "isn't he a rare bird?" And then there was the famous episode of McClellan refusing to meet Lincoln in McClellan's home[54]. Lincoln only statement in response to McClellan's behaviour was, "It was better at this time not to be making points of etiquette and personal dignity." Lincoln could transcend the snub, because to him the indignity of the snub was minor than the greater cause.

Self-absorbed and insensitive, McClellan seemed totally unaware that in a democratic society military commanders were subordinate to elected authorities, and he felt no need to keep the President informed. Aware of his own limitations in military matters, Lincoln continued to bear with McClellan in spite of persistent demands from Congress to remove him.

Later on May 4 1862, with Lincoln's direct involvement, Norfolk, Virginia, was recaptured by the Union army under Secretary of the Treasury Salmon P. Chase. But Lincoln would not allow this victory to be used to discredit McClellan. "I will not hear anything said against General McClellan, it hurts my feelings," Lincoln rebuked someone who made a derogatory remark of McClellan.

But McClellan was not so generous to Lincoln. In his capacity as the Commander of the Army of the Potomac, McClellan insisted on reversing some of Lincoln's recent decisions. Reluctantly Lincoln went along with McClellan's recommendations.

Yet, complaining to newspaper reporters of the way he had been treated by the administration, McClellan said, "honest A has again fallen into the hands of my enemies and is no longer a cordial friend of mine." McClellan went on to speak of the overwhelming superiority of the

---

[54] See chapter 19, 'THE BEST WAY TO EAT AN ELEPHANT', pg. 313

Confederate army, and spread the word that the Lincoln administration was ignoring calls to strengthen his army.

All this while, Lincoln continued to read with painful anxiety the telegraphic dispatches from McClellan's headquarters. Those messages were filled with repeated excuses for not advancing and their constant complaints. The weather, wrote the general, was impossible; rains made mud bogs of the roads and repeatedly washed out all his bridges. Wryly Lincoln observed that the weather did little to restrict the movement of the Confederates, and he jokingly noted that McClellan believed that the rain fell more upon the just than the unjust.

Lincoln needed McClellan to launch an assault on Richmond, the Confederate capital. It was important to keep the momentum going and the spirit up. The Confederates needed to know that at any cost the Union would be preserved. There was another motive behind the push on Richmond. Lincoln has been quietly planning a change of strategy for the war; he has been working on the now famous Emancipation Proclamation, an order to release Blacks in the South from the scourge of slavery and making them free to join the Union army, if they so wish. He had majority backing of the Congress, and all he needed was a victory to precede the announcement of the Emancipation Proclamation. To that extent, Lincoln could bear with McClellan, however ill-advised and impetuous McClellan was.

Later, in 1862, even as Lincoln replaced McClellan, he told reporters that his decision "had nothing whatsoever to do with making or unmaking any General in the country." It had to do with a higher goal, preserving the Union. Until his very end, Lincoln believed that forbearance towards those who differed in belief was a moral, social and political imperative for all.[LIV] [LV]

3. ARRIVAL

Lincoln's fatalist belief sheds light into one of the greatest character traits displayed by Lincoln. He could forgive wrongdoers. He could separate what men did and the need to judge them for it. Imagine this: If conditions, circumstances, laws or fate forced someone to behave in harmful ways, then can you condemn him for it? How can we hold someone to account if it was outside someone's control to do the things we do? This view of justice set Lincoln free from the need to censure or punish others.

This capacity for compassion was a common trait among all the Being Leaders at the peak of their lives. To forgive, you must free yourself from your conditioning. The wounds that you have inherited should not become the judge of your choices. Through the prism of your wounds, you cannot find understanding for others. Hurting others is simply a demonstration of your capacity to hurt, it does not show the worthiness of your cause or the strength of your leadership. It simply tells your wise opponent that you are simply a victim of your pain. After all, your pain is seeking its counterpart through the pain of others. It finds its validation through seeking a perverse pleasure in seeing others suffer.

Mandela, before going to prison, saw only the differences among different peoples. With the South Africans of Indian origin, the Coloured and the communists, he could only see what made their legitimate needs different from those of the black South Africans. He saw that their skin color was different, their life circumstances were different, their financial status were different, their ideologies were different and so were their aspirations in life.

The emotional and passionate Mandela before his long prison term could not see the things that made all the non-white South Africans the same. Their sufferings were the same. Their indignities were the same. The South Africans of Indian origin and the other Coloured South Africans also had to carry identification passbooks as the black South Africans had to. They could not vote either. The best schools and Universities in South Africa were not open to the Indian and Coloured South Africans. Justice was delivered to all non-white South Africans based on the colour of the skin, not on the merit of the case.

The Mandela who came out of prison twenty-seven years later did not let his *conditioned self* respond to the indignities of South Africa. Instead, he sported the Highest Ideal of a rainbow nation where all South Africans—Black, White, Indians, Coloured—have the same rights and lived a live of dignity. It is true that black South Africans were the worst affected by Apartheid, but prison awakened Mandela to the plight of all non-Whites. He did not let his responses be guided by his hurt, rather by his awareness.

Out of prison, Mandela's forbearance was not limited to non-white South Africans. He could transcend his wounds to feel the same way about his oppressors as well. Recollecting his experience in Robben Island at the hands of the brutal prison commander Piet Badenhorst[55], this is what Mandela had to say: "These men were not inhuman, but their inhumanity had been put upon them. They behaved like beasts because they were rewarded for such behaviour. They thought it would result in a promotion or advancement."

"He was a better man than how he had behaved. His motives were not as cruel as his actions. No one is born prejudiced or racist. No man," Mandela suggests, "is evil at heart. Evil is something instilled in or taught to men by circumstances, their environment or their upbringing. It is not innate. Apartheid made men evil, evil did not create Apartheid."

---

[55] See chapter 4, 'THE FIERY ORDEAL THROUGH WHICH THE BEING LEADERS PASS', pg. 59

3. ARRIVAL

"They were simple, uneducated men who had been inculcated in an unfair and racist system since they were children. Almost all were from poor families, an upbringing not all that different from most of the prisoners."

In spite of the many betrayals and the political back-stabbings Mandela experienced from the last Apartheid president, F.W. de Klerk, Mandela could feel compassion for de Klerk. Mandela noted in his autobiography that during the negotiation process for a new constitution, de Klerk had simply acted in his own interest and that of his political followers. The political landscape had prevented de Klerk from rising above the pettiness. In spite of his self-centered interests, de Klerk had shown some integrity towards his own community.

The Being Leaders had an unparalleled capacity to accept that each individual was doing his best in any given moment. As Mandela recognized about Badenhorst, humans are only limited in their nobility by their consciousness. The Being Leaders believed that given greater maturity, all men have the capacity to rise in decency. This quality of the Being Leaders' Noble Creed gave them the tremendous capacity of discriminating the doer from the deed. The Being Leaders would condemn the deed without condemning the doer.

In the sarcastic words of General Jan Smuts, the head of the Apartheid Transvaal government, a South African province, about Gandhi: "He is fighting injustice while he loves the human."

Gandhi took effort to understand the long journeys of the British administrators who controlled and administered pre-independence India. In his letters and during his appointments with the British administrators stationed in India, Gandhi held deep conversations with them. He felt a genuine interest in their lives. He noticed that there were more similarities between the British administrators and the Indians than there were differences. Their outlook towards life and their love for their family was not any less compared to what Gandhi felt himself.

Away from his wounds, Gandhi understood the indoctrination that the British administrators have undergone under the monarchy in Britain, and how that indoctrination has created within them an image of India. He took time to learn about the system the British administrators grew up in. He understood that they were a product of a highly hierarchical society where it was demanded of them that they sported unquestioned loyalty to an inaccessible and far away monarchy. To be chosen as a representative of the monarchy was a prestigious assignment, and it was incumbent upon each administrator to prove themselves.

There is a French saying, "tout comprendre, c'est tout pardonner". To understand all is to forgive all. This is indeed true when it comes to the Being Leaders. They wanted to understand their adversary not just because they wanted to overpower them, but also to forbear with them.

20.1 ACCEPTING IMPERFECTION

Ulysses S. Grant led Union forces to victory in the Civil War earning a reputation as an aggressive commander. In July 1863, Grant defeated Confederate armies and seized Vicksburg, giving the Union control of the Mississippi River and dividing the Confederacy in two. After the Battle of Chattanooga in late 1863, President Abraham Lincoln promoted Grant to commander of all of the Union armies.

As genius as Grant's skills in warfare were, so little was his communication with the elected representatives in Washington.

3. ARRIVAL

"Grant is a very meagre telegrapher and stenographer. He does not write to me very much." When Grant was not communicating very much with Lincoln, he could forbear with Grant's idiosyncrasies. When Grant was criticised for his reckless advance in the bloody battles, Lincoln responded, "I cannot spare him, he fights." When Lincoln was told by some of Grant's critics that Grant drank too much, Lincoln is supposed to have responded: "Let me know what brand of whiskey Grant uses. For if it makes fighting generals like Grant, I should like to get some of it for distribution."

The Being Leaders could look beyond the imperfection of those around them. The Being Leaders saw people for what they had within than for what they lacked. We all know the saying, 'to be human is to be imperfect.' This belief underpinned the Being Leaders' mastery.

If we contrast that statement against the obsession of most leaders today with addressing the weaknesses of their staff you can recognize an instant distinction. Training and development today is so oriented towards eliminating the weaknesses of employees lest these weaknesses should impede the performance or productivity of the employee. That approach makes for good employees, high in productivity and generally non-disruptive to the flow of organizational activities and non-intrusive to the harmony between staff.

Such an approach though does not create greatness. It is when a leader harnesses his Unique Gift, champion Life Purpose, be guided by his Highest Ideal, live his life in alignment with his Noble Creed, and yield his fullest potential that he achieves greatness. This he cannot do by focussing on his weaknesses. Where does the list of weaknesses end? Never. When one weakness is fixed, there is another seeking your attention.

Capacity for Compassion and Forbearance

To recognize and accommodate the imperfections of humans is a hallmark of a Being Leader. A true leader can dispassionately observe—free from the entanglements of his conditioning or ideologies—that no one race or no one nation or no one organization is all evil. From within each race or nation or organization, you will encounter those who are driven by their fear or identity needs, as you will encounter those who are propelled to serve and care with love and compassion.

Gandhi did not see all of the British empire as evil and all British as bad. During the second Anglo-Boer war from 1899 to 1902 between the British Empire and the Dutch settlers in South Africa, Gandhi felt that he should side with the British. India had wilfully fought on the side of the British in the first World War. Similarly, he felt that India should lend its support to the British during World War II. Their cause seemed righteous.

When you are ideological you will perceive the world as being black or white. You will perceive any agency as either your friend or your enemy. You will experience life as a constant battle between good and evil. All situations will seem to you as a conflict between the divine and the demon. That is a simplistic view of life. While certain actions from individuals might seem objectionable, their motives might warrant sympathy. Sometimes the reverse is also true.

The Being Leaders experienced life as an ongoing path of integrating the various lessons so they could rise for the greater good. They saw life as a process of integrating the darkness with a wholesome light. Their noble pursuit was not one bent on destroying the opposing forces, rather showing them the path of goodness. Dr. King famously stated that his movement was not about annihilating the enemy through hatred, rather converting them through love.

They could forbear things that were against their belief systems. When the AIDS epidemic was ravaging the young population of the nation,

3. ARRIVAL

Mandela took a position towards eliminating its scourge. Mandela's successor Mbeki, on the other hands, was caught up in his ideology against AIDS. Mbeki maintained that AIDS was an act of God and a punishment for the erring. While Mandela had given support to AIDS prevention and restitution and aided the distribution of drugs to the needy, Mbeki, caught up in his ideology, could not see the suffering of AIDS patients with forbearance and compassion. He ended up blocking the distribution of life-saving drugs within South Africa.

Imperfections in others are not easy for most to grasp. But when you are able to see all the imperfections and recognize the inherent humanness about the grays, you not only understand the motives of those involved, you accept that it is human conditioning to be propelled by self-interest. That understanding throws open your heart in compassion and forbearance to make you in that moment a Being Leader.

21. EPILOGUE

"With great power comes great responsibility," French writer Voltaire once said.

We are constantly looking to unleash our immense human potential. We first longed to stand on our own two feet, and once that we achieved, we moved on to run and jump.

We did not stop there. We climbed the highest mountain. Then we learned to fly. Today, we have mastered the ability to reach outer space. At each step, we naively thought that we had reached the summit of a human feat. And we rejoiced. Until someone new captures our collective imagination by scaling new heights. Then we forget the previous champion. This cycle of evolution continues.

However, with the Being Leaders we know that humanity has attained the peak of personal mastery. They did not attempt this climb to the summit for the sake of glory, nor for the thrill of conquest, nor to test their peak performance. They scaled summits for our collective cause. They did it to save humanity. They owned the responsibility that they were bestowed, and they wielded their spiritual powers.

The Being Leaders got where they were through a hard journey in life. They were the unlikely heroes plucked out of nowhere. Often against their own volition, they were compelled to take on great challenge and suffer greatly. In that process, the Being Leaders had resurrected themselves and went through a path where they overcame many demons and reached a place of personal mastery.

They loved all of the human race. They believed in the solidarity of all humans, and accepted no differences in colour or race. They sought to make every human better and happier. They sympathised with the poor and the downtrodden. In listening to the pain of stricken soldiers, in holding the hand of an aged black man, in smiling or giving a word of encouragement to a little child, the Being Leaders gave evidence of their largeness of spirit.

The Being Leaders met their responsibility with a resolve that did not give in, and they imparted justice without retribution. They resisted injustice without vengefulness, they endured suffering without complaints, they brought the best out of warriors without intimidation, they liberated the oppressed with malice towards none, and they carried humanity unto victory without pomposity.

Unlike other leaders, the Being Leaders are not just any leader, they are the bonds that hold our noblest ideals together. There is a golden thread that connects us with these noble leaders, in spite of all our differences. That is why they are in our textbooks. Our bedtime stories are filled with the grandness of their feats and the generosity of their spirit. They populate our collective imagination, trigger our greatest aspirations and tickle our childhood fantasies.

X   X   X

You are an immense spiritual force.

You have within you all the resources you need to become a Being Leader. The necessary life experiences are already within you and the opportunities to learn and apprentice are all around you. You simply need to seek it.

Life itself is your greatest apprenticeship. Consider it your most exposing thesis. All the homework is included within it, and all projects are contained therein. Life is the Google and the encyclopaedia of learning.

Epilogue

All you need to do is to hold the Being Leaders close to you in your awareness. Simply in your practice of holding them in your awareness, their power will rub off you. You will experience the transformative power of their principles. Their enormous sacrifices will find their resurrection through you.

Then you become immortal; as immortal as the leaders examined in this work. The Being Leaders can never die, because in their brief lives they have shone the immense power of our spirit. Every time you choose to embody the mastery exposed in this work, you will shine the same immense power of spirit. As a result, you will step into that same immortality that the Being Leaders enjoy.

The day you claim the path of the Being Leaders, you have planted within you the seed of transformation. That transformation begins internally, within you, and then slowly spreads amidst your relatives and friends, and into the collective. And when the lives of those around you are exposed to your ideals, they will eventually begin to reflect those ideals as well. The process gradually widens its arc to embrace your organizations and your society, and in time perhaps the world. We need no further proof of this than the lives of the Being Leaders, which after decades, reach us today, across the continents.

You cannot beat the Being Leaders, but you can match them. So I call on you to match them. There are opportunities to step into greatness all around you. Once, while Gandhi's train was pulling slowly out of a station, a reporter ran up to him and asked him breathlessly for a message to take back to his people. Gandhi's reply was a hurried line scrawled on a scrap of paper: "My life is my message."[LVI]

So I end this work with this prayer;

> *"Let the lives of these great Being Leaders elevate us, to the realization in ourselves of the spirit which animated them.*
>
> *Let us go on to fulfill the mission for which the Being Leaders have taken the first step.*
>
> *Let us rise to the task the Being Leaders have called us for, of being the model of a pure and ennobling civilization.*
>
> *Let us dedicate ourselves to be that which they have been, let us prove worthy of the Being Leaders' sacrifice."*

22. REFERENCES

- **10 Qualities that Made Abraham Lincoln a Great Leader** by Catherine L. Moreton, J.D.
- **101 Selected Sayings of Mahatma Gandhi** by Irfan Alli
- **A Testament Of Hope: The Essential Writings and Speeches of Martin Luther King, Jr.** by Martin Luther King
- **Abraham Lincoln: A Biography** by Benjamin P. Thomas
- **Abraham Lincoln as a Man of Ideas**: Allen C. Guelzo
- **Abraham Lincoln: Preserving the Union**, A&E Home Video (ASIN: B0002V7NUM)
- **Abraham Lincoln: Redeemer President** by Allen C. Guelzo
- **Abraham Lincoln, the War Years** by Carl Sandburg
- **Abraham Lincoln: The True Story of a Great Life** by William H. Herndon And Jesse W. Weik
- **An Easy Burden: The Civil Rights Movement and the Transformation of America** by A Young and Quincy Jones
- **Black Confederates and Afro-Yankees in Civil War Virginia** by Ervin L., Jr. Jordan
- **Chained Together: Mandela, De Klerk, and the Struggle to Remake South Africa** by David Ottaway
- **Charisma: 10 Leadership Lesson from Gandhi's Life** by Maxwell Leader
- **Congressman Lincoln** by Chris DeRose
- **Conversations With Lincoln**, by Charles M. Segal
- **Conversations with myself** by Nelson Mandela
- **Crisis of the House Divided**: Harry V. Jaffa, published in 1959
- **Crusader without violence;: A biography of Martin Luther King Jr.**, by Lawrence Dunbar Reddick
- **Gandhi and India's Independence**: Wynnewood, Pa. - Schlessinger Media (DVD)

- **Gandhi on Non-Violence: Selected Texts from Gandhi's "Non-violence in Peace and War"** by Mahatma Gandhi (Author) and Thomas Merton (Editor) 1996
- **Gandhi, The Movie**: Sir Richard Attenborough, 1982
- **Gandhi: The Power of Pacifism** by Catherine Clement, (1996), New York.
- **Great Negroes Past and Present** by Russell L. Adams, Afro-Am Publishing Co., 1963
- **Higher Than Hope: The Authorized Biography of Nelson Mandela** by Fatima Meer
- **I Have a Dream: The Story of Martin Luther King** by Margaret Davidson
- **I HAVE A DREAM: Writings and Speeches that Changed the World**, by Martin Luther King Jr., edited by James M. Washington
- **Killing Lincoln: The Shocking Assassination that Changed America Forever** by Bill O'Reilly and Martin Dugard
- **KING: Go Beyond the Dream to Discover the Man**. DVD, HISTORY Channel, ASIN: B0016PDZEQ
- **King Remembered** by Flip Schulke
- **Leading the Mahatma Gandhi Way**: Low K. C. P. (2010), Leadership & Organizational Management Journal, Volume 2010 Issue 2, pg. 110 - 117
- **Life on the Circuit with Lincoln** by Henry C. Whitney (Author)
- **Lincoln: A Life of Purpose and Power** by Richard Carwardine
- **Lincoln, Land, and Labor**, by Olivier Fraysse
- **Lincoln and the Economics of the American Dream** by Gabor S. Boritt
- **Lincoln at Gettysburg: The Words that Remade America** by Garry Wills
- **Lincoln Nobody Knows** by Richard N. Current
- **Lincoln Speeches** by Allen C. Guelzo and Richard Beeman
- **Lincoln's Boyhood**, by Van Natter & Francis Marion. Public Affairs Press, Washington, 1963

References

- **Lincoln's Emancipation Proclamation: The End of Slavery in America** by Allen C. Guelzo
- **Lincoln's Greatest Speech: The Second Inaugural** by Jr. Ronald C. White Jr.
- **Lincoln's Tragic Pragmatism: Lincoln, Douglas, and Moral Conflict** by John Burt
- **Lincoln's Youth: Indiana Years, Seven to Twenty-One**, by Louis A. Warren
- **Long Walk to Freedom: The Autobiography of Nelson Mandela** by Nelson Mandela
- **Mahatma Gandhi: Nonviolent Power in Action** by Dennis Dalton
- **Mahatma Gandhi: Pilgrim of Peace**, DVD, BIOGRAPHY Channel, ASIN:B0002V7KVO
- **MAHATMA GANDHI: The Life and Times of a Modern Legend**. KULTUR, DVD, ISBN: 0769786647
- **Mandela** by Ann Kramer
- **Mandela** by Donna Faulkner
- **Mandela** by John Vail
- **Mandela** by Peter Hain and Desmond Tutu
- **Mandela: Long Walk to Freedom**. DVD, ASIN: B00HE11L7O
- **Mandela: My Prisoner, My Friend** by Christo Brand and Barbara Jones
- **Mandela: The Authorised Biography** by Anthony Sampson
- **Mandela's Way: Lessons on Life, Love, and Courage** by Richard Stengel and Nelson Mandela
- **Martin Luther King, Jr.,** (electronic resource), Great Neck Publishing
- **Martin Luther King, Jr.: The Making of a Mind** by John J. Ansbro
- **Martin Luther King Jr.: The Man and the Dream,** DVD, BIOGRAPHY Channel, ASIN: B0002V7NZ2
- **Martin Luther King Jr. Day** by Linda Lowery

- **Mentor Graham: The Man Who Taught Lincoln** by Kunigunde Duncan and D. F. Nickols
- **My Philosophy of Life** by M. K. Gandhi and Anand T. Hingorani (Editor) (1961), Pearl Publications Pte. Ltd.: Bombay.
- **Nelson Mandela** by Kadir Nelson
- **Nelson Mandela: Journey to Freedom**, DVD, BIOGRAPHY Channel, ASIN: B0002V7NUW
- **Nelson Mandela: The Man and the Movement** by Mary Benson
- **Nelson Mandela Speaks: Forging a Democratic, Nonracial South Africa** by Nelson Mandela
- **Pilgrimage to Nonviolence: On Gandhi's Legacy** by Martin Luther Jr King and Carson Claybourne
- **Presidency of Abraham Lincoln** by Phillip Shaw Paludan
- **Strength to Love**, by Dr. Martin Luther King Jr. New York, Harper & Row, 1963
- **Stride Toward Freedom: The Montgomery Story** by Martin Luther King Jr. and Clayborne Carson
- **Team of Rivals: The Political Genius of Abraham Lincoln** by Doris Kearns Goodwin
- **The Autobiography of Martin Luther King, Jr.** by Clayborne Carson
- **The Collected Works of Abraham Lincoln**, by Roy P. Basler
- **The Essential Gandhi: An Anthology of His Writings on His Life, Work, and Ideas**, by Mahatma Gandhi & Louis Fischer
- **The faith of Abraham Lincoln**, by David Raymond Taggart
- **The Fundamental Leadership Wisdom of the Bhagavad Gita:** Low K.C.P. (2011), Business journal for entrepreneurs, Volume 2011 Issue 1, pg. 90 – 100
- **The Inner World of Abraham Lincoln** by Michael Burlingame
- **The Life Changing Lessons And Story Of Martin Luther King - The Fight For A Dream** by Anthony Taylor
- **The Life of Abraham Lincoln** by Isaac N. Arnold (1994)

References

- **The Life of Abraham Lincoln: From His Birth To His Inauguration As President** by Ward H. Lamon
- **The Long Walk of Nelson Mandela** by pbs.org
- **The Measure of A Man: Dr. Martin Luther King Jr., The Christian** Education Press
- **The Real Lincoln: A Portrait** by Jesse W. Weik and Michael Burlingame
- **The Sayings of Mahatma Gandhi** by Mahatma Gandhi and Peter H. Burgess
- **The Soul of Abraham Lincoln** by William E. Barton
- **The Struggle Is My Life** Paperback by Nelson Mandela
- **The Trumpet of Conscience** by Martin Luther King Jr.
- **The Writings of Abraham Lincoln** by Abraham Lincoln and Steven B. Smith
- **We shall overcome: Martin Luther King, Jr., and the Black freedom struggle** by Peter J. Albert, Ronald Hoffman
- **What Manner of Man: A Biography of Martin Luther King, Jr.** by Bennett, Lerone, Jr., Johnson, 1964
- **Where Do We Go from Here: Chaos or Community?** by Martin Luther King Jr., Coretta Scott King and Vincent Harding
- **Why We Can't Wait** by Jr. Martin Luther King Jr., Harper & Row, 1963
- **With Malice Toward None: The Life of Abraham Lincoln** by Stephen B. Oates

---

[I]   **Mandela's Way: Lessons on Life, Love, and Courage** by Richard Stengel

[II]   **Gandhi**, by Dwight Macdonald, Politics, December 1948, www.unz.org

[III] Adapted from the research done by **The History Connection** (www.thehistoryconnection.com)

[IV]   **Our Fiery Trial: Abraham Lincoln, John Brown, and the Civil War Era** by Stephen B. Oates

[V]   Quoted from **Martin Luther King, Jr.: A Biography** by Roger Bruns

[VI] **Let The Trumpet Sound: A Life Of Martin Luther King, Jr.** by Stephen B Oates

[VII] **The Autobiography of Martin Luther King, Jr.** by Clayborne Carson

[VIII] **Mandela** by Martin Meredith

[IX] Adapted from **'Gandhi, the Man'** by Eknath Easwaran

[X] **The Heart of Lincoln: The Soul of the Man as Revealed in Story and Anecdote** by Wayne Whipple

[XI] **"That Disgraceful Affair," the Black Hawk War**, by Cecil Eby

[XII] **Lincoln** by David Herbert Donald

[XIII] http://en.wikipedia.org/wiki/Satyagraha

[XIV] **Gandhi: The Man, His People, and the Empire** by Rajmohan Gandhi

[XV] http://www.unfetteredmind.org

[XVI] Adapted from **'Abraham Lincoln and the Doctrine of Necessity'** by ALLEN C. GUELZO

[XVII] **Citizen King**, DVD, by Noland Walker and Orlando Bagwell

[XVIII] **The Power of Non-violence** by Martin Luther King, Jr.

[XIX] Adapted from **Mandela's Way: Lessons on Life, Love, and Courage** by Richard Stengel

[XX] http://teachingamericanhistory.org/library/document/the-power-of-non-violence/

[XXI] Adapted from **Humble Leadership: Being Radically Open to God's Guidance and Grace** by N. Graham Standish

[XXII] http://www.ihrf.com/messages/tribute-to-mahatma-gandhi.html

[XXIII] Adapted from **'Gandhi, the Man'** by Eknath Easwaran

[XXIV] http://mlk-kpp01.stanford.edu/index.php/encyclopedia/encyclopedia/enc_sit_ins/

[XXV] **The Last Hours Of Mahatma Gandhi**, by S. Murphy (http://www.mkgandhi.org)

[XXVI] **The Life and Death of Mahatma Gandhi** by Robert Payne

[XXVII] **The Autobiography of Martin Luther King, Jr.** by Clayborne Carson

[XXVIII] http://www.encyclopedia-titanica.org/titanic-survivor/arthur-godfrey-peuchen.html

[XXIX] **The Mission of Abraham Lincoln: A Sermon Preached Before the Fourth Baptist Church** by Jeffery Rueben

[XXX] Adapted from **Mandela** by Martin Meredith

References

[XXXI] **The Mission of Abraham Lincoln: A Sermon Preached Before the Fourth Baptist Church** by Jeffery Rueben

[XXXII] **The Compassionate Universe: The Power of the Individual to Heal the Environment** by Eknath Easwaran

[XXXIII] **American President: A Reference Resource**. Miller Center, University of Virginia. www.millercenter.org

[XXXIV] Adapted from '**The War Over King's Legacy**', by Vern E. Smith and Jon Meacham

[XXXV] **The Life and Death of Mahatma Gandhi** by Robert Payne

[XXXVI] **A Call to Conscience: The Landmark Speeches of Dr. Martin Luther King Jr.** by Clayborne Carson, Kris Shepard and Andrew Young

[XXXVII] **Great Soul: Mahatma Gandhi and His Struggle with India** by Joseph Lelyveld

[XXXVIII] http://library.ucsc.edu/content/free-nelson-mandela

[XXXIX] http://www.sahistory.org.za/topic/negotiations-and-transition

[XL] Adapted from http://www.aucegypt.edu/gapp/cairoreview/pages/articledetails.aspx?aid=69

[XLI] Adapted from **Encyclopaedia Britannica**

[XLII] **Great Soul: Mahatma Gandhi and His Struggle with India** by Joseph Lelyveld

[XLIII] Adapted from '**Gandhi, the Man**' by Eknath Easwaran

[XLIV] Adapted from '**Gandhi, the Man**' by Eknath Easwaran

[XLV] Adapted from http://en.wikipedia.org/wiki/Chauri_Chaura_incident

[XLVI] Adapted from **Mandela** by Martin Meredith

[XLVII] http://www.sparknotes.com/biography/mlk/section8.rhtml

[XLVIII] **The Compassionate Universe** by Eknath Easwaran

[XLIX] Adapted from **Mandela's Way: Lessons on Life, Love, and Courage** by Richard Stengel

[L] **Mandela's Way: Lessons on Life, Love, and Courage** by Richard Stengel

[LI] Adapted from **Mandela** by Martin Meredith

[LII] **Gandhi: An Autobiography, The Story of My Experiments with Truth** by Mohandas K. Gandhi

[LIII] **Lincoln** by David Herbert Donald

[LIV] **Lincoln** by David Herbert Donald

[LV] **Abraham Lincoln and the Doctrine of Necessity** by ALLEN C. GUELZO

[LVI] **Gandhi, the Man** by Eknath Easwaran

CPSIA information can be obtained
at www.ICGtesting.com
Printed in the USA
LVOW13*1445300317
529060LV00010B/181/P